JUAN MARTÍN DEL POTRO

THE
GENTLE
GIANT

SEBASTIÁN TOROK

JUAN MARTÍN DEL POTRO

Originally published by Spanish under the title
EL MILAGRO DEL POTRO

Translated by Luis Rossi
with assistance from Haley Hunt

To Renata, my light, motor and sweetest weakness.
To Sole, for his long love, company and complicity.
To my old ones, Alicia and Julio, for the love, the values and the care.
To my brothers Nicolás, Lau and Candy, and my nephews Santi
and Bianquita.
To the memory of the grandfather Pedro, buddy and eternal reference.

Contents

Acknowledgements

To Andrés Prestileo, for his solidarity, friendship, balance and help in the moments where my fingers became numb.

To Franco Davin, Martiniano Orazi and Marcelo Gómez, for the trust.

To Gabriela Sabatini, Ricardo Darín and Pablo Trapero, for the support and the warmth.

To Alfredo Bernardi, the coach, for the affection, teachings and valuable peripheral vision.

To Bernardo Paredes, for his kindness, witty nature and collaboration in the sierras of Tandil, between tennis and Salamines.

To Mariano Acosta and Claudia Ferreyra, for the strength and for opening your heart to this stranger.

To Daniel Arcucci, for his rich and immediate contribution from Maradona.

To Diego Morini, for making a giant like Ginobili participate in the work.

To Pablo Gianera, one of the first who convinced me that this was possible.

To Miguel Bossio, Gustavo Goñi, Tato Aguilera and Ángel Núñez, for the help with the Titan and El Flaco.

To Fernando Pedersen, for the logistical support in Tandil.

And Carlos Losauro, my deceased former writing teacher, who is with me always in my journalism duties.

Introduction:
Four Snapshots

One

Seriously? Roman named his dog Palermo? Tell me it's not true. It can't be. Some bad rumors around the La Boca neighborhood are saying so…But, seriously? It's alright if they don't like each other but he can't name his dog like that. That's cruel. I just don't believe it.

The shimmering hallways inside Melbourne Park look like the inner tunnels of an anthill on the opening day of the Australian Open, the first major tennis competition of the season. Tennis players, male and female, family members, trainers, promoters, journalists, ball boys, former players and security guards are all packaged together, coming and going in dizzying fashion. The scene is like a Disney park of tennis, where languages, routines, clothes and humors are mixed.

It is the second half of January 2010 and Juan Martín del Potro is in Australia as the winner of the previous major singles championship at the U.S. Open four months earlier. The man from Tandil, Argentina should look radiant, excited to once again challenge the top players in men's tennis. However, he is worried. Something is not working well with his body. His right wrist, that unleashes his powerful forehand, hurts. At times, it hurts a lot. He fears that it could be something severe (so much so that later on he would have to have surgery in the United States).

Before Juan Martín entered the locker room, he saw the author of this book, who had covered his career since he was a young player for *La Nación* newspaper in Argentina. Del Potro abruptly stopped and asked if what was said about his Argentine football idols. It is true?

The short tempers between Argentine football stars Martín Palermo and Juan Román Riquelme had been public for years. Their differences were irreconcilable. And many fans, lovers of the goals of the optimistic No. 9 and the exquisite technique of No. 10, refused to accept certain stories, some of them enhanced by controversy. That was, no doubt, false, but somehow it had settled. The striking thing, in the specific case of del Potro, was that in the midst of the medical evaluation of his wrist in Melbourne and the tension leading into a Grand Slam tournament, he could isolate himself from the whole world of demands to show his more earthly and spontaneous side.

Del Potro is a football fan, an even bigger fan than he is of tennis. He practiced it as a boy at the Independiente club of Tandil, even before picking up a tennis racket. He enjoys it as an adult, going every time he can to La Bombonera to watch the Boca Juniors team and even playing "picaditos" – or friendly pick-up games - with friends at home. The most popular sport in the world cheers him up, makes him happy but also infuriates him. He can be competing anywhere in the world and, still, be aware of what happens in Argentine football. He can even take the time to write and send an email complaining about some failure by a referee in a match by River Plate, the archrival of his beloved Boca Juniors team._

Soccer also makes you scream like a child. Like on Tuesday, June 22, 2010 when del Potro went crazy in front of the television when Palermo, his friend and inspiration, scored a goal against Greece in the World Cup in South Africa. "This is great! It's incredible. We went out to party and shouted from the balcony with my friends. I know how he fought every blow that life gave him; that's why I got excited," del Potro wrote in an email to me a few hours after the match. It became more understandable the meaning of that frank and surprising question about the world of soccer from the Australian Open, in the middle of the craziness of a Grand Slam tournament. Soccer is a subject that he likes to discuss. In this case, it is something that he turned to for a distraction from the ghosts and bad thoughts that would start to enter his mind.

Two

It was an ideal afternoon. Almost all the courts of the Buenos Aires Lawn Tennis Club were occupied by members, who were closing out the year playing tennis. On Friday, December 28, 2012, del Potro was the No. 7 player in the world and sat in one of the rooms of the historic club.

"I spoke with the captain, Martín Jaite, and I communicated my decision for next year, which is to focus on the ATP Tour and not Davis Cup," he said to a small group of media, confirming rumors that had been circulating for weeks. "The end of the year filled me with hope that I can fight for the No. 1 ranking. I am 24 years old and it's a moment where I have to make some decisions. The decision is not to play Davis Cup for 2013. I know that I cannot make everyone happy."

His relationship with the Argentine Davis Cup coaching staff and with the leadership of the Argentine Tennis Association was shattered. It had been weeks since del Potro was considering moving away from the team and yet had not announced it. That's why, that day, when he left the club after doing so, he was relieved, despite knowing the weight that would fall on his back in an impulsive and unresolvedly successful country, which had not yet won the blessed (or damn) Davis Cup.

"I cannot conform to everyone," added del Potro, who was accompanied by Franco Davin, his coach but also his trusted confidant. The Davis Cup would, for a long time, be an issue that Juan Martín would not allow him to freely enjoy the circuit and that would put him in uncomfortable and tense situations, some of them enhanced by his own silences, mood swings and distrust, even with some who showed him respect and approached him with good intentions.

Three

The squeak of the alarm broke through the silence of the wide and luminous house facing the sea. It's 7:30 am – not the time for lazy people. Orange juice, cereals, yogurt and toast - a little of everything, not more than enough – is served. Martiniano Orazi, the physical trainer, is an earlier riser than all the other inhabitants of the house. He is already in the garden, adjusting his watch. Del Potro, trying to wake up, soon joined him, walking through the small door and on to the beach.

The scenario is ideal for an elite athlete who intends to train with absolute freedom. On these first days of November in 2014 the beaches of the Argentine coastal town of Cariló is still deserted. The idea is to run for 50 minutes and return, and then continue with on-court training with Davin, his coach, at the Cariló Tennis Club. Juan Martín warmed up his arm before punishing the ball with such fury that the noise of the impact was louder than the chirping of the birds. There were few witnesses of those first blows by del Potro. One of them was Santiago, a 14-year-old who knew that his idol would be there. He managed to convince his parents to let him miss his history, mathematics and plastic classes for the day to watch.

All of the training is part of a kind of "pre-season" for del Potro for the 2015 season after the Argentine had been off the ATP Tour for almost a year after surgery on his left wrist. After the practice, del Potro invited three journalists to live with him for two days in this house he rented for two weeks on the Atlantic coast, south of Buenos Aires.

"I'm going to make three serves to each one of you," he said to the journalists. "If they manage to return at least one ball, I'll do the roast tonight; if you cannot, then you do it ..." Del

Potro smiled as he issued the challenge. The journalists accepted. The first service, on the deuce court, was hit with such force out wide that it is impossible to stop, especially for an amateur. The second, from the same side of the court, was a hammer down the middle. It did not even gain a reaction from the returner as the ball hit the back fence as another ace. "Well, the last one is going into the body," he warned. The racket blocked the blow and the yellow sphere, almost in slow motion, crossed from one side of the net over to the other side into the court. The challenge was won and half fulfilled, because the one who took control of the barbecue was one of del Potro's childhood friends, Martín Bertrand. Juan Martín was responsible for cutting the meat, putting the dishes and cutlery on the table and helped distribute the different cuts of meat and achuras. This was followed by ice cream, the chocolate cake that Juliet, his sister, prepared, and the jokes about old poker games with Davin.

"I cried a lot," del Potro said the next day during the interview for *La Nación* newspaper. "After surgery on my right wrist, even in my worst nightmare, I thought I was going to have to go back into an operating room. But the setbacks make you stronger and more mature."

He was 26 years old and, despite his career obstacles, radiated enthusiasm. He left for a few weeks to get away from the madness of Buenos Aires to think and breathe in the sea breezes and continue to work on his fitness and form.

"I want to be able to go to parties in my house and participate in toasts to my trips to play in tournaments and to have good energy and be healthy in my tennis career for a long time, but unfortunately that was not the case," he said. "Instead, in 2015, I would go through two more surgeries on my left wrist."

Four

"Here you can really hear the silence, it is not a lie," said del Potro. And he is right. If there is a way to hear the silence, the scenario is ideal. Only the bark of Caesar, the family's Newfoundland breed dog, broke the almost sedative environment. On one side, the mountains; on the other, fences and thick, old trees.

With a beard of a few days and a tired face, Juan Martín was once again the host, this time in his house in Tandil, Argentina, located in the touristy area of town. The previous day, del Potro was cheered by a crowd at the Municipal Palace, celebrating winning the silver medal at the Olympic Games in Rio de Janeiro. Music was at full volume and cries of hysteria and applause accompanied him in the reunion with his neighbors. But now, it was just him, Mauro Rizzi, the photographer from *La Nación*, and the author of these lines. After the seemingly never ending surgeries and anguishing recoveries, Juan Martín had managed to return from sporting death (and he still had to obtain the Davis Cup, no less).

"I was confident that one day there would be some light at the end of the tunnel. And with that hope I went ahead," said del Potro. "Today, I enjoy a present that I can't compare with any other moment in my life. I learned that many times the mind dominates the body and self-love and the heart do incredible things."

Although new epic episodes would soon be built, that tennis player who had gone through the worst that an athlete can suffer, had already won and defeated the demons. The miracle of del Potro, the gentle giant, had already materialized.

Sebastián Torok
Buenos Aires,
April 2017

1

Trials and Triumph

The six-foot, six-inch body frame was collapsed face down on the bed frame, completely covered by a blanket. A bit of natural light entered from a blind slot. The cold morning advanced. But Juan Martín del Potro had no intention of getting up. He had been awake for a long time. Think, ask questions and answer them mentally. He cannot get rid of the demons. The head worked like a locomotive out of control on rickety rails.

He could feel a throbbing in his left wrist. It hurt, especially on the wettest days. It was silent but for the sound of the building's electric intercom. He did not have the courage to pay any attention. The doorbell kept screaming but he did not answer. His cell phone rang and chimed but he paid no attention. The next day, this same situation repeated itself. And again the next day. And the one after that.

"Until my hand stops hurting, I do not want to do anything," the anguished tennis player said before a visit by his coach Franco Davin and physical trainer Martiniano Orazi, the same men who worked with him since 2008 and helped him win 18 titles on the ATP pro circuit, including the U.S. Open in 2009.

By mid-2015, del Potro had undergone three surgeries on the left wrist in a short period of 15 months. The torture did not disappear.

"I did not have the courage to run or to hit balls. The future seemed truly dark," del Potro said. "I was down, depressed. There was no way to lift it because it was really bad."

He had already made two attempts to return to tennis and had to make a third, with the question of not knowing if he could continue playing.

"It was a very big wear. It was several months like this," said Orazi, Juan Martín's trainer for more than seven years. "It affected us a lot emotionally, not only from the working point of view. He was our life; it was the family first, and then him. We went to his apartment and we tried to get him out. I saw him broken, crying many times. We tried to distract him for a while in the morning, a little while in the afternoon or to wake him up if he did not want to get up. We could not plan anything. It was a total uncertainty. He did not have that energy that characterized him so much. And it was understandable."

***

The six-foot, six-inch frame was again collapsed, but this time only centimeters from the Olympic rings painted at the bottom of the court. The body was face up, arms extended above the head and the eyes filled with moisture. The Olympic Park in Rio de Janeiro was like Carnival itself. It was the Sambadrome roaring in August, off schedule.

The scoreboard on the side of the court revealed the final score of the Olympic men's semifinal match – del Potro defeating Rafael Nadal 5-7, 6-4, 7-6 (7-5), clinching for the man from Tandil a second Olympic medal to go with his bronze from 2012 at the London Games. However, this medal has a greater flavor and triumphant aroma than the bronze from four years earlier. The Argentine, wearing a light blue shirt, white shorts and yellow dazzling shoes, stood up, greeted the Spanish legend whom he just defeated, then the chair umpire. He returned to the center of the court, where he knelt, covered his face with his hands, bit his lip and contemplated the delirium.

"Deeeelpo! Deeeelpo! Deeeelpo!" Hundreds of Argentines showered their hero with cheers and chants. Del Potro again spilled his body on the court. As a passionate football fan, he then was encouraged to do something he saw many times in English Premier League matches: he ran through the photographers' area and threw himself to the public. He surrendered to the tide of hands and arms that want to reach him, squeeze him and celebrate with him.

"Not in the best dreams did I imagine this," said del Potro. "It's a story that is more like a movie. It's impossible. A year ago, practically, I did not have the energy to get out of bed or start the day."

However, tennis - and life - reserved for him an opportunity once again for greatness. Still dazed and uncertain, he spotted his chance, took it and fed it, day after day.

"Enough, I have to get up," del Potro finally said to himself while in the depths of his gloomy pit of depression. He started to test his body, to go for a jog and began to watch what he ate to control his weight, which was increasing week after week. But del Potro only thought of ... how he would announce his retirement.

"I was very sad, very lost, very empty," he said. He was just 26 years old, but he felt chained. He could not find a way to recover his skills, his vocation and the encouragement that accompanied him since he was a boy when he began to hold a tennis racket on the brick dust courts of the Independiente club in Tandil. It was not an economic issue, the possibility of losing sponsors or running out of the juicy tournament guarantees; it was clear that neither del Potro nor his family would have financial problems in this life, nor in the next. This was about something else: not feeling free, not getting the fuel for motivation, not being able to play with that addictive adrenaline that sustains athletes.

"There comes a point in your career where you end up hating adrenaline," said Argentine tennis great Gaston Gaudio to *La Nación* magazine in 2014, ten years after his win at Roland Garros. "You say: 'I do not want to have that feeling in my chest anymore of not being able to breathe before playing a game.' But you stop playing and that's the only thing you miss! I think he's already a chemist, it's like the body needs him."

Not drinking from that indispensable concoction for athletes dehydrated del Potro. It weakened him so much that it left him lethargic.

"I cannot get up one more day in this state, sad and crying because my wrist hurts and I cannot hold a racket. It cannot be. I cannot anymore," Juan Martín told his friends and relatives, explaining why retirement was a close consideration.

However, there was a day when del Potro woke up with an optimism that he had not had until then. It was sunny. His wrist did not hurt. He sensed a signal that, even through the years, he did not know how to specify. It was as if an angel asked him for his last attempt, the final effort. He took a bath, looked for sports clothes that he had not worn for a while and dressed. He had breakfast and then went down a few floors to the gym of the building where he lived, near the old zoo in the neighborhood of Palermo. It started little by little. He sweated again. He got excited. He returned the next day and then the next. He tried to control his anxiety. He tried to take slow but firm steps, without rushing.

A few months earlier, del Potro had tried to play and entered the Miami Open. Inside, Juan Martín knew that he was wrong to try and play and that he would have to reenter an operating room, which would require another distressing layoff from tennis. Even so, he wanted to compete to see if that way he could get rid of the pains and fears. The effect, regardless of his first-round loss the Canadian Vasek Pospisil by a 6-4, 7-6(7) margin, was the opposite. It was devastating. The hand and the mind no longer worked. The ghosts in his head were haunting him without abandon.

"I had hit bottom, again," he said.

He had just reached the shore after a long swim between storms in seas infested with sharks and he did not want to face this again. He must be smart and, above all, patient.

"I am more determined than ever to return," he said. "No more doubts or questions. It will be a new career for me. Three operations on the left wrist and one on the right." I do not know how many similar cases there were in tennis. I only know that when I have a thought in my head, I will work to make it happen or with everything that is within my reach."

Facebook was the primary communication method for del Potro during these difficult times, but his messages were encouraging. Those who know del Potro well all agree that he does not stop with any task that he sets his mind to, whatever it might be. It is worth digging a bit into that aspect of his personality to begin to understand the origin of his fabulous capacity for improvement.

"What defines Juan most is his head," said Marcelo Negro Gómez, the childhood coach for del Potro from Tandil. "What he has inside, what he thinks. Damn it, in a good way, when it focuses on a goal."

In an anecdote, he explained it in more depth.

"Once we were in Tres Arroyos and he was playing the end of a G3; He was little. He was eight, nine years old. At that time he also played soccer. We go to the tennis tournament and in the semifinals it was already weird, he told me that his belly hurt. 'What's wrong with you?' I asked. 'I do not know if I can play the final,' he replied. I thought it was very strange, because he wanted to beat everybody. The final Sunday arrived and he asked me what time it was. 'Over there if it's earlier, better, because it's not so hot' he asked me... I looked at him, I did not understand why there were so many questions and comments. He played and lost 6-0 and 6-1. 'Come on, come on, let's go home,' he said to his father and me after the match. 'No, stop, let's eat something,' del Potro's father said. 'No. We will eat at Tandil,' Juan replied. Well ... we went back to Tandil, we traveled 180 kilometers and at three in the afternoon ... he went to play a football final. He had not told us anything! We wanted to kill him. Well, that's what he is and it was always the same. Once something gets in his head, he does not stop: he organizes himself to fulfill the objective and tries to achieve it as he is."

Already without a coaching staff, del Potro found Rolando Schiavi, the former defender of Boca Juniors and then coach of the reserve division of the Auriazul club, a partner with him to help him with his physical recovery to get back into shape to once again play professional tennis.

"Today Juan Martín is coming. We are going to run for a while on the court," Schiavi told Daniel Cinti, a physical trainer in youth soccer and a Boca reserve for more than a decade.

When the tennis player arrived at the Pedro Pompilio complex, Cinti made himself available and gave him some initial guidelines. During the first ten minutes of jogging around one of the courts, del Potro, wearing some small protection on his left wrist, literally drowned. He felt -- and was -- heavy, uncoordinated and agitated. He was sweating more than usual. However, he was not discouraged.

A few days later, he returned. The training increased to 40 minutes, with ten extensions (past one hundred meters, a brief recovery and back out).

"It was wrong. He was barely a professional athlete," said Cinti. His physique had suffered a lot and it showed. But it is also true that bodies have memory, especially high performance athletes. With small steps, del Potro was feeling better.

"Juan Martín had to recover the strength he had lost," Cinti said. "Our goal is to improve resistance, coordination and build a basis for what would come next. Of course he wanted to recover, but he did not know how the body would respond in the future. He wanted to, but he started at the bottom of the sea. He did not know what was waiting for him."

It started, really, from scratch, and in less than two months he made substantial progress.

"Working with him, it was easy for me to see that he was a special athlete... a real elite athlete," Cinti said. "With these type of athletes, you do not have to tell them to run more or do more push-ups. It's the other way around. You have to actually tell them to stop. You should never underestimate these type of athletes with this mind set."

With more confidence in his physical abilities, del Potro chose to isolate himself for a while in Miami. In the humid subtropical climate of Florida, del Potro decided to become more familiar with his racket in a city where he owns a condo in the Brickell area of downtown. It's an area where it is not unusual to see famous people, including other well-known athletes, shopping in the supermarket, eating in a restaurant or standing in line in a cafeteria like any anonymous person, a situation that for this tennis player was ideal in his search for privacy.

In his suitcase, del Potro packed a physical fitness regime provided by Cinti. Day after day, del Potro sent him his records and fitness updates so he could monitor his progress. Matias Apodaca, a kinesiologist from the world of rugby who was recommended by Davin, accompanied del Potro to the United States.

Another important member of his team while in Miami was the former touring pro Jimy Szymanski from Venezuela. Born in Caracas in 1975, Szymanski reached a career-high ranking of No. 160 in 1999 and won the bronze medal at the Pan American Games in Mar del Plata in 1995. He played in 28 Davis Cup ties, two of them against Argentina.

Living in Miami with his family, Szymanski became friends with Davin and, in the days when he was coaching Russian players Maria Kirilenko and Nadia Petrova, he took advantage of combined men's and women's tournaments to leave the Russians during some meals and dine with Davin, Orazi and, of course, del Potro. This is where his relationship with del Potro began to take shape.

"When Juan Martín arrived in Miami, he called me and said: 'Jimy, I'm going to go see the doctor (Richard Berger from The Mayo Clinic in Rochester, Minnesota) following my recovery, do my physical preparation here and I would like you to help me with tennis. Are you interested in helping me?'" Szymanski said. "I replied that I would do it with great pleasure. And we started. For me it was also a great learning experience."

Although Szymanski was aware of the limitations that the Argentine had during the early stages of his comeback, he found himself entrenched with an even more difficult panorama.

"Juan Martín had a kind of inner voice speaking to him at all times, transmitting fears to him," Szymanski said. "It was not easy."

One might think that del Potro's first shots were on the courts of the Crandon Park Tennis Center, where the Miami tournament was held, or on the Key Colony apartment complex, a few minutes away on Key Biscayne. However, this was not the case. They were in a much more reserved place, away from any intruder who could photograph or film - at the Continuum South Beach, an exclusive oceanfront condominium where Szymanski taught some private lessons. When del Potro began putting together his bag the night before his return to the court, he noticed that of the six rackets in the bag, only two where strung! It was enough for the first day. Then he threw a headband, a pair of wristbands and antivibrators with the image of a four-leaf clover. He began to remember certain routines that he had lost during his absence. He began to get goose bumps.

Del Potro was enthusiastic with the endurance exercises on the beaches, swimming and jogging in different urban circuits, but he was terrified by how the left wrist would respond when he started to hit balls.

Beyond the confidence that Dr. Berger tried to transmit to him from Minnesota, Juan Martín rehearsed his first shots with colored balls and without pressure, typical of the "Play and Stay" program, designed to encourage practice among young children.

The first day, he hit only 30 balls. The second day, he hit just 40. On the third day, he hit 50.

"Juan Martín had the wrist super bandaged and protected," said Szymanski. "It looked like Robocop. When I went to the gym to lift weights, I pulled and pulled hard, and the wrist held up well. But his biggest fear was inside the court. The conflict in the head."

The initial full-on tennis practice was supposed to be about 30 minutes and at a slow pace. However, it ended up being an hour and a half, and with good intensity. This practice session was on court No. 10 at the Tennis Center at Crandon Park, where it looked significantly less glamorous than during the Miami Open. Some of the courts were not painted, the bathrooms were locked up, there were no commercial tents and the extra stands of seating that towered above the permanent structure of the stadium were absent.

"He was hitting the crap out of the ball," said Szymanski. "He had a lot of frustration, which was logical. He had reached a very high level in tennis and from one moment to another he was without tennis. It was pure fire; He would often insult, curse, but that was a good sign. I was very involved but the key was going to be in his head, in the switch of his mind."

Back in Buenos Aires, satisfied with the progress he had made in Miami, Juan Martín used social media to tell his fans about his first on-court training sessions.

"In the first rallies it seemed to me that instead of a racket I had a hammer. I made the movements as if they were in slow motion," he published. However, above all, he wanted to convey a sense of certainty. "All the effort I do, since I made the decision of the last operation, it is to return to the circuit. The only uncertainty is the date of the tournament. There is no doubt that I will return, the question is when and where."

A few days later, he hit his backhand with two hands once again. And he planned a new stage for his comeback training, in his hometown of Tandil. Del Potro was in full pursuit of hitting his two-handed backhand with as little pain as possible and in the most natural way he could. He dedicated himself to strengthening his forearm and wrist, so as to be able to achieve it. But during most practices he had to rehearse the shot since he had to make a technical alteration to how he would hit his two-handed backhand. He had to hit it more flat so that the wrist was rigid and did not rotate. He needed to have as little movement as possible.

"These days are like returning to my childhood with Negro Gómez when I first learned to hit the ball. I thank you that throughout my career you have always been with me, learning alongside me," del Potro told the local Tandil media.

The man who had trained Juan Martín as a boy was helping him again. Gomez was coordinating del Potro's training sessions on a cement court at a hotel in La Elena, a young neighborhood in the mountain town. His sparring partner was Alejo Prado, a player from Tandil who achieved ATP points, played on the Futures tour and then dedicated himself to playing club tennis in France.

Del Potro and Prado first came to play together when del Potro was 18 and Prado was 15. It had been years since they had seen each other and even more since they shared the same court. When Gómez summoned him to hit with del Potro, Prado did not hesitate for a moment. Juan Martín's wrist was still inflamed and he had to ice it in the middle of the practice. He hit his two-handed backhand with extreme caution.

"He hit a backhand with two hands and then one with slice," said Prado. "He took care of his hand and it was fine."

Del Potro soon returned to Buenos Aires, where the development team of the Argentine Tennis Association, with Daniel Orsanic, Mariano Hood and Sebastián Gutiérrez, took over in Buenos Aires what Gómez had done in Tandil.

"I came across an athlete who really wanted to, but who had spent a lot of time inactive and had a logical frustration because of the uncertainty," said Orsanic. "His mood was not the best and he was not going to be until he was certain that he could compete again at a good level. It was a difficult process, because as soon as he wanted to train a little more, his wrist would become more inflamed."

The hard court at the Argentine Tennis Club was the setting for the training sessions in Buenos Aires. Some of the practices were with juniors promoted by the Argentine national association and others against fellow ATP player Leonardo Mayer.

"I trained with Juan during his times of uncertainty," said Mayer. "After we would hit, when we sat down to drink some water, he asked me about the speed of his shots, if he felt he lost velocity. He was not training full-time at that time, but it didn't show."

When pain in his wrist persisted during the last fortnight of the year, it undermined del Potro's confidence and he stopped his tennis training for the rest of the year. He returned to Tandil to celebrate Christmas with his family and, although he stopped practicing tennis as a precaution, he did not abandon his physical training. At different times of the day he went running through some of the more pleasant parts of Tandil. However, impatience, after so many months of preparation and effort, began to weigh on him.

At times, he felt stuck. "I had to make decisions," he said. "I needed to keep moving forward and renewing my energy."

After analyzing many different people to incorporate into his team, del Potro made a very important decision: he selected Diego Rodríguez, an expert in physiological kinesiology, to be part of his team.

Born in 1971 in Gualeguaychú, he was much more than the physiotherapist of his countryman David Nalbandian, the 2002 Wimbledon runner-up, but he had been "out of the loop" in tennis for three years.

"Before moving on, Juan, I want to ask you something specific. Do you really have the desire to return to tennis?" Rodriguez asked del Potro during their first meeting.

"Yes. Obviously, yes. Otherwise, I would not be looking for alternatives and solutions," answered del Potro.

"Then, if you have the desire, I will accompany you in everything," said Rodriguez. With that, the bond was sealed.

Evidently, the man from Tandil had clicked on his mind and turned to another system of prevention and training.

"Seldom was I with a patient who was so convinced of what he was doing, even with the limitations he still had," said Rodríguez of del Potro.

Many were surprised that del Potro chose to work with someone who had done so for so long and with such good chemistry with Nalbandian, who was his historic archenemy. "Personally, I was not surprised, because I am a health professional, with experience, and many years had passed since David's retirement," said Rodríguez.

Rodríguez and another team physiotherapist, Germán Hünicken, insisted on detecting the risk factors that del Potro had in his body that caused the discomfort in his wrist. They found answers and everything began to flow.

"We explained to him why his wrist hurt and he understood and that gave him peace of mind, because despite the inconvenience, he knew that he was not going to break anymore, since he was working on what caused the injuries," said Rodriguez. "Once you're healthy, you can think about competing. If you do not have your health, you do not have anything. Juan was fine, so he tried to forget about the nagging pains and worked on other parts of his body that were not in optimal condition. He began to tolerate pain."

"It was difficult to find people with so much experience in Argentina that would help me overcome my pain in the wrist, improve my strength and the stability in my hand," said del Potro. "And Diego helped me in many different areas that I needed. We think long-term and between the two of us, we set the goal of finishing out the year without any health issues."

Rodriguez offered Juan Martín a good amount of tools to prevent injuries, recover and regenerate his body after his efforts. This was how stretching, cryotherapy and bandages and tapes were incorporated into the tennis player's routine. It was nothing mysterious, no magic solution, but no less productive.

"There are some tennis players who need a long ice bath and others where a quick one minute is enough," said Rodríguez.

Cryotherapy sessions are used in a regenerative way, looking for a vascular effect, a kind of cleaning of all the waste 'products' that the athlete generates with their physical activity. In addition, the ice baths have an analgesic purpose and leave the body as regenerated as possible for the next day's effort.

The Rodriguez methodology for del Potro included breathing and body posture repair as well as yoga. Juan Martín began to feel more comfortable and physically more confident.

"The breathing techniques and the different postures have an origin in yoga but we have adapted them to the needs of tennis," said Rodriguez. "The posture does not lie. It reflects the real suffering that this human being has. It is body language. What we did with Juan was to locate his body in more efficient positions, which spent less energy, so that it would not deteriorate so quickly. All that came from a well-applied biomechanics."

Since del Potro did not see improvements via conventional physical treatments, he opened himself up to these new methods presented by Rodriguez.

"I focused more on the spiritual part," said del Potro. "Then I started with breathing and with other types of exercises in the gym. I found a new way of training that it allowed me to get the best out of my career and not only to recover from my wrist problems, but also to be healthy. Yoga is already part of my training and the kinesiological treatment of the wrist, which is not only what you imagine, with a device with magnets. I was incorporating into my life and it is something routine, which makes me feel calm."

In any case, the process of caring for the wrist was not minor. Actually, it was much to the contrary. On a daily basis, the 2009 U.S. Open champion invested between five and six hours undergoing different manual therapy treatments. Rodríguez, a specialist in kinefilaxia (prevention and treatment of injuries through movement), had a thought: in tennis, nobody hits the ball with force only with the wrist, elbow or shoulder; tennis is a transfer of forces from the feet to the racket, in which the wrist is one more link. A link that suffers because it is weaker. After the wrist and feet, there is nothing else to compensate for.

"The mistake was to think that the problem was only with the body," Rodriguez said. "What we had to guarantee was that these transfers of forces were made efficiently, economically. And that's how it was done."

It was common knowledge that del Potro and Nalbandian did not get along and were like water and oil. However, according to the kinesiologist, both are united by their common search for excellence.

"There are things that make you realize why they are so good at what they do, although with different styles," said Rodriguez. "Juan and David are both extremely demanding. They were always thinking about how to improve and challenge themselves all the time. That unites them."

Meanwhile, del Potro improved day after day. Those close to him who were with him during these training sessions at the Argentine Tennis Club likened him to a caged beast with the desire to go out and compete. Once the Australian Open was over, after consuming all of the attention in the tennis world in January, Juan Martín started to plot when he would return to the circuit. Physically, he was at a very good level; the drive and the serve retained the power of fire. He only lacked the match practice where he could correct things that had gone awry and learn to compete again in an official arena.

On Wednesday February 3, del Potro, ranked No. 1,041 in the world, took a huge step to his return to tennis. By video message, in the same way he sadly announced his third wrist surgery the previous June, del Potro announced that in a few days he would play again at the ATP 250 in Delray Beach, Florida. It was no accident that his first event would be in Florida. In February of 2011 it was there where he won his first title after the nightmare of his first surgery on his right hand that kept him off the tour for eight months. That title was one of the most emotional wins of his career.

"We have been waiting for this call. We are happy to know that we can have you back here," said Mark Baron, the director of the Delray Beach Open. The tournament already had Milos Raonic, Grigor Dimitrov, Bernard Tomic and Ivo Karlovic in its field but del Potro would really move the needle of interest.

"I still do not know how many tournaments I will play, because it will depend on my health and my physical condition," said del Potro in a three-minute video that immediately went viral. "Just thinking that I'm going to put on the headband, enter a court, make the sign of the cross and look at the sky is exciting, In this time I had a lot of mental ups and downs and complicated moments and almost thought of giving up. But it was too early to throw in the towel."

Orazi, who after disengaging from del Potro's team, was thrilled with the announcement.

"I lived almost eight seasons next to Juan and we were like nomads, because we traveled eight months a year," he said to *La Nación*. "We made many memories together, good and bad. I know him as my son. He deserves to finish his career when he decides. He is already winning when he returns to the court. He is really going to enjoy returning to do all of his small routines such as assembling his bag, putting on his headband or getting warmed up before a match. His return will be great for Argentine tennis."

Independently of the fact that there was no contract between the two, Orazi still helped Juan Martín by supplying him with physical routines and advice.

Tuesday, February 16, 2016 was not another day in the life of Juan Martín del Potro. It marked his first ATP Tour match is 327 days when he faced the American Denis Kudla, ranked No. 65, in his opening round match in Delray Beach. The match was a success for del Potro, more than just his 6-1, 6-4 victory in one hour and one minute.

"I am impressed by the level that I showed tonight, by winning and by the way I played after almost a year without playing," he said. "For being my first match, I was happy.

Winning was a relief, because I doubted many times if I was going to be able to return."

"I want to play tennis for many more years," he continued. "The wrist is fine. I have no pain outside what is normal."

That night in the Delray Beach, the stadium was jammed with Argentines who cheered and chanted endlessly for del Potro. "My next opponent? I don't know... I spent two years at home watching 'The Simpsons,'" joked the tennis player, referring to his second-round opponent John Patrick Smith of Australia, ranked No. 135 in the world and fresh off beating Ivo Karlovic in the first round.

Del Potro went on to reach the semifinals in Delray Beach, also beating Jeremy Chardy of France 6-2, 6-3 before losing to the American Sam Querrey 7-5, 7-5.

After a short break back in Buenos Aires, he returned to the United States to participate in the first Masters 1000 of the year in Indian Wells. In the Californian desert, he won a match against American Tim Smyczek and, in his first match against a top ten player, he fell to the Czech Tomas Berdych, ranked No. 7 in the world, 7-6(4), 6-2. In that match, especially in the first set, the respect that del Potro held from a top opponent like Berdych was still evident. The trip continued in Miami, where del Potro eliminated Guido Pella, at that time the highest-ranked Argentine player in the world at No. 39 by a 6-0, 7-6(4) margin. In the second round, he was set to face Roger Federer, but the Swiss was forced to withdraw with a stomach virus and could not play. Instead, Horacio Zeballos was inserted into the draw against del Potro as a "lucky loser" and proceeded to beat his countryman 6-4, 6-4.

"I did not even know what color it was," del Potro joked when he started training on red clay courts for the pre-French Open European swing of the circuit. It had been since Rome in 2013 when del Potro last played a tournament on the red clay surface that he was raised on, but likes the least. Juan Martín was very encouraged having overcome one of the biggest obstacles in his life and returning to competition but he still did not feel fully satisfied. Self-demanding to the fullest, it did not give him any grace to lose against players whom he previously won without much of a struggle. Before traveling to the clay tournaments in Munich and Madrid, a childhood friend Manuel Mallo made public a video that del Potro had sent to a WhatsApp group that showcased the internal struggle that he still felt.

"And any day, gray and with a lot of rain, a video comes to the group of friends. You think it is one more but you realize that it is a friend of yours giving a more than important message," Mallo wrote on his Facebook wall. In the video it shows the tennis player looking at the camera on the phone and saying: "This is so, guys. One is alone in the gym. There is nobody. There is little desire to train, to get out of bed and not having anyone there for motivation makes everything much more difficult. But pride and self-love are much stronger and I am here thanks to you, who are my friends, and they always bank me when I was very bad. So, now all the effort is so that they can enjoy watching me play and for many more years we are all together fighting because I can be happy inside the court. I send a hug to everyone. If it goes well, great. And if not, let them rest assured that they gave everything."

Throughout the year, the video went viral and was even put forward as an example for motivational talks for corporations. Months after the video was released, del Potro explained more about how the video came to be. "It was during my recovery period," he said. "Without a coach or physical trainer, self-love has to be very great to get up in the rain, cold and wind knowing that you have to go running and go to the court. It was hard for me, it really cost me a lot because doing it alone was more complicated and that day was on the video and it went like that. I decided to record that video knowing that people could take me seriously or they could joke with me for a whole year, It was so sincere and my friends got so much from it and that is why it went viral. A lot of people came up to me to talk about it and I even got videos from people talking about how they were inspired by my words."

In Munich, where it was very cold for the season, del Potro won two matches, one of them over the German Jan-Lennard Struff in his first three-set match in his return. He lost in the quarterfinals to another German Philipp Kohlschreiber. In the Masters 1000 event in Madrid, already with a ranking of No. 274, del Potro won the biggest match of his comeback over No. 14-ranked Dominic Thiem of Austria 7-6(5), 6-3. Thiem was fresh off reaching the final in Munich the week before, buoying del Potro's confidence. After losing in the second round to American Jack Sock, del Potro decided not to play at Roland Garros and instead prepare for the grass-court season.

"My team and I decided that this is the smartest thing," del Potro said.

The grass court swing ended up being very productive for Juan Martín. In Stuttgart, he reached the semifinals after winning big matches against No. 18-ranked Gilles Simon of France and No. 36-ranked Grigor Dimitrov of Bulgaria. At Queens Club, del Potro drew a first-round match against the six-foot-10 inch John Isner, one of the few players taller than him on the ATP Tour. Isner fired 25 aces and won 7-6(2), 6-4. However, it was at Wimbledon where del Potro began to flirt with returning to the top of the game. It was 894 days since he last played at a Grand Slam tournament at the 2014 Australian Open and it was his first appearance at the All England Club since he reached the semifinals in 2013. He lost in the third round to No. 30-ranked Lucas Pouille of France, but defied the odds to upset the No. 5 seed Stan Wawrinka of Switzerland 3-6, 6-3, 7-6(2) 6-3 in the second round.

"Del Potro is back," said Wawrinka without any resentment over the loss.

"After my last surgery, this is like my second or third career in my short life," del Potro said. "It's a great feeling for me. I feel alive."

Wimbledon officials showed del Potro immense respect by allowing him access to the "A" locker room reserved for the 32-seeded players, where del Potro was located during his last visit to Wimbledon. His locker neighbors were Novak Djokovic and Jo-Wilfried Tsonga.

July marked the celebrated return of del Potro to the Argentine Davis Cup team in their quarterfinal against Italy. He had to make a sudden change of surface from the grass of Wimbledon to the slow clay of the Baratoff Club in Pesaro, Italy, a serene city located on the shores of the Adriatic. Del Potro still did not want to play a best-of-five singles match on clay and opted only for doubles duty against the Italians. He and Pella paired for an important 6-1, 7-6(4), 3-6, 3-6, 6-4 win against Fabio Fognini and Paolo Lorenzi. The following day, Federico Delbonis clinched the 3-1 win for Argentina, moving the team into the semifinals against Great Britain. It marked the first time del Potro had played Davis Cup since 2012 when Argentina lost to the Czech Republic 3-2 in Parque Roca in Buenos Aires, a series that ended up breaking the relationship between Martin Jaite, who was the Argentine captain, and with the leadership of the Argentine Tennis Association.

"Emotionally I live each match as if it were the last of my career," del Potro said. "It is physically and mentally exhausting for me at the moment. It is very difficult to forget the problem in my wrist. When the ball comes to my backhand, it's hard not to think about a lot of things, how to do the technique, hit hard, slow or slice."

Was hitting his backhand exclusively with one-hand only an option? "Technically, it's impossible at this point," said del Potro, who had always hit his backhand with two hands. He would persist with the two-handed backhand, even though the wrist problems would not allow him to do so without pain.

The tennis player returned to Argentina after Davis Cup and settled a few days in Tandil. Between rest, roasts and bike rides through the mountains, he understood that the best thing for his schedule would be to skip tournaments in Washington, D.C. and Canada. He wanted to make sure that he would be healthy enough to play in the Olympic Games in Rio de Janiero, where he would use a protected ranking to gain entry and qualify.

"Going to the Olympic Games in Rio is an award that I give to myself after so much effort and for having managed to return," said Juan Martín.

Astonishingly, del Potro drew world No. 1 Novak Djokovic in the first round, a rematch of their bronze medal match from the 2012 Olympics in London.

"Well, I'm going to tell my friends to prepare the barbecue for Monday night," del Potro said to his inner circle, with humor, on the tall prospect playing the dominant Djokovic, who had just completed a sweep of all four Grand Slam tournament titles in a 12-month period by winning the French Open two months earlier.

In a clash of the highest level, del Potro shocked the tennis world by upsetting Djokovic 7-6(4), 7-6(2) in two hours and 27 minutes. The Serbian did not travel to one of the most festive corners of South America to simply dance samba. Even if there were no ATP points awarded in Rio, Djokovic was seeking the title that was missing from his brilliant career: the Olympic gold medal. Djokovic's disconsolate crying when leaving the central court of Barra da Tijuca was a symbol of his immense disappointment. Del Potro had guts and never gave up. He hit demolishing serves at 130 mph. There were no service breaks, but the Argentine had seven break point opportunities. He turned a deaf ear and nothing took him out of focus, not even the Brazilian fans cheering Djokovic's points as if they were goals from Pelé or Neymar.

"I find it hard to believe what I achieved," del Potro said in the mixed zone following the upset victory. "I just didn't want Djokovic to beat me badly. It was a disappointment when I saw the draw, but I'm learning that things happen for a reason." Del Potro's voice was breaking and he showed great strength in holding back tears.

As if it had been necessary to add a bit more drama to del Potro's day, it started when he was locked in an elevator in the

Olympic Village for 40 minutes. A power outage caused him to be trapped and was out of communication with a mobile phone signal. Unable to do anything, he sat on the floor, resigned, until members of the Argentine handball team managed to rescue him. In 2009, during the Australian Open, del Potro suffered a similar panic. It was at night and the Tandilian returned to the five-star hotel in Melbourne where he was staying, pressed the button on the 28th floor and suddenly the light went off, the system was cut off, an explosion was heard. Desperate, he made calls and they eventually were able to get him out....two-and-a-half hours later. His rescuers had to destroy the roof of the elevator car to pull him out.

"I was stuck, without light, and the emergency button was not on," said del Potro of his Australian Open elevator odyssey. "Nobody answered. My voice broke. I ran out of air. I thought I was dying."

This new frightening experience, but in Brazil, could have knocked him out of focus, but Juan Martín took it as a new obstacle to avoid, something he was used to.

"What happened to Juan in the elevator in Rio is very psychological," said Patricia Wightman, head of the Department of Psychology of the National Center of High Performance Sports (CeNARD) and present in Rio during the Olympic Games. "It could have generated a panic attack or have awakened the tiger, as it finally happened. In that place, Juan reacted with anger and that helped him. He has a maximum reference, which is God. He always crosses himself. He is a boy with an important spirituality. Here the Iceberg Theory applies very well: what is above the water is what is seen and what is below is the root. What is sought in an athlete is peace, ease and strength. And below, there is depression, fear, tension and confusion. In the case of Juan Martín, he managed to keep the energy that gave him the restraint."

Following his emotional win over Djokovic, del Potro did not let down. He proceeded to beat Joao Sousa of Portugal, Taro Daniel of Japan, Roberto Bautista Agut of Spain and, in another torrid performance, Rafael Nadal of Spain in the semifinals. In the final, which was a best-of-five-set affair, del Potro finally relented and lost to Andy Murray, the defending gold medalist, in a titanic four-set match 7-5, 4-6, 6-2, 7-5 in four hours and two minutes.

"I never cried so many times in so few days," said del Potro of his eight-day run to the silver medal. "I'm going to my country with a medal. I left everything on the court. I did not have any toenails left. It was the most important week of my career, even higher than when I won the U.S. Open."

There were two factors that weighed heavily in the final: the magnificent performance by Murray, who was playing some of the best tennis of his career having just won Wimbledon for a second time en route to clinching the world No. 1 ranking for the first time three months later and the physical and emotional exhaustion from del Potro.

"Athletes like Juan defy the odds, break the limit and the molds," said Rodriguez. "Injuries are often the language the body uses to tell you that something is malfunctioning. He put things to work in harmony and it ended up paying off."

During the Olympic award ceremony - the podium was completed by Kei Nishikori of Japan, who beat Nadal in the bronze-medal match – Murray said to del Potro, "You deserve it" of his accomplishment and his success, showing his maturity and forgetting their rivalry from the junior days that was not always pleasant.

The inspiring silver medal performance from del Potro at the Olympic Games made a huge impact in his home country. The television ratings were extremely high. Tennis fans followed closely as well as those who did not even know that tennis rackets had strings. It created excitement about tennis in Argentina and brought many people to start to play tennis again or to learn to play. The demand for tennis classes and the court rentals increased at least 30 percent following del Potro's Olympic run. This sort of phenomenon was noticed, above all, in clubs that did not have membership but those who rented courts by the hour and offered open individual or group classes. The explosion occurred in Buenos Aires, but also in the interior of the country. It is true that the spring weather starting in September encourages gets more people to be active and participate in sports, but, following the inspirational achievement by del Potro in Rio, phone calls and emails into tennis facilities doubled. In several clubs, parents arrived with their children hand in hand explaining to the teachers, "My boy saw del Potro play and he wanted to start."

With his Olympics over, del Potro returned to Argentina to be celebrated.

"Now I know that tennis was waiting for me," del Potro said on Monday, August 8 in the halls of the InterContinental Hotel in Buenos Aires during his brief passage through the city. The next day, his hometown of Tandil received him as a true hero. Some 10,000 people populated Plaza Independencia and gave him a moving moment when he came out to greet his fans from the balcony of the Municipal Palace. This time there was no parade for him as they did in 2009 when he won the U.S. Open. Del Potro was exhausted and wanted to avoid complications and uncontrollable crowds. But he did not stop shuddering.

"Do not make me cry once again, enough tears," he pleaded, when in front of the crowd the well-known local journalist Claudio Andiarena, acting as an announcer for the event, reminded him of the constant support of his parents while also mentioning his deceased sister. "Silver medal, heart of gold" was one of the many signs among the crowd of varied ages. As the Tandilians themselves recognize, the city tends to be somewhat cold and distant in terms of popular recognitions. However, at that time, it was paralyzed in celebration of their hometown hero's performance at the Olympic Games.

When Juan Martín was playing the Olympic final, Tandil was almost completely transfixed on the match. Del Potro's efforts inspired almost everyone in the town, especially the students of the San José school, the same one that he attended for many years.

"For the boys he became a giant," said Beatriz Etcheber, del Potro's teacher in sixth grade. "They saw him on TV. They saw him triumph. They saw his fighting spirit. Generally in the student's notebooks, we have them write positive news of the day or good things that have happened, and many times they are about sports. And they have written about Juan Martín in their notebooks many times. The children are drawn tiny and Juan Martin is like giant next to him...There you realize how they see him... Huge, huge, huge. They drew pictures with tennis rackets even though they do not play tennis. That was part of the contagion. When I saw the drawings, I would say: 'Ah, you are going to play tennis.' However, the majority would tell me 'No, but let's go like Delpo.' Imitation at that age is something magical. In the world we live in, with the kids stuck with computers, getting kids excited about sports is spectacular."

Almost at the same time he arrived in Tandil, del Potro received notification that he received a special "wild card" invitation to play in the U.S. Open, despite his ranking at the time not allowing him to automatically qualify. His status as a former U.S. Open champion and based on his results at the Olympic Games accorded him the exemption. Making sure he would be healthy and rested in New York, he withdrew from the event in Cincinnati.

"What happens if after I receive a wild card and I lose in the first round? Or if I play against Sam Querrey and defeat an American? It is a decision that can make many Americans disappointed," he said.

After beating countryman Diego Schwartzman in his opening round match in New York, the Tandilian drew American Steve Johnson, seeded No. 19, and, perhaps upsetting some Americans, defeated him 7-6(5), 6-2, 6-2. He next defeated the No. 11 seed David Ferrer of Spain and benefitted from the No. 8 seed Dominic Thiem quitting with an injury in the second set of their fourth round match. The run of del Potro came to an end in the quarterfinals where he lost to the No. 3 seed and eventual champion Stan Wawrinka 7-6(4), 4-6, 6-3, 6-2. Ranked

No. 142 at the time, del Potro became the lowest ranked player to reach the U.S. Open quarterfinals since Jimmy Connors, ranked No. 174, did so in 1991. When del Potro was finally eliminated – at 1:20 am local time in New York - the Argentine received a magnificent ovation at Arthur Ashe Stadium, so much so that Wawrinka paused to allow for Juan Martín to have his moment by himself after the match with the crowd in New York.

"I know I can still do more," del Potro said. "I have a lot to improve on my backhand. Physically, I was not prepared to play a five-hour match at a Grand Slam. The good thing is that I'm not satisfied."

After the U.S. Open, del Potro's ranking moved up to No. 64. It seemed incredible, but of course del Potro still could do more. Next came the semifinals of the Davis Cup against Great Britain at the Emirates Arena in Glasgow. The opening match of the series would see a rematch of the Olympic final with del Potro facing Murray and this time Juan Martín got a bit of revenge, beating Murray 6-4, 5-7, 6-7(5), 6-3, 6-4. It was one of the biggest matches of his career considering the opponent, the stage and being a visiting team in front of 8,000 partisan spectators rooting against him. Juan Martín had not played a five-set match since he lost to Bautista Agut in Australia in 2014 and he had not won a five-setter since 2010, also in Melbourne, when he beat James Blake. That he managed to sustain the energy and electricity in his legs during the five hours and seven minutes he ran in front of Murray is another miraculous achievement. It was the first time Murray had lost a Davis Cup match on home soil.

Argentina finished up 2-0 on Friday as Guido Pella beat Kyle Edmund, but the British equaled the series with the doubles successes of brothers Andy and Jamie Murray beating del Potro and Leonardo Mayer, and on Sunday's first singles point where Andy Murray beat Pella. It was Mayer who won the heroic third clinching point defeating Daniel Evans that propelled Argentina into their fifth career Davis Cup final and the third for del Potro.

"It went better than we could imagine," said del Potro. After such wear, del Potro returned to the country to celebrate his birthday on September 23 and went to La Bombonera to see the Boca Juniors football team play, one of his most favorite pastimes. With the Davis Cup final against Croatia in Zagreb looming in the future, del Potro confirmed that his next three events would be Shanghai, Stockholm and Basel. In Shanghai, he lost in the first round to the Belgian David Goffin, ranked No. 12, and in Basel, the hometown of Roger Federer, he lost in the quarterfinals to Kei Nishikori of Japan, ranked No. 5. But in the middle of these two events, del Potro did something he had not done in 1,017 days – win an ATP tournament. He won the event in Stockholm, played at the Kungliga Tennishallen, a very traditional venue in the Swedish capital with wooden seats. He beat the American Jack Sock in the final 7-5, 6-1 to win his 19th career ATP event and his first since Sydney in 2014. He received the Percy Rosberg winner's trophy, named for the renowned coach of Swedish all-time greats Bjorn Borg and Stefan Edberg.

"In these thousand-odd days that passed without titles, I experienced the worst things that a human being and an athlete can face - frustration, anguish, sadness," said del Potro.

His performance was overwhelming: he did not lose a set the entire tournament and only lost serve one time, against Grigor Dimitrov in the semifinals.

In Stockholm, del Potro was accompanied by Daniel Orsanic, the captain of the Argentine Davis Cup team. Orsanic, who prayed that his team's main figure would not suffer as much as a scratch before the final, was surprised with the competitive ferocity from his main charge.

"Juan Martín is a great competitor," said Orsanic. "The tournament had some uncertainty because he was bothered with the wrist a little. But he was encouraged after each match. When he won the semifinals, he was a little more concerned. I asked him if he was OK and he said, 'Tomorrow I will tell you.' After the final I asked him the same question, he looked at me, smiled and said, 'Now I do.' Those great athletes, who are above all of the others, have that something extra."

Orazi, who spent so much time at del Potro's side, never doubted him. "Juan is addicted to winning," he said. "Win and it becomes more demanding. I'm sure that personality helped him recover after suffering through so many setbacks. The bar is set very high for him although sometimes you have to know how to have more patience."

Said Davin, "Inwardly I never thought he could retire. I always thought that I would keep fighting to get back, even if it was complicated. When one falls from the place of elite in which it is and not by losing it in the field but by an injury, it is hard. It is difficult to put in your head that you are a 600, a 700, an 800 of the world. Go play a tournament and instead of giving you the main court, you get the 40, that instead of sending you a car to look for you at the hotel, you have to go by bus, they do not give you a room for you alone and that is to share with your coach ... The circuit is cruel in that sense. You're a number."

Del Potro arrived in Croatia ranked No. 38 in the world (he started the year ranked No. 590 and had dropped to No. 1,045 by February.) He had been voted by his fellow competitors as the ATP Comeback Player of the Year at the ATP World Tour Awards, an award he had already won back in 2011. Although the season was much more wonderful than he even imagined, he wanted to put a cherry on the top of this comeback season with a win at the Davis Cup in the last competition of the year.

The Zagreb Arena became the theater of dreams for the Davis Cup, the coveted sports trophy that Argentina had yet to win. On November 25, Marin Cilic opened the series by defeating Federico Delbonis in five sets. Del Potro then equaled the final after defeating Ivo Karlovic 6-4, 6-7(6), 6-3, 7-5. It was the first point contributed by Juan Martín in a Davis Cup final after falling in one match in the 2008 final against Spain in Mar del Plata and in his matches in the 2011 final also against Spain in Sevilla. On Saturday, Cilic and Ivan Dodig left Argentina without any margin for error after beating del Potro and Mayer 7-6(2), 7-6(4), 6-3. Cilic and Dodig had much more doubles experience as a team than the two Argentine singles players and it showed in the key moments of this straight-set win. Sunday, November 27 was judgment day for the Davis Cup. On this day, del Potro wrote one of the most moving chapters of his tennis career by defeating Cilic, the No. 6 player in the world, 6-7(4), 2-6, 7-5, 6-4, 6-3 in four hours and 53 minutes. It gave life to the Argentine team and set up the decisive match to decide the Cup. Delbonis put the final strokes of blue and white paint on the glorious victory for Argentina when he stunned Karlovic 6-3, 6-4, 6-2, establishing the definitive and glorious 3-2 win.

"Thanks to those who did not let me retire, I was very close to not playing anymore, and well... here I am," said del Potro after his win over Cilic, where he trailed two sets to love.

With Diego Maradona jumping and cheering in one of the corporate boxes of the stadium, Cilic was making a martyr of del Potro with his great serve and his ability to move his opponent from side to side on the baseline. Cilic tried to not hit more than two shots in a row to the powerful del Potro forehand so that he could not find any confidence or rhythm. The Croat fans cheered loudly in the stands and relished at Cilic's play. They started to savor the thought of Croatia winning a second Davis Cup title, the first coming in 2005. This strategy worked well for Cilic... until the start of the third set.

Del Potro, who was playing for the first time for all three days in a Davis Cup series, asked to go to the bathroom. He returned fresher after a few minutes, started serving and won the third point of the game with a spectacular "Great Willy" between-the-legs "tweener" lob winner. The shot electrified the stadium and the Argentine fans while causing a shock to Cilic, despite his big lead. After this jewel of a shot, del Potro took a few seconds at the back of the court, wiped the sweat with the towel and remained half-crouched, thinking. "It cannot be that I have to do this to sustain the dream. Does the blessed Davis Cup cost this much?"

From there, the match turned dramatically. Del Potro, who up to that point had an 8-2 head-to-head match advantage in previous matches with Cilic, began to dominate with his forehand, took the net, hammered his serve and capitalized on some of the small hesitations from Cilic, who was born just five days after Juan Martín. Del Potro lost his serve at the start of the fifth set, but found a way to break back immediately for 1-1. Each player held serve with confidence until the Croatian, again, showed his doubt and double-faulted away the eighth game to give del Potro a 5-3 lead in the decisive set. As with their match in the semifinals of the Orange Bowl boys' 14-and-unders in 2002, del Potro was the was the last to smile and clench his fist. He sealed his miraculous victory with a hard serve to Cilic's backhand that the Croatian softly hit into the net. The Argentine team and fan base erupted into an incredulous and euphoric celebration. Del Potro had dressed up as a superhero once again.

There was a moment, in the middle of the raucous atmosphere in the first set, which was a distinct moment that reflected the character of the "Gentle Giant" del Potro. Just 18 minutes into the match at 3-1 in favor of Cilic, del Potro walked over to a ball girl in his corner and asked how she felt. She had just been hit in the stomach by one of Cilic's near 140 mph serves. He asked her how she felt and got a brief positive response. The girl was uneasy and clearly holding back tears. Del Potro, with concern, signaled to the chair umpire that she should be replaced. The girl, touching her belly, agreed and went to the side of the court. Walter Alfonso, the masseuse of the Argentine team, handed her a bottle of water. The spectators, Argentines and Croats, cheered Juan Martín's behavior.

It is difficult to find comeback stories similar to that of del Potro in tennis. There is the case of the Croatian Goran Ivanisevic, who after losing three Wimbledon finals was stricken with a bad shoulder injury and in 2001, after a receiving a wild card and being ranked No. 125, finally won the title at the All England Club. Also, the Austrian Thomas Muster, who was hit by a drunk driver before the final of the Miami Open in 1989 and spent months in a wheelchair, only to return and win Roland Garros in 1995 and become the No. 1 player in the world in 1996. However, the comeback of del Potro eclipses even these two great stories. The magical and successful return of Federer to the circuit in the first three months of 2017, after being off the tour for six months, is not quite as dramatic. Standing up after being on the edge of the cliff of despair is for a few, for people with a special drive and a supernatural inner strength. Those athletes who get out of the dark depths become examples for many to follow and draw inspiration from. Like Bethany Hamilton, who in October of 2003 at only 13 years old, lost her left arm when a large tiger shark attacked her while resting on her surfboard on the beaches of Kauai, Hawaii. Hamilton was predicted for a bright future in the sport and most thought that the accident would end her career. But after the amputation, the American returned to surf in a month and in 2005, adapting some techniques for her new condition, she won the national 18-and-under competition in the United States. Her biography *Soul Surfer: A True Story of Faith, Family and Fighting to Get Back on the Board* was a success and was adapted into a movie. The meaning of resilience is valuable.

According to the Royal Spanish Academy, the word "resilience" means "the capacity of adaptation of a living being in front of a disturbing agent or adverse situation" or the "human capacity to assume with flexibility extreme situations and overcome them." According to the Academy, it is among the most searched terms, but the word is difficult to pronounce in Spanish.

"I learned the meaning and I felt very touched with what it represents, with all my history, with everything that happened with my return to tennis," del Potro said. "That word defines what my life has been."

It is not by chance that during the Olympic Games in Rio, the tennis player became friends with Santiago Lange, a legend of Argentine yachting and a highly respected figure worldwide. Almost a year earlier, Lange, a father of four children, overcame the battle of his life, beating lung cancer. In the Brazilian waters of the Guanabara Bay Lange and Cecilia Carranza were crowned Olympic champions in the Nacra 17 mixed class. When the doctors informed him of what he was suffering from cancer, he was in total denial. He could not understand why since he was such a healthy and athletic person. But he accepted it and battled it. Like del Potro, Lange's is an example of perseverance and courage. One of the customs that Lange has is watching videos of Federer and Nadal on YouTube. But not images of matches, but press conferences or interviews._He identifies with the way of life and the vocation they have. He loves tennis and has a great admiration for del Potro.

"I have followed Juan Martín's entire career," he said. "Everything he did is awesome. In general, I'm impressed by the rhythm of the professional tennis players, who finish a tournament and the following Monday they are in another country competing. It's admirable compared to any sport. But I understand that many times the mind and body require us to rest. Juan suffered in his inactivity, but I'm sure that the rest also helped him to load the batteries."

"Sport helps overcome traumatic issues," he continued. "Two months after finishing the Rio Games, without any pressure, I started running and I swear I could not, it was incredible. I started to ride a bicycle and I did some really bad times. The strength that motivation gives you is key. The case of Juan Martín is the best example."

The six-foot six-inch body frame was scattered on the box spring of the bed. The face was staring straight up with eyes open. It is the month of December of 2016 and from a slot in the blind on the window, rays of the summer sunlight of Buenos Aries entered the room. There were no more demons speaking to del Potro. The alarm did not need go off. Del Potro prepared to get up, but out of nowhere a tennis memory appeared in his head. He paused and smiled. He got up and the day began. He was at peace.

2

The Growth of the
Wild Beast

T andil is a town located in the center of the province of
Buenos Aires at the foot of the Sierra Mountains. Located
230 miles south of the city of Buenos Aries, the city was
part of Argentina's industrial eruption in the 1960s and 1970s.
Metalúrgica Tandil, created in 1947 for the smelting of auto
parts, became an emblem of the town and revolutionized a
territory that consisted almost entirely of agricultural livestock.
During that manufacturing explosion, the company created a
large amount of jobs that boosted the local economy. It came to
have more than forty engineers and two thousand workers. The
magnificent writer Osvaldo Soriano, born in Mar del Plata but
settled in Tandil since he was 19 years old, worked as a night
watchman in that metallurgy plant. In the same company, in the
mid-1960s, the popular actor Victor Laplace specialized in gray
smelting and participated in the manufacturing circuit of exhaust
pipes and cylinders. It is no coincidence that at the highest point
of the Villa del Dique, a place where locals and tourists pass

daily, they erected a monument to the Smelter, made of grey iron, rising four meters and weighing 5,500 kilos. The sculpture shows a worker casting molten metal. During these industrial times, working in metallurgy in Tandil represented one of the best possible labor exits for locals.

For decades, working at the Metalúrgica Tandil represented one of the best labor opportunities for settlers. However, during Argentina's economic crisis and the fall in exports to Brazil, the production decreased considerably in comparison to the Golden Age.

Living in Tandil used to mean listening to the drone of combat airplanes that furiously pierced the clouds. Apart from accommodating a delegation of the Argentinian army in the city, an air force military base was also established in the late 1940s that, over time, became very important strategically in the nation's military defense. During the Falkland Islands war with Britain in 1982 (known as the "Islas Malvinas Conflict" in Argentina), the base in Tandil had a lot of activity as many pilots involved in the conflict were stationed there. One of the 649 Argentinian fighters who died in the Falkland Islands war was José Leónidas Ardiles, who died May 1, 1982 when a British Harrier missile demolished the plane he was piloting before he was able to eject. Jose had adopted Tandil as his home and is included in the list of national state heroes. He also was the cousin of Osvaldo Ardiles, the very famous soccer player and member of Argentina's 1978 World Cup champion team.

"He was a second cousin whom I never met," said Ardiles to the magazine *El Gráfico* in 2010. "He was a pilot and I didn't know about his death at that time, moreover since they said the British had Argentine prisoners, my uncle went to England several times after the war to find out what happened. He never had the answer until one day I received a letter from the pilot who brought down the plane. This man knew of my uncle's inquiries and wrote to me what happened: that my cousin had not had the chance to eject and died. It was a very emotional letter and a gesture I valued very much. And then I told my uncle."

Ardiles was a member of the Tottenham Hotspur football club in England, but due to the war and the abuse he received from British fans, transferred out of England to play for Paris Saint Germain.

During the emotional time the war lasted in Tandil, bombing simulations occurred often. With a major air base in the city, it was very likely to be a target of British forces during the conflict. In the evenings, one would hear the sound of the old siren of the daily Nueva Era, a medium founded in 1919 and whose building is in front of the Plaza Independencia, the main square in the city. Citizens had to turn off the lights in the houses and buildings. Civil Defense personnel had designated heads of each block to organize the different blackouts.

The Mirage airplanes that were stationed in Tandil flew for a last time in November of 2015 when a ceremony was held to bid farewell of the place, in front of retired pilots, families, technicians and neighbors from the city. A big plaza on the street Fuglal 1100 was named in honor of Jose Leonidas Ardiles. The green space that features games for kids is located in the Falucho neighborhood, which is the precise location of where Ardiles chose to live in Tandil.

In the neighborhood, built between 1975 and 1978 by the Falucho Cooperative Housing, two, three and four bedroom houses were built. At first there were not too many amenities in the area and the first settlers were civilians of the Air Force and the Army Battalion, but the possibility of acquiring housing there was then extended to neighbors in general.

In 2017, the Falucho 1 community was mainly a middle-class neighborhood with serene blocks filled with trees, mainly Acacias or Tipas, with paved streets, with all the services and some shops. A thick domestic plum tree with purple leaves painted the front of a modest house with roof tiles at 231 Rubén Dario Street. A wooden garage, a small garden in the front without security bars, a few windows in the front and the walls painted in green. Nothing flamboyant. This was where Juan Martín del Potro grew up. He lived in this modest area during his childhood and teenage years with his parents, the veterinary doctor Daniel Horacio del Potro and his wife Patricia Lucas.

Juan Martín was born via C-section on September 23, 1988 at the Tandil Sanatorium. Eduardo Diez was the 71-year-old obstetrician of Juan Martín's mother Patricia for not only during labor of the baby that later would become an elite tennis player, but also in the births of her two daughters, Guadalupe, one-and-a-half years older than Juan Martín, and Juliet, the youngest of the house.

The life of del Potro was linked to sports since he was a boy. "I dream more about soccer than about tennis," he said. "I dream of making plays in the Bombonera, about making goals, knocking walls with Martin Palermo, one of my idols," he said as an adult and already an accomplished professional player. "But as a kid, I also fantasized about playing tennis and some of those fantasies I accomplished."

Between his house in Falucho 1, the Club Independiente on Avellaneda Street and the San Jose College, behind his school, there was a radius of no more than twenty blocks. This was the circuit that Juan Martín played as a boy.

"I was a child with a lot of conditions for sports," he said. "I had a really good physique for my age and was well coordinated. But the biggest difference I had was mentality." In that, he surpassed his classmates and was always 100% competitive.

"His parents would always go to accompany him whenever he played, this was important," remembered Fernando Aramburu, coaching director of the Independiente children's football team (five against five players), where Juan Martín played between 1996 and 1998. "In a small reduced field I put him in the middle; some people started comparing him to Claudio Marangoni, the tall and elegant midfielder who shined for Independiende de Avellaneda and Boca in the 1980s."

In those times at the Balcarce Racing Club, they organized national championships, which were attended by teams from the region, such as Mar del Plata, Buenos Aries and Rosario. The curious thing was that in 1998 del Potro and future Barcelona soccer star Lionel Messi competed in the same tournament but they did not come to face one another since they were in different divisions.

"Juan was a bug," said Aramburu. "His head wasn't like others. He saw the game, he knew how it was played, and he had fun and was an excellent teammate. In a school tournament in Tandil, we needed one more player in the first half and we won 3-0, and during halftime he tells me: Vasco, want me to be the goalkeeper the second half of the game? Sure, with the body he had in those small nets he would just laugh about it. They didn't score a single goal on him and that's how we finished the game."

Del Potro's team won many tournaments during this time period. Of his soccer skills, Aramburu said that del Potro could "head the ball really good and kicked like a mule. He had an enormous foot; at the age of ten he already wore size 13."

From one day to the next, the life of del Potro's family suffered an abrupt and tragic turn. His older sister was killed in a car accident. Juan Martín was also traveling in the vehicle and was no more than two-and-a-half years old at the time. The tragedy became a topic that all those closest to del Potro avoided bringing up, unless Juan Martín himself talked about. What's more, many learned of the sad situation much later when he incorporated the custom of making the sign of the cross after his wins on the tennis circuit.

"My sister is very important to me. I make a gift to her in each match, the sign of the cross," del Potro said to La Nación magazine in August of 2013. "I have beautiful memories. My family and I don't like to talk about it, but it's very special. I know that she takes care of and guides me, and that always gives me strength."

Some months after the accident, tennis came to the life of Juan Martín. In a time of profound grief in the family, Juan Martín was enthusiastic in pursuit of soccer, but his parents understood that it would be healthy to add another activity, as to channel all of their energies into sport and have the least amount of time for negative thoughts.

This is how Nancy, Patricia's sister and Juan's godmother, approached him one day at the Club Independiente tennis school, which was led by Marcelo Gómez at the time. When she arrived at the club, the tennis class was about to start. "Juan plays soccer here in the club, but he also wants to try out tennis," Nancy explained to Gomez. She gave Juan Martín a kiss and left him there.

The philosophy that the Tandil school had with every little boy who joined was to give him time to try out.

"I put him to practice in front of the wall since he already hit the ball really well," said Gomez. "I asked him if he ever played before on a court and he said no, but that in his house he would practice hitting against the garage door. Juan was six years old and I already realized he had potential."

As the classes continued, Juan Martín stood out in the clinics and in games such as "Around the World" where one hits the ball and runs to the other side of the net to join in a line on the other side of the net again and again and again.

"I realized that he played really well and could be fit to play competitively," said Gomez. Del Potro moved quickly from the pre-competition group to the competitive group. His new classmates were between the ages of 11 and 12 and he was barely eight years old. Nevertheless, he seemed like he was ten. "That let me put him against older players," said Gomez.

During his young years of pure recreation, del Potro combined tennis and soccer.

"He played well with the ball. He would take advantage with his physique," said childhood friend Matias Petersen, one year older than Juan Martín but no longer in contact with the tennis superstar.

"On the field, he played in the front and for his great height, he had good technique and good movements. He was never a child who would draw attention to himself. He was just one of the guys," said former teammate Nicolas Trasante. Del

Potro's teachers at the San Jose school agreed and depicted him as a respectful, low profile, disciplined, happy and cheerful young man who completed his tasks, even when sports dominated his days.

"I remember him with a great passion for soccer; he followed Boca a lot," said Beatriz Etcheber, a sixth grade teacher of Juan Martín. "At the time they were collecting albums of figurines, he liked the drawings of Dragon Ball Z. He was a hard worker and he never skipped out on a single day. His parents never asked me to come pick him up sooner. What he could not do was make compromises for the school plays since he couldn't comply with the school schedules. His mother, who taught at various places in the city, insisted that he study.

The loss of his sister, according to Etcheber, did not cause trauma to his school development. "He never was a sad kid, always full of friends and happy," she said. "To my students I usually tell them that sports entertain and unite but also heal. I think that sports really helped Juan to heal. His growth in tennis helped him a lot and his family too, because the tragedy that happened to them was very, very sad."

There were several nicknames that Juan Martín had as a boy; Stick, since he was tall and thin; Trilli, a deformation of Del-Potrillo; Fatigue, because he was big and his movements looked slow. "As a child he didn't like to put in the effort, like everyone who is talented," said Gomez.

But little by little he became more focused on tennis and practiced every day a little more. The coach did not increase the contact with Juan Martín's parents until he was about eight years old and the improvement in his racket skills became clear. At a young age, del Potro began to compete and achieved great results. "His father started to get excited and that led us to get to know each other," said Gomez. "When the situation started getting serious we started getting together more. In fact, a lot of mornings I would meet with him at his veterinary office to talk and plan out his next steps. They were middle-class workers. They didn't have much to spare and neither did I."

As the months passed by, tennis started consuming the soccer player's time and dedication. Juan Martín went to compete on the 11-field team but he barely played a handful of tournaments before completely leaving soccer.

"There came a time where he had to choose," said Trasante, one of his soccer buddies. "To not let down his soccer buddies he tried to do both, but it was impossible. He was accommodating, maybe he was missing one of the two weekly workouts or when he didn't have to travel on the weekends for tennis, and his father brought him to the games. He was very useful to our team, he made a great difference, but he just couldn't keep doing it. He couldn't be in two places at once."

And then came the fateful decision day. "One day, he went to practice with his father and, a little sad, he told us that he was traveling and that he had chosen tennis," remembered Aramburu.

Del Potro played his first national tennis tournament in Argentina at the age of seven in the city of Bragado. From age 8 to 9 and until he was 13 and 14, he spent a lot of time training and perfecting his shots and movement on the court.

"This is an age in which all of your energies can go astray but the only thing he thought about was tennis," said Gomez "And I was quite devoted to what he was doing because I wasn't married and still had no children and I had time to give. So on a Sunday morning, I heard the landline phone ring from my house because at that time we had no cell phones and he said 'What are you doing Negro, are we going to train?' It was a Sunday at 11 am! It was a call out of context; we never discussed playing at this time. He said he wanted to practice some strokes. He was ten years old! I was young; I wanted to do it so I went. He excited me and pushed me because we came up with goals together and achieved them. I would travel and work with Juan Monaco, who won all the national titles in the 12s and also the 10-and-unders with Juan Martín, so it started to be complex for me too."

The first years of competitions were very difficult. Negro Gómez, already very involved in the diamond in the rough project that was del Potro, asked his father, a greengrocer, to borrow the Fiat Duna used deliver merchandise, to transport del Potro to different regional tournaments. The car ended up with 300,000 kilometers before being replaced by a Renault Kangoo van. They also traveled in the Volkswagen Polo belonging to Juan Martín's father.

Bernardo Palace, a player three years older than del Potro who traveled and played in many of the same events as the future champion in the junior days, said that the green car of del Potro's father was unforgettable.

"It seemed as the car was cooking," he said. "When he would start it up there was a lot of smoke, it was incredible."

The del Potros did not have money to spare. Many times they would go the all-you-can-eat buffets and since Juan didn't have money for his drink, he would go to the restroom and drink water out of the sink. As a kid he was always wearing tight clothes and a normal tennis racket. In that era, to have a Nike shirt you had to move the heaven and the earth, especially in the center of the country.

"One day we went to a tournament in Rafaela in my parents' Kangoo," said Gomez. "The trip was 800 kilometers from Tandil to there and we would drive with Juan Martín sleeping on a mattress in the back of the truck. When we were driving through Cordoba, we got stopped by some tough police officers who asked for car documents and we were fined for speeding because supposedly it was an urban area and we were supposed to drive slowly. But it was an area with only one tire shop and an empty warehouse! The town was ten kilometers down the road. After the discussion, we continued, arrived at Rafaela, and then returned to Tandil and two months later my father got a ticket. He almost killed us! After he lent us the car, we came back with a ticket."

It was common for del Potro to stay in family homes during some of his junior tournaments outside of Tandil. While most of the boys were lounging in bed, del Potro had already gotten up, had breakfast, and was ready to leave for the club. He was reserved and somewhat timid, but took advantage of every minute of training. It was like he was already programmed to compete.

Del Potro was already molding a fierce personality. At times, he looked like a veteran of a thousand battles. Gaston Chiumiento, born in Los Polvorines and three years older than Juan Martín, went on to play in Futures events and club tennis in Germany. He was not able to make it onto the ATP Tour but was inspired by the young Juan Martín.

"I was playing a tournament that gave out ranking points for South American tournaments on clay courts at the Vicente Lopez club that no longer exist," said Chiumiento. "It was a random draw and in the first round I was put against del Potro. Almost no kid my age (14 and 15 years old) knew him. I thought it was just a normal case where they would put a younger kid to play against an older one to warm up. 'He won't last half an hour against me,' I thought. I went to get the balls and waited for him on the court. He arrived and I asked if he was del Potro, like the draw said. 'Yes,' he responded, dryly."

They started to warm up and when del Potro came to the net Chiumiento started to hit balls hard to his body to try and intimidate him. However, this attitude did not have any effect. He saw that the tennis player in front of him was actually really good. He wouldn't miss a ball and his shots were fast and accurate. The match started and it was close. Chiumiento couldn't get ahead so he tried to assert his experience by talking to Juan Martín during the changeovers.

"Where are you from?" Chiumiento asked.

"Tandil," said del Potro, sharply.

"Who is your coach?"

"Gomez."

The match continued. Chiumiento used to play well in that division, he felt comfortable. However, that day was the opposite.

"What are you doing playing in this category?" The older of the two insisted.

"The Argentine Tennis Association put me in a higher level because in my category I won easily," said del Potro, always looking forward.

They kept playing. Juan Martín already had the nuances of a professional player: he was organized, he had his towel, his drinks and he was serious. They sat down again and before Chiumiento could ask a new question, del Potro interrupted him.

"Excuse me. I do not usually talk to my opponents during matches."

With great effort from both sides, the match ended with Chiumiento winning, but he never forgot that day. What's more, he arrived at his house and the first thing he told his family was the demeanor of del Potro's serious, skinny face. They did not face each other again.

Sports journalism gave Miguel Ángel Calvo the opportunity to get to know players in Tandil who stood out at a young age. As the editor of the local newspapers *El Eco* and *La Voz* and founder of the magazine *Tennis Tandem*, he was among the first to interview Mariano Zabaleta, a standout Argentine player who ranked as high as No. 21 in the world in 2000. Then came Juan Monaco, who ranked No. 10 in the world in 2012. Then, del Potro arrived.

"From a young age, they made him play up in the older divisions," said Calvo. "He was so good that winning 6-0, 6-0 against players his own age didn't give him any experience. The shift took place in a G3 tournament, in Coronel Suárez. At no more than 11 years old, he played in the final against another boy from Tandil, Matías Magnasco, who was 14 and two heads taller, and Juan Martín won. It was very striking. At the time, I spoke with his father. It meant a lot; everything had clicked for Juan Martín. He always kept moving forward, there was never a setback in his career, except later, due to the operations on his wrist."

"Juan was very docile about everything," he continued. "He paid a lot of attention to Negro Gómez. Eventually I ended up interviewing him in the living room of his house in the Falucho 1 neighborhood, surrounded by the trophies he had won. But at first, he was not used to my questions, did not say much. He just gave short answers. He was surprised to see his photo in the newspapers. He was rather shy as a boy, but once, before an important match, he told me something that stuck with me. 'I know my serve is not going to be broken.' He was a winner since he was a kid."

As del Potro enjoyed greater success in junior tennis, he began to convince himself that tennis could be his career and way of life, especially during a South American 12-and-under tournament in Porto Alegre, Brazil. The national Argentine team, captained by Juan Carlos Yunis, finished as runner-ups with Juan Martín, playing No. 2 singles, winning most of his individual matches and was awarded as the most valuable player. The competition was played by zones and the two winning countries, Argentina and Brazil, faced off in the final.

"The team lost the final because the Brazilians drove them crazy and insulted them," said Gomez. "'Argentines are shitty, they're jerks,' they shouted, even at young del Potro. I almost threw punches at people. The police came and it was a big controversy. In the third set, Juan could not take any more of the nerves and suffocating heat. He actually fainted and did not finish the match. He was lying on the floor and got taken out on a stretcher. The tournament ended, we went back to the airport and saw José Luis Chilavert, the famous Paraguayan football player, and I said: 'Look, Juan, there's Chilavert, let's take a picture with him.' I liked how he stopped. Juan was with the second place medal hanging on his neck, so Chilavert asked us where we came from and we told him what had happened. He was waiting for the same plane as us and told us: 'That's what you have to get used to, because if you do something right there are many people who are envious and will try to say bad things, to make you perform badly. But that strengthens me. You do not know the things that people tell me behind the bow, and I don't give it any importance. You have to do the same.'"

Juan Pablo Yunis, the son of the team captain who played No. 1 singles on the squad, recalled that Juan Martín was an "introverted" boy, who was always "one step ahead" in tennis, and was always excelling.

"He was good from a very young age," he said. "He was not someone who burned out at the age of 16. He maintained his progress. Since he was a boy, he made it look easy, with great timing and good coordination despite his height."

Yunis, whose uncle Francisco coached standout Argentine players Carlos Berlocq and Renzo Olivo, remembered the afternoons at the tournament in Porte Allegre where they took advantage of the Gremio Náutico União club's huge pools to take a swim and stop thinking about tennis for a while.

"The local crowds at that tournament were…intense," he said. "Some smoked in our face when we approached the fence to look for a towel, to try and intimidate us."

Back in Buenos Aires, it was the tennis player himself who stated that he wanted to dedicate more time to tennis training and drop out of school. First, he told his coach, and then his father. The hardest part was convincing his mother, who, on top of it all, was a teacher.

"But are you crazy? Do not even think of it! What will you be, a donkey?" Patricia del Potro cried when the three of them told her the idea.

As a boy, Juan Martín did not like his mother to watch him play matches. He adored her, but her presence made him nervous, even though the woman did not express her opinions. His father would accompany him to the tournaments, but he would sit some distance from the court where his son played and did not say anything, win or lose. Gómez said that Daniel del Potro never approached him with technical questions. He also said that from the beginning, he said he would not travel abroad and that he wanted Gomez to go with him.

"Many sacrifices were made for him to travel," said Gomez. "I was very hard working. When I left for a month to Europe with Juan, I left my wife here with nothing, with a hundred pesos. I knew he was playing for me, I knew that the boy was going to be really good. We did not have sponsors. It was difficult to raise money, the family helped, the trips were very hard. We went to the cheapest hotels there were. It was very hard because he suffered. We went to some good caliber tournaments and the rest were too expensive to attend. And Juan wondered why we could not do this or that, why we could not go to another hotel and it was hard to explain, because he was a kid. It was a huge responsibility to be abroad with him being so young."

Juan Bautistia Barboza, a year older than del Potro and born in Olavarría, played junior tennis along with del Potro. He and Juan Martín knew each other well and trained together. At the ages of 12 and 13 years old, they were the No. 1 and No. 2 singles players on the Federation Center team and used to get good results.

"Juan was disciplined," said Barboza. "He did what he was told and that was very important for his development. He was different and it was noticeable that if he encountered no pain along the way, he would be very good. He did not like to train very much, but he competed very well."

As a junior, del Potro had a predilection for steak and sneakers, both of which he cared for as if they were a pirate's treasure. Omar Téllez, secretary—and often captain—of the Federation Tennis Center, remembered a junior match of del Potro's where he was being beaten easily, which was a rare event.

"I went over and asked him what was wrong, if he felt bad," he said. "'Do not worry, I am studying,' he told me against a fence. He had lost the first set, but then won 6-0 and 6-1. He had those options as a boy, putting the ball where he wanted, at a faster pace than the rest. And physically he took advantage because at ten years old he was more than ten centimeters taller than the other players in his division."

Daniel del Potro asked Téllez to protect his son if there was any talk in the group about the death of his older sister.

"Juan suffered a lot," said Téllez. "The few times he talked about the subject, he cried. We all supported him."

In September of 2000, del Potro played in an international junior tournament sponsored by Nike in Sun City, South Africa, a place similar to Las Vegas located 190 kilometers from Johannesburg, with luxury hotel complexes, casinos, golf courses and artificial beaches. The entire area is located in the middle of the African savannah with a stifling tropical climate. Juan Martín, Negro Gómez and Juan Pablo Armado, a player two years old than Juan Martín, all traveled to the event. It became a custom for Spanish players to get together to chat and relax with the Argentines. Among the Europeans was Rafael Nadal, who swept the 14-and-under division. It became a tradition to meet in the hotel rooms to watch movies and the kids would sometimes get into trouble. In was here where the relationship between Nadal and del Potro started to form. They even went on a safari together, among lions, elephants and rhinos.

The tournament ended for Juan Martín in very unusual circumstances. He was winning in the final of the 12-and-under division by a 6-1, 5-2 and 30-0 margin when his opponent, the Australian Todd Ley, was stung by a bee. The match was then suspended for 15 minutes so that he could receive medical attention. And, when play resumed, the Argentine could no longer play the same and lost 1-6, 7-5, 6-2.

During that trip to South Africa, Juan Martín brought gifts to some of his school teachers back home. José Passucci, general director of the school and, at the time, del Potro's history professor said, "At the time when he began to travel, he came to school sporadically. But what really caught my attention was that he was catching up right away. He was always available and earning good grades. That intention to fulfill responsibilities, sports and studies was a concern of his parents."

However, Juan Martín's interest in learning about math and science started to wane. After his outstanding performance in South Africa, sponsors began to take an interest in him. His mother Patricia began to understand that it might not be possible for her son to go to school every morning. She began to look for alternative programs so he could study remotely.

Del Potro was a very active boy who was always trying to play or compete. He challenged even Gómez in tennis. "When he was 12 years old and I was close to losing, I did not play him anymore," said Gómez with a smile. He played mini-tennis, basketball, cards and raced in swimming. And there was always some reward at stake: a soda, an ice cream or a cookie.

"Once we went to play the tournament Les Petits As in France and they left us at the airport about 20 hours before the flight departed," said Gomez. "The number of card games we played--al truco, Escoba, Chinchón—in that free time... was crazy. We played for one euro and he was owing me 50. He focused on something and wanted to do it. And if he lost, it was worse, because he wanted to play you again. And again, and again. He was 12 years old and I was an adult, so it was very difficult for him to win. But he insisted, he insisted. It was a setback. But for tennis that characteristic was good, because if he lost, he would get angry on court and tell you: 'In the next tournament I want to play against him again and beat him.' He was obsessive. He loved the challenge of trying to beat the best or the oldest. And of the great players, it was the same. His challenge was always to beat Roger Federer, Andy Murray, Novak Djokovic or Rafael Nadal. Winning against the No.50 in the world did not interest him. He was already mature for his young age. He made me think of a much bigger player, because he had thoughts of being one of them."

During his training, del Potro competed mostly against better and older players. He played up in the 12-and-under division when he was young and would beat 14-year-olds when he was a 12-and-under player. At the age of 13 in 2001, he won the 14-and-under stage of the COSAT circuit in Argentina and Colombia but, being self-critical, felt discouraged because he did not do well as well in similar tournament in Europe. He began to rethink several situations that he explained with great clarity.

"I did not have my act together," he said to *El Eco de Tandil*. "I have many friends and I have a good time with them. We get together and I like to share the same things and there came a practice where I was thinking that afterwards I would play with all of them without paying attention to my obligations. To win in tennis, one must sacrifice many things, like missing parties with friends."

He was barely 13 years old, 13…and he already reasoned that way. He felt and accepted the tradeoffs.

"The pressure exists and I know that both my family and friends or my coaches are quite aware of me, but the real pressure I put on myself and it does not bother me," he said. "On the contrary, if I did not have it, I would be stuck."

In 2002, del Potro's conquests extended to Chile, Uruguay and Brazil. In the middle of the year, he was ranked No.1 in South America. But it was not a simple matter to participate in these tournaments. Argentina was going through a deep economic and social crisis and the del Potro family juggled to try to pay the expenses. After the tournament in Paraguay and the financial constraints, Juan Martín had already planned to return to Tandil, but received financial help from the father of Daniel Vallverdú, who over the years became the coach of Andy Murray and Grigor Dmitrov among others.

"I was lucky and I found very generous people," he said. "In Paraguay, when playing doubles, I became friends with a Venezuelan boy, Vallverdú. We won the 16-and-under title and his father offered to pay me everything so that I could travel to Brazil for two weeks. A phenomenon, a gesture that is not forgotten. Thanks to the help I went and won the two tournaments, the Gerdau Cup in Porto Alegre and the Banana Bowl in San Pablo. In addition, we left as doubles champions at the Banana Bowl."

And he went further, with a maturity that exceeded his young age: "I had to get my act together, each game I knew that maybe it was my last. I have no support from the Association or a sponsor. Everything was done with effort."

On June 6 of that season, after del Potro won his first title in the 16-and-unders, an article in *El Eco de Tandil* newspaper was written about him titled: "Del Potro, Always The Best." And the text described what was already palpable about its virtues: "The fields of the University Club of Mar del Plata witnessed the phenomenon of del Potro, who, other than the quarterfinals against Damian Listingart, devastated every opponent who crossed his path. In the final, the crowd waited for the favorite of the match, Matías Gianella, to prevail, but he could do nothing to stop the attack of the Tandilense, who made the upset almost a formality and sealed the match with a convincing 6-0, 6-1."

Also in 2002, with 34 official matches and 33 victories and clearly one of the top Argentine junior players, Juan Martín traveled to Europe, on a scholarship, to compete for five consecutive weeks between July and August in four countries: France, Holland, Belgium and Germany. He won the title in Des Hauts-de-Seine, in the French community of Rueil Malmaison (Kei Nishikori was one of the players he defeated along the way). He also won the title in Hasselt, in northern Belgium. Immediately, the Prostejov World Cup arrived. As the No.1 singles player on the Argentine team, Juan Martín put up a terrific performance to help the team rank third among the sixteen participants of the tournament in the Czech Republic. He won in four of the five singles matches he played and triumphed in all five doubles matches. In that contest, del Potro played with a Head brand racket. Representatives from Wilson saw him play and the following year, began a sponsorship agreement with him. The sponsorship, after some see-sawing, continues in the present day.

In the 1980's, Professor Juan Carlos Menchón, who worked for the Independiente soccer team, joined the Pérez Roldán tennis school and was one of the first in the country to put together a specific physical preparation system for this sport. His son, Ignacio, followed the same path and, while studying, helped his father at the academy of the Tandil club. There, Menchón helped to train Juan Mónaco, Machi González and del Potro among others. He put a lot of effort into preparing Juan Martín for the physical demands required to excel in tournaments across Europe. In return, the young tennis player recognized Menchón publicly in the local media.

"He always cared about me, wrote me mail and also left me with a training plan," said del Potro. "There are times when in practice one complains of being tired, but all the effort that is invested ends up becoming a great support."

After an extremely productive season, his last goal remained: the Orange Bowl in Miami. Del Potro had already beaten most of his potential opponents, but Negro Gomez, before traveling to the Ezeiza airport in Buenos Aires, and from there to the United States, demanded a bit of restraint.

"Juan has many possibilities and expectations are high, but the idea is to go and play, with the ambition to get as far as possible without having the extreme pressure of having to win this or that," he said.

On November 20, Juan Martín packed his bag and, among the clothes, shoes and rackets, placed two objects that served as his good luck charms: a necklace of beads that had been purchased the previous year in Europe and a rosary that Julieta, his younger sister, had gifted him. Before playing in the Orange Bowl, he had planned to participate in the Eddie Herr tournament in Bradenton and the Prince Cup in Miami, all on hard courts.

"I know it will not be the junior tour, there will be many of the best in the world, but I like it, it's what I want, to measure up against them," he said. "I have plenty of confidence. If I put everything out on the court I can win, or I can lose. But it will be because the other player played better than I did."

Before leaving for the airport, he took a photograph that would eventually cover the editorial offices of the newspapers and websites: at the front door of Negro Gómez's house, with his right arm resting on the chest of his dad's polo and a racket emblem hanging from his left shoulder. In the photo they both smile, as though knowing what would come in a few weeks.

It was not the first time del Potro had played in the Orange Bowl: in 2001, he reached the quarterfinals. In 2002, on Christmas Eve, he arrived as the No. 12 seed, but he did not care about favoritism. With courage and a strong mind, he knocked off his opponents one by one. In the semifinals, he gave a real beating to the No. 1 seed, the Croatian Marin Cilic 6-1, 6-3. In the final, the Tandilian was challenged by the Russian Pavel Chekhov but it was the Argentine who posed with the trophy, as per tradition, with the cup full of oranges over his head, after triumphing 6-2, 7-6(5). Del Potro became part of a list of winners that also included fellow Argentines Guillermo Vilas, Gabriela Sabatini, Guillermo Coria, Brian Dabul, Patricia Tarabini and Florencia Labat.

At that time, journalists at Argentine newspapers received the results of international tournaments through three ways: by the news agency cables, by fax, or directly by calling the tournaments. That December, something special happened: Alfredo Bernardi and Marcelo Maller, journalists who covered tennis for the newspapers *La Nación* and *Clarín*, respectively, individually called the Orange Bowl offices. They were informed that del Potro had lost in the quarterfinals. But, at the beginning of 2003, José Luis Tata Echegaray, director of Head for Argentina, the racket brand Juan Martín was using at the time, called Bernardi, surprised, to ask why an article about del Potro's victory had not been published. After the journalist's astonishment and the explanations of what had happened, on January 28, *La Nación* published an article entitled "The news that escaped," where the story was told. And it was noted: "He traveled in silence, with a low profile and returned with all the glory and with the trophy."

The big tournament victory began to accelerate the talk about what Juan Martín should do with regard to school. Back in Argentina, a barbeque was organized to celebrate the end of the school year and, above all, to discuss and try to devise a plan for next season. Everyone attended the barbeque, including Juan Martín's parents, Negro Gómez and both Menchóns. Each gave their opinion. Patricia, who had many doubts, had been in charge of finding out more about homeschool programs.

"She was convinced and became more open to the idea of home school," said Gomez. "She started looking at programs for Juan Martín and found the program SEADEA (System of Distance Education of the Argentine Army, created in 1989), which ended up being a solution."

Said Nacho Menchón, "What helped Patricia reach her decision, I think, was the desire of her son to devote more to tennis. With the good players, they are their own engine. It's a characteristic. Others you have to push. The good ones are marking with you their desires to improve. They see what other players are doing outside of training."

The more hours Juan Martín spent training, the more the plan intensified. He left the Independent Academy program to do something more personalized. This included Gómez, naturally, and also Menchón for the physical part. It was time to make another leap. And finally, there were changes in Juan Martín's school plan. He left San José in the second year of high school and enrolled in the distance system.

In November of 2009, after del Potro's life changed after winning the U.S. Open, María Angelica Scarpelli, then coordinator of SEADEA, published a letter in *La Nación* entitled 'Un ejemplo.'

"Mr. Principal:

In February 2003, a young man from Tandil came to our institution to pursue his secondary studies. Why did a 14-year-old boy want to study in a system of distance education? Long hours of training and participation in national and international tournaments prevented him from studying at school. He did not have the status that he has now earned, but the morality and commitment that characterize him. During the years he studied with us, beginning in December of 2006, he never failed to comply with his academic obligations. He was one of the hundreds of boys and girls who travel through our virtual classrooms: athletes, musicians and artists in general who, in addition to a strong commitment to their field, are committed to their formal education along with others who do so for reasons of health, geographical isolation, or living abroad. Juan Martín del Potro is our pride and has become a symbol of that Argentine youth that we want to highlight."

In 2003, the windmill continued to rotate with intensity. Del Potro won the prestigious Avennire tournament in Milan in the 16-and-under category that was once won by Bjorn Borg, Stefan Edberg and Ivan Lendl. In the final, Juan Martín defeated Cilic once again 6-4, 6-3 (he had previously sent Italian Fabio Fognini packing earlier in the tournament). In that season, he began to get involved in the first level of pro tennis on the ITF Circuit. Between August and September, he played in three "Futures" events in Argentina, losing against Diego Cristín, Pico Mónaco and Juan Ignacio Destefano. Of course, not everything was optimistic and joyful. Juan Martín, between the ages of 14 and 15, greatly missed his family every time he traveled. But he really suffered, even when he was accompanied by Gómez, a second father to him.

"Once in Italy at an event, they gave us lodging in a small town of 500 people called Cividino," said Gomez. "Ugo Colombini, who was Juan's manager, managed to book our stay there. We stayed in an apartment that was depressing, without windows, dark…We arrived at night. There was a church, some city buildings, a supermarket, a pizzeria, and a telephone which was on top of these shops. You had to buy a card to use the phone, which was difficult to use. We were going to buy something to eat but everything was closed. We went back to the apartment and there was only one package of noodles. I boiled water in a pot and we ate them without sauce, without salt, without butter, without anything. We went to bed and Juan started to cry, badly. I was in the bed next to him and I said to him: 'Well, Juan, stay calm, tomorrow we will talk with your father, if he sees we are having a bad time, we will go back.' This was a lie. We had to travel for six more weeks. He had to try to play as much as possible. He cried all night. I sat on the bed with him and tried to calm him down, but I could not. He was almost 15 years old and I was 33. I had no experience. This was my first time in Europe. The next day I called his father and said: 'Daniel, your son is crying, he is depressed. What do I do?' And he replied: 'Keep him there, try to calm him down.' After he began to settle in, we met some friends and he calmed down little by little. It was a very tough tour, but we endured."

Apart from financial limitations, del Potro's program was derived from a philosophy that had produced good results, such as the Tandilian school of tennis. In the tournaments played around the country, while some coaches accompanied five or six players, Juan Martín was accompanied by a coach (Gómez) and a physical trainer (Menchón).

"We were all convinced and eager," said Menchón. "We did not take it as a risk. Negro had been a little limited working with Pico Monaco because the weak economic structure of the country had pushed him to have to go abroad to train. We all saw a possibility to transcend. Juan went to tournaments and played in the heat, he trained more hours than most…Maybe he caught others' attention, but not because of us, because Guillermo Pérez Roldán and Zabaleta came to see him. He was consistent emotionally, even though he had some bumps, but they were a product of his age."

According to those close to del Potro during the time when he competed on the Futures tour, he was not very interested in winning in South American Tennis Federation events. His motivation was different. He wanted to try to be one of the best players in the world. When competing in Argentina, he thought about playing in Europe and the United States.

"He analyzed a lot when he traveled," said Menchón. "He always compared himself with Novak Djokovic and Andy Murray and Gael Monfils."

On May 10, 2004, at 15 years and just over seven months old, del Potro earned his first ATP point. It was in a Futures event in Argentina with $10,000 total in prize money at the Highland Park Country Club of Pilar. There, del Potro overcame world No. 1,048 Matías Niemiz in the first round 6-4, 6-2 to become the youngest Argentine professional player.

"His celebration was not euphoric, he took it easy, as if winning many more points would come," said Niemiz.

During that season, del Potro played seven more Futures events, but continued playing on the junior circuit as well. He was a finalist in the Bonfiglio event on red clay in Milan and played in the junior French Open, where he lost in his opening round match to South Africa's Fritz Wolmarans, and at junior Wimbledon, where he lost in the second round against the American Scoville Jenkins. At the junior U.S. Open, he drew Andy Murray in the first round and lost 6-0, 6-1.

On the Futures tour in Campinas, Brazil, del Potro showed again that he did not scare easily. In November, already with two points on the ATP Tour and ranked No. 1,318 in the world, he had to match up in the first round against Henrique Mello, a local player who had been born in that area of the state of San Pablo. As expected, the crowd harassed the Argentine from the first game. Del Potro ended up winning 6-0, 4-6, 6-4 and, as soon as he won, he threw his racket up in the air and shouted: "For you, Maradona!" The police had to escort him off the court because the Brazilians wanted to lynch him, literally.

At 15 years old, almost a decade after denting the door to his house in the Falucho 1 neighborhood with tennis strokes, del Potro had not stopped growing or improving. Sometimes he had to jump thorny obstacles and sometimes he progressed naturally. He was ready to take a new step in his career.

3

The Initial Ascent

Mariano Zabaleta and the Moroccan Younes El Aynaoui hit their last groundstrokes of their first practice session of the day on the hard court inside the University of Tandil's gym. The practice was part of a demanding preseason workout preparing for the start of the ATP Tour circuit in 2000. A thin and good-looking boy observed this practice session with great attention and heard a question directed at him from Argentina's No. 1 player.

"Do you play tennis? Do you want to rally a little?"

The boy, just 11 years old, accepted. He took a racket and started hitting the ball. He did not miss on either the forehand or the backhand. He just did not miss.

"Look at this kid, Eduardo! Look at him!" Zabaleta shouted to his coach, Eduardo Infantino. At 21 years old and ranked in the top 35 on the ATP Tour, Zabaleta worked with Infantino for several seasons and would go on to reach his best ranking of No. 21 during their partnership. Infantino, curious about what Zabaleta was saying, came to check out del Potro. Physical trainer Horacio Anselmi, who worked on many projects with Infantino, also joined. Indeed, they were in the presence of discovering a new talent.

"What's your name?" asked Infantino.

"Juan Martín."

"And the last name?" The coach insisted.

"Del Potro."

The moment is a treasure in the memory for Anselmi.

"He was a boy with the characteristics of successful athletes: he was quiet, self-absorbed and introverted," said Anselmi. "This is a norm with great individual athletes. Time went by, of course, at some point, I told him and his father that something serious had to happen for him to not reach the top 10. I also warned them that he would have to take care of certain physical aspects throughout his career, because of the fragility of some parts of his body."

Anselmi, part of the physio staff for the Boca Juniors soccer club in Argentina for more than 30 years, said he was very impressed the first time he laid eyes on del Potro.

"From the first moment, I was really struck by his attention," he said. "He had a coordination and concentration of another level. He was not a little boy with a fixed gaze. He was not scattered. And you do not have to be a tennis expert to realize that his shots almost always landed in the same part of the court. His strokes sounded clean and he moved towards the ball without waiting for it. His feet were extremely large for his age and yet he was not clumsy."

While going through that stage of training, del Potro underwent some tests of endurance with Anselmi, who, later in 2006, would be his official physical trainer when Infantino became the young player's coach. Anselmi followed the same routine when evaluating these young athletes: making them throw stones.

"It was one of the tools that I used," he said. "And obviously, Juan Martín sent the other athletes to the hill of the devil. That is a characteristic of great athletes. I remember telling him that I liked fishing and that he would probably throw the rod too far. He threw those stones 50 percent farther than the rest. That spoke to his coordination and his power. When someone is good at throwing stones, as an athlete the talent is clear and it is a check payable to the bearer."

Navigating the seas of the lower-level ITF Futures and Challenger tournaments was not an easy feat for del Potro, even with his vast talent and potential. Unexpected obstacles were added to the challenges already on the road map.

January of 2005 was, literally, a disaster for him. He spent the first few hours of the New Year in San José, Costa Rica participating in the Copa del Café, a traditional tournament that has been played since 1965 on the courts of the exclusive Costa Rica Country Club. Juan Martín, at 16 years old, defeated all of his opponents to reach the final where he faced the Dutchman Robin Haase. The match, on a night with very unpredictable weather conditions, began with Haase winning the first set 6-3. The second set went the way of the Argentine, also 6-3. In the final set, Haase leveled the match at 3-3 but gave del Potro an advantage when he hit a ball out on break point. The Argentine shouted and clenched his fist because he was now ahead 4-3 and had the chance to go up 5-3 if he served well. However, unexpectedly, although the line judge had called Haase's ball out, the chair umpire Rodolfo Chacón corrected the shot as good. Juan Martín was furious and began to argue with Chacon, but this did not change his decision. The public, who unanimously supported the Tandilense, began to whistle their displeasure with the chair umpire. It was a total embarrassment. From there on, del Potro lost his concentration and the fight was against the umpire and not Haase. It ended with del Potro losing the final set 6-3.

"Argentino came to the Coffee Cup but was robbed," was the title of the journalist Harold Leandro's article in the Costa Rican newspaper *La Nación* in San José.

After such sloppy calls, the rain caused the match to stop twice, until the organizers had no other choice than to move the match to an indoor court in the same complex. Both players accepted the new conditions, since the next day they had to fly to other tournaments (del Potro was heading to a Futures in El Salvador). The match ended at 1:05 am on Monday, January 10.

Bernardo Palacios, who had trained as a boy with del Potro in Tandil, was one of the witnesses of that unpleasant experience. What's more, he continued working at a tennis academy in Costa Rica. And that was how, on one particular day, Palacios was preparing to start a class with a new student. When he saw him arrive, he froze, remembering he knew the boy from somewhere. And yes…it was Chacón, the controversial umpire, who, far from being inflexible in that final, confessed: "That day I made a big mistake. I do not know what happened to me. It came out of my mouth to say 'Good;' I saw the ball like that, I swear. Poor Juan Martín…I will always remember the damage I did to him without meaning to."

In December of 2009, del Potro and some close friends chose Guanacaste Beach, on the Pacific coast of Costa Rica, to relax. The Costa Rican press, upon learning of the presence of the new U.S. Open champion, looked for him in the airport, but they barely got a few words out.

"Everything was very nice, beautiful places. I missed the flight to Buenos Aires. Bye," del Potro merely said, behind dark glasses, before getting into a taxi. Better not to stir up what had happened five years before…

Thiago Alves was born in São José do Rio Preto, a town in the populous state of São Paulo in Brazil. Almost six years older than del Potro, his best individual ranking was No. 88 in 2009, but he retired because a right shoulder injury took him out of the sport, so he instead started a tennis school. Right-handed with a two-handed backhand, Alves defeated the Argentine for the first three times they went head-to-head (in 2004 at a Futures in Santos, Brazil and in 2005 in Futures events in El Salvador and Guatemala) and he did it again in October of this last year at the Challenger in Quito. Juan Martín, at least, took revenge by winning the final of the Futures Chile 2 at the Palestino Club. A week before, in Santiago, the Tandilense had won his first professional championship, also in Chile, defeating the local Jorge Aguilar 6-4, 7-6(6).

Alves had a method for rattling players with less experience: by playing shots that took his opponents several meters behind the baseline. This tactic was especially effective on slower courts. With del Potro, despite the fact that he managed to beat him four times, he found it difficult to put his strategy into practice.

"The first time we faced each other, I was coming back from a shoulder injury, but I was still playing at a good level and had been competing for two months," said Alves, who played Davis Cup for Brazil in 2008 and 2013. "When I saw that I had to play against a 15-year-old boy, I imagined it would be an easy match. But we started playing and I was not able to take that statement back. He stayed in front of the baseline, and I put up with a lot of shots before winning the third set in a tough match 6-7, 7-6(5) 6-2. We played many more times. He already had the winning mentality and was ready to be great. He was a very calm and focused boy. He did not hit as hard as today, but I was impressed that he always tried to play modern tennis. Also, he did not give any games away. He already behaved like a professional. He did not look like a junior."

While maturing and building his big personality, del Potro did not go unnoticed by his peers because of how he acted on and off the court. Juan Bautista Barboza, who practiced often with said: "Nobody wanted to face him on court. Almost everyone wanted to kill him, because he was superb, which is typical of a good tennis player. Off the court, it was quite different. But when he played, that was the only thing that mattered to him. He was very clear about what he had to do, and between Negro Gómez and his father, they had it under control. A great advantage he had in his career was that he almost never traveled alone. Once, when I was 15 years old, I traveled alone to Brazil to play for a month. I returned with my head on fire, I came back to my house and did not want to play anymore."

Germán Gaich, a Spaniard who reached No. 740 in the rankings in 2009, had the pleasure of beating del Potro a few times in junior events and was impressed with the potential of the young boy.

"Juan, since he was a boy, was very intense on the court," he said. "He did not want to lose for anything in the world. He was extremely competitive. We killed ourselves playing against him. He was a good person and did not have bad intentions. His father accompanied him to all the tournaments. He was very overprotective. With Juan, we made jokes. Once, I grabbed a pen and drew an obscene figure on his racket string and he did not realize it. He started playing and people in the audience laughed. Later, when he realized what was on his racket, he wanted to kill me."

During the difficult financial times, Palacios brought a Bartom portable stringing machine along with del Potro to save money from the tournament stringing service. It was carried like a suitcase and weighed five kilograms.

"Juan had a mentality superior to the rest. He understood the game, he knew when you were going to get angry and did not get intimidated," said Palacios. "In 2004, he played a Futures event in Brazil and I started winning 4-1, but I got angry quite easily. He knew it, and waited, patiently, to sidetrack me. He ended up beating me 6-4, 6-2."

But who really represented karma for del Potro during his training and transition to professional tennis was Juan Pablo Armado, who was two-and-a-half years older than Juan Martín and lived in Mar del Plata. Far from being enemies, there was a friendly bond between them, because when del Potro competed in the seaside town, he stayed at Armado's house.

"We slept in the same room, we got up together, we had breakfast and after a while, we had to face each other in the final," Armado said. "That happened several times. I won a lot of matches, like 20. He did not miss a ball, but he did not serve strongly and it was easy to attack on him. He had a good backhand and was a great competitor. I don't know what happened, but even if he started beating me, I would come back. I did not feel that our rivalry was a classic or anything like that. Perhaps because one of us was from Tandil and the other was from Mar del Plata, two nearby cities. One could think that there was some feuding between us, but he did not feel it that way. I would never have imagined when we were kids, the level Juan Martín would reach. It's a phenomenon. We have traveled together in the same car many times to tournaments in Cordoba or Buenos Aires. We left Tandil first and continued on the same route to Mar del Plata. He was already a fierce competitor. He did not like to lose anything."

Said Negro Gomez, "Juan Martín hated with all of his heart to lose to Armado. Besides, Armado beat him and enjoyed telling him: 'I have you as a son.' Those matches were tremendous."

November of 2004 was marked by fire in del Potro's mind because, after taking so many losses, he managed to finally beat Armado for the first and only time. The score was 7-5, 6-4 in the first round of the Futures event played on red clay in the Rosario gym and fencing club.

"It was a very emotional match because of the history between them," said Ignacio Menchón, at that time Juan Martín's physical trainer. "They played with good sportsmanship, having played against each other so many times. But when Juan won, Juan Pablo told him something like: 'Well, at last you beat me…I want a rematch soon.' And Juan Martín replied: 'I do not think so…you will not be able to get revenge anymore, because soon I'm going to stop playing these tournaments.' And it happened like that, because Juan Martín's level continued to rise and they did not face each other again. Juan Pablo had a good career, but not of the magnitude of Juan Martín. That revenge never came."

Armado reached his best ranking on tour as No. 225 in July of 2009, shortly before del Potro won the U.S. Open. He played until he was 27 years old, when osteochondritis forced him to retire. Together with an engineering friend, he started a sports management company that received advertising in different international markets. But one day, a Russian millionaire client hired him to develop his young son's tennis career in Dubai. Armado travelled to the Emirates in January of 2015 and settled in as a resident. He has had some eccentric side projects, such as giving tennis lessons to a businessman who had a loose tiger in his garden, or being hired by a sheik for five hours to help him buy tennis gear.

Indeed, Armado was left with the desire to have the rematch. On May 1, 2005, del Potro won his third Futures title, but his first in Argentina. He defeated Damían Patriarca 6-0, 3-2 by retirement in the final at the Jockey Club of Córdoba.

"La Voz del Interior," the Cordovan newspaper titled their article about the Argentine's victory: "Del Potro stole the scene."

"Tall and slim, with a young face, weary and good-natured, he demolished opponents until he won his third final of four at this level of tournaments. Undoubtedly, he was a different player," wrote the journalist Fabián Sacarelli in the article about del Potro's standout week, where he beat, among others, Leonardo Mayer and Horacio Zeballos.

After that victory, the Tandilense played another Futures tournament at the Cordoba Lawn Tennis Club, and immediately after traveled to in Europe. First, he played in the Roland Garros junior championships, where he fell 6-4, 6-2 in the quarterfinals to a more experienced junior player from Scotland named Andy Murray. It ended up being the last junior match of del Potro's career. The next year, del Potro would qualify for the main draw. After his junior swan song, del Potro reached two consecutive semifinals at Futures events in Italy: Verona and Bassano. He then never competed at that level again, moving up next to play on the Challenger level, first in the town of Reggio Emilia, where he lost in the semifinals to Martin Vassallo Argüello 3-6, 6-0, 7-5. He also played in the final in Campos do Jordão and the semifinals in Belo Horizonte, both in Brazil, until he captured his first title on the Challenger Tour in Montevideo, Uruguay.

Negro Gómez soon became known as one of the best coaches in Argentina. Having carved, like the best craftsman, a precious stone like del Potro was a great achievement for the coach. Of course, he also fully dedicated himself to the project. He pushed himself to the limit, until he no longer could.

"Everything revolved around del Potro," Gomez said. "I left my family for him. I went to the tournament in South Africa for two weeks and left my wife with my 10-day-old daughter. My son started walking and I did not see him because I was with Juan at a tournament. Those are the things one expects later, when the player matures, is great, and retires, and says: 'This person sacrificed a lot of things for me.' While they are playing they do not realize it, because they do not have time."

"Juan Martín gave me great satisfaction," Gomez continued. "In a tournament in Bahía Blanca we were sitting together scouting an opponent, because he liked to analyze his opponents, and he said: 'This kid plays well, but if you trained him he would be much better.' That stayed with me. It was a nice recognition, in his way of speaking. Then, when he grew, that changed. It happens as it does with parents. You go from being the idol, to an asshole, to having no idea of anything in life. That was what happened next, that broke our relationship, and sent him back to Buenos Aires to train for a few months. There are things that I do not compromise on."

During a few months of that season, Juan Martín left Tandil and settled in a small area of the Recoleta neighborhood along with Menchón, who was responsible for taking care of him. Del Potro was afraid of walking along in the Federal Capital, so Menchón accompanied him to the bus stop. They took route 130 together, which left them a few meters from the Buenos Aires Lawn Tennis Club. Juan Martín was going to train at the National School of the Argentine Tennis Association there and his physical trainer continued to work in those communities, gyms, and pools. In front of the building where they lived, there was a butcher shop. Menchón and del Potro both became good clients and friends of the owner. What's more, Juan Martín often expected that Menchón would come from working with other athletes, to working with the employees in the shop. Juan Martín felt good about being in the butcher shop. It created a sort of connection to his maternal grandfather, who was known for looking after the local Villa Italia shop in the Tandil neighborhood.

Also, the butcher's brother had a pizzeria and del Potro, passionate about sweets and desserts, got used to bartering tennis hats for dulche de leche. The tennis player spent much of his free time with Leonardo Mayer, who also attended the AAT National School. Many days at noon, they went to the supermarket in that area, saw what was being offered in the food court, and had lunch.

"Juan was very quiet, maybe that's why we got along so well," said Menchón. "For those things in life, it took me a long time to go back to that neighborhood after we left. And the boys from the butchery remembered and said, 'To think that skinny boy was Delpo.' Everything was put together, based on the belief of Juan Martín's father that he would become a great tennis player. They say you have to plan for and visualize the end result it will happen and it was like that. He was armed with all of the resources, with the intention of what he was after. There were indications that he was different, yes, but the certainty that he was going to make it big…was relative. Looking at his everyday life, it's easy to say he was special. But there were a lot of guys that were very good and did not make it. At the stage where I was with Juan, when he was between 14 and 17 years old, there was a marked difference with those players in Europe, like (Gael) Monfils, Murray, and Djokovic. Their games were superior. That worried Juan a little. He wondered if he would ever match their level. 'These skinny boys play like something else,' he said. Time showed that he was up for the challenge."

At that time, many specialists in racket sports were uncertain about the effect of del Potro's height. They thought it would be a real disadvantage. However, the Tandilense was very willing to work and adapt his physique to a high level of competition. Menchón was convinced that his training on red clay helped him directly in that way. The training and coordination work on that surface required strength and endurance.

"If you analyze the movements of Juan Martín and compare it with players of similar height, he is a star," he said. "Obviously, if you compare him with David Goffin, Juan moves like a tractor, but the Belgian is about 20 centimeters shorter. I was with him when he won the Challenger in Montevideo. Because of puberty, he still did not have enough muscles, but when he started to become much stronger, the footwork he had practiced helped him to become accustomed to his size. For a long time, he said he was 1.92 meters tall, when in fact he was about 1.97. Now, he is 2.02 or 2.03 meters tall. It's a complex experience for players who are tall. Today, it is very normal to see very tall players, like Marin Cilic, Milos Raonic and John Isner. But before, when Juan Martín was 17 or 18 years old, it was not so common and his build was considered atypical of a tennis player. As a child, he carried the pressure of everyone. Really, we had to see if he would have the ability to play with the cards stacked against him in the pros, which is not the same."

But sure enough, that boy, ebullient and self-assured on court, had a treasure in his racket and his mind. He was a very valuable treasure.

4

A Polished Drive

Wimbledon's press room was always jammed packed with journalists every time Roger Federer sat down for a press conference. It was, however, an unusual circumstance when he sat down in this environment frustrated under his white cap adorned with his signature "RF" logo. As the No. 2 seed and defending champion, Federer had lost in the quarterfinals to Tomas Berdych 6-4, 3-6, 6-1, 6-4.

The great Roger was furious inside; he showed it with his eyes. It was the first time since 2002 that he did not reach the Wimbledon final and was forced to wait, at least a year, to try to match Pete Sampras as a seven-time champion at the All England Club. As if this were not enough sporting torture, Federer felt acute back pain in the match, converted only one of the eight break points he was able to muster and, above all, had been punished from all angles by Berdych, then ranked No. 13 in the world.

Hours later, *The Guardian* newspaper published: "Berdych hit 21 winning shots from the baseline, burning the grass with a fast and flat blow that made Federer shake when he hit the ball."

Downcast, waiting to be somewhere else, Federer heard a question that led him to address, immediately, the response to another figure.

"Some of these big, flat hitters seem to be having an effect on you. Do you need to alter your game to adjust to that?" was a question from one of the journalists.

Federer, a winner of 16 major singles titles at the time, took a few seconds, thought, and, despite the fact that the Czech's cannon shots still resounded in his mind, he put Juan Martín del Potro as the standard for big hitters on the ATP Tour.

"If I'm healthy I can handle those guys, you know," he said. "Obviously it's a pity that del Potro is not around, because I think he would have a run at world No. 1 or a run at another Grand Slam. It's unfortunate for him."

During those days in 2010, del Potro was off the circuit, recovering from surgery on his right wrist. This was not enough, of course, for him to be forgotten on the ATP Tour. It is curious, but the version of the coup that came, without a doubt, one of the most explosive in the history of tennis, as the Argentine, at first did not have much pepper. And the only things that provoked del Potro were jokes, insecurities and headaches. When he was a boy and Marcelo Gómez polished him with a chisel in the clay courts in the Independiente Club in Tandil, del Potro was already different than the rest. Not only because of the competitive attitude and the power he showed at such a young age, but because of his movements. Tall and slim like almost no other boy in his class or division, the movement of his arms and legs did not go unnoticed. His limbs were like the blades of a windmill. When you are a child, or above all, a pre-adolescent, some comments or jokes can be cruel and harmful. One does not have much awareness of the effect that a comment out of place can have on someone else. Del Potro had a flat forehand, with very little topspin, and the boys his age—and also the biggest ones—told him it was "horrible."

"Everybody, even the players, told him that his forehand was ugly, but because it was different," said Gómez. "They burned his mental state badly and many did it out of envy, because they already saw that he was going to beat them all. There were a couple of Colombian and Venezuelan guys who he played against in the tournaments and they told him that he could not play. It was a disaster. Juan had many doubts about his forehand and hearing criticism of it did not add to his confidence. Juan was very upset by what he was told. He was always annoyed by that, all of his life, and he did not like it when they criticized or called him out for how he played."

According to Gómez, some coaches—Argentines and foreigners—who saw the potential in del Potro also criticized him and told him that he needed to make adjustments with his forehand. However, this was with the best intentions and with future partnership opportunities in mind. Officials with the Nick Bollettieri Academy in Bradenton, Florida in the United States wanted to accept him, but they could not get him to come.

While shaping his own philosophy as a coach, Gómez, the creator of del Potro, understood that in the near future, tennis could go down a path that was not exactly that of the traditional Argentine school. That is to say, in modern tennis there was no place for strokes with massive topspin.

"I was convinced that tennis would be dominated by those who hit the ball flat and hard," said Gomez, who went on to become a developmental coach with the Argentine Tennis Association and also his nation's Fed Cup team captain. "It was the time when Andre Agassi and Pete Sampras were still active. In addition, I saw that in the future the game was going to be played more on fast and hard courts. I saw that the red clay had an expiration date. So, although Juan Martín handled himself very well on clay, evidently he had to play a modern, flat tennis game."

Convinced, Gómez proposed to Juan Martín a series of technical modifications to look for that offensive nuance designed for hard surfaces.

"At that time, Juan was a boy and could freely try whatever he wanted," said Gomez. "He played with topspin but then we armed him with a flat forehand, with a classic grip, with the idea that he would take the ball on the rise and come to the net. I liked that and we started to practice it."

This was a stage for stroke development and for creativity, without the severe pressures that were approaching. But when del Potro started competing on the Futures tour and his game was already beginning to make noise, he began to play the high and deep balls with that flat drive that he was trying to perfect every week. Of course, as Juan Martín still did not have the strength he would have later, those shots from his opponents challenged him, left him out of breath and pushed him behind the baseline where he could not attack. And he suffered. Then, during this transitional time in his game while he was gaining muscle strength and physically growing, he returned to hitting the ball with more topspin. However, this was just for a short time when he was 16 and 17 years old. It was like a momentary inversion. He took a step back but del Potro was quite clear about moving forward.

Already flirting with becoming a top professional, del Potro was an ardent competitor. Between 2004 and 2005, he managed to move up more than 900 spots in the ATP rankings. Specifically in 2005, he finished as the youngest player in the top 200 at No. 157 in the ATP rankings at the age of 17. During this season, he also won his first Challenger series title. It was in Montevideo, Uruguay on the red clay at the Carrasco Lawn Tennis Club on November 6, after beating Serbian Boris Pashanski 6-3, 2-6, 7-6(3) in the final.

"My biggest idol is Marat Safin and from my country, David Nalbandian. I would like to one day be able to play like them," del Potro said on December 15, 2005 after being invited to participate in the Peugeot Cup, an exhibition event that brought together the best Argentine players—and some foreigners—like the Brazilian Gustavo "Guga" Kuerten—at the Buenos Aires Lawn Tennis Club. "I try to imitate the ease with which they play, the concentration they have. When they are mentally strong, it is impossible to beat them."

In the qualifying round of the event, del Potro lost to Agustín Calleri (who was 12 years older, and by then No. 52 in the ATP rankings) by a 3-6, 6-3, 6-1 margin. In any case, the result was not important. He was already beginning to be noticed among the older players. Juan Martín wanted to train with all of the greats and he got a lot out of practice. He was trying to improve all the time.

"He drew attention because of his focus despite being so young," said Argentine player Martín Vassallo Arguello, a top 50 player in 2009 and a training and doubles partner of del Potro despite being nine years his senior. "He always played to win. If he lost, he always wanted to play again. His forehand was already flat. And the most valuable thing is that he played with it at a time when Argentine tennis was not so clear about the path he was taking."

"Until that moment, he was a great competitor," said Argentine compatriot Pablo Fuente. "He entered the court and fought like he had a knife between his teeth. He moved very well for his height, and he hit a big backhand, but at that time, he did not earn so many points with either his serve or his backhand."

Born in Necochea (a city on the Atlantic coast, located about 170 kilometers from Tandil) and eleven years older than Juan Martín, Fuente built his tennis career in Futures, Challengers and European clubs. He met del Potro almost by chance, in 2005, when he traveled for two months to Tandil to do a pre-season with Máximo González, another player born in the mountain town.

"One day Negro Gómez came and told me he had a kid who played well and asked if he could play with him for a few days," said Fuente. "I did not know Gómez well and Juan Martín even less. We started to play a set and he hit a shot into the street. He went to go get it, but he didn't immediately return. I was about to go out of the court and make sure he was looking for the ball and finally, after ten minutes, he comes back. I wanted to kill him! I look at Negro, as if to say: 'What is he doing?' We continued training. At first, I had a brazen attitude. But later, over the days, we forged a good relationship. He was going to a Futures event in Chile and I was going to the club matches in Europe for eight months. He was worried, he said: 'It's going to go badly, they're going to kill me with sticks.' I told him: 'No. Calm down. You're playing well.' It seemed to me that he played well for his age. I went to France and, at the time, I looked at their results and I saw his name under 'Champion,' 'Champion,' 'Champion.' I could not believe it."

Fuente coexisted perfectly with del Potro's uncertainty and maturity.

"I was with him when he stopped being a baby and became a man," he said. When he returned to Argentina after his experience in Europe, at the end of 2005, Fuente received a call from Daniel del Potro, Juan's father, with the proposal to join his training team.

Del Potro had returned to training at his home club after spending six months in Buenos Aires at the AAT National School run by Gustavo Luza. He maintained his relationship with Gomez, but there was still some instability in his game. For that reason, in part, another person needed to step in and enter the team to act as a sparring partner and also to moderate specific circumstances.

Fuente found in Daniel del Potro's offer an opportunity to start learning the job where he could continue a life in tennis in the near future—as a coach—and accepted. He helped the Argentine in the 2006 preseason and began to travel to some tournaments, alternating and sharing trips with Gomez. That season, del Potro began to transition quickly into becoming a professional tennis player.

A first opportunity to play in a main draw ATP event happened in early 2006 in Viña del Mar, Chile on red clay. He defeated the Spaniard Albert Portas, ranked No. 117 in the world, 6-2, 6-2 in just 55 minutes. Four years earlier, Portas had been ranked No. 19. A few days later, Martín Jaite, the tournament director of the ATP event in Buenos Aires, give him a wild card invitation to play and del Potro took advantage. He made a good impression in his first-round match against Spain's Juan Carlos Ferrero 6-2, 4-6, 6-4, in two hours and 17 minutes.

"Del Potro battled an adversary who had played more than 450 matches on the major circuit, and won 11 titles, including one at Roland Garros," the newspaper *La Nación* reported. "His opponent was No.1 in the world and is now ranked No.18. This match exhibited some of his strengths, a very good two-handed backhand, a strong drive, and some signs of youth—hasty decisions. Ferrero, when he had to step on the accelerator, did not hesitate. At 4-4 in the third set, he unbalanced del Potro with two impeccable returns and found the necessary break to pull ahead."

Said Fuente, "Juan had a lot of nerves before the match. If my legs were shaking, I can't imagine his…he played the feature match, with the court full and everyone watching him as a great Argentine prospect. But since he hit the first ball, I noticed a total change. We were with Negro Gomez and we looked at each other. There, really, I took into account how good he was."

Fuente welcomed the teenager del Potro to his home in Necochea for many weekends, where the Argentine also had close relatives. Even when he was in the coastal city, del Potro called Fuente several nights to ask if he had contacts in a local nightclub in order to be allowed to enter without having to wait in line.

"It was comical when that happened, because I would call a friend and say: 'Che, let it go; remember that this kid is going to be good.' I was not contracted with Juan, I was free to tell him anything. At that time, he began relationships with girls and, being older than him, I advised him a bit. As if I were an older brother."

While del Potro continued to advance, improving his ranking and competing against more experienced professionals, Gómez and Fuente confirmed that his strokes still had their weaknesses.

"There was a flaw but it didn't hurt much," said Fuente, later the coach of Juan Ignacio Chela when the Argentine reached the quarterfinals of Roland Garros. "It was with his forehand grip that he used to prepare for the shot but it was that blow started to beat the better players."

Even so, del Potro continued to improve and move his way up in the tennis world. He passed a major psychological test in a three-set match in the final round of the qualifying rounds at Roland Garros after playing in many Challenger-level events with little luck and not being able to earn enough ATP points to earn a direct entry into Grand Slam tournaments. The final-round qualifying match was against a Frenchman Ludwig Pellerin and del Potro was terrified.

"I saw him in the locker room and the tears fell," said Fuente. "I told him 'Rest assured that you are going to play this tournament a thousand times.' In the end, he played a spectacular match, he got into the main draw where he played Ferrero again in the first round. He lost (6-3, 2-6, 6-2, 6-4) but he played very well. Everyone congratulated him."

However, in the midst of del Potro's satisfaction of qualifying on the Grand Slam stage, the fragilities of his efforts returned.

"Well, Juan Martín, with that forehand we're not going to beat anyone," said the Italian Ugo Colombini, who was already his manager, without a filter.

"But you can't come to me and say this! Everyone congratulates me except him. What happened?" del Potro said, offended, not wanting to look at Colombini.

That French Open marked a pivotal point of "before" and "after" for del Potro. Several adjustments were going to happen. That's why, after those days in Paris, Eduardo Infantino, from the tennis program in Tandil run by Raúl Pérez Roldán, became Juan Martín's main coach. Infantino previously worked with Nalbandian, Mariano Zabaleta and Younes El Ayanoui. He had already collaborated with Gomez a few years ago, but now he would be in charge of taking the reins of the thoroughbred horse that had the potential to win many races.

Fuente continued to be part of the group for a while, and Gomez, who felt tired after so many years of effort, continued as a sort of advisor. One of the first changes that Infantino worked on was his forehand, gradually altering the grip.

During that 2006 season, del Potro began to feel the pressure of the expectations on his shoulders. He started collecting small financial guarantees to play events despite the fact that he had not yet won any ATP titles.

"Everyone tells me I'm a phenomenon but, in the end, if I cannot win matches, I won't reach the top 100," del Potro mumbled in front of his team. To add insult to injury, in the midst of his search for a tennis identity, Juan Martín had reactions that sometimes hurt him. This happened at the Biella Challenger in Italy, one week after Roland Garros.

"Win a match, win another, hit the forehand well, moving forward, without twisting the grip. Until he has to play with Simon Bolelli in the quarterfinals," Fuente said. "In the warm-up, Colombini arrived on the court and Juan saw him and started to rally and I noticed that he automatically changed his grip and started hitting like before he did before working with Infantino. I said to Eduardo: 'What are you doing? He's changing the grip back.' He started the match, lost the first set, looked to Ugo and threw him off the court. He lost the match, finished about nine o'clock and then we went to practice until like 10:30 pm, hitting the forehand flat as we did before. Juan respected Infantino very much, but he had had that attitude towards change because he was a very spiteful kid. You did something to him and he remembered it. He had in his memory what had happened at Roland Garros."

Del Potro finished the season ranked No. 92, becoming the youngest to finish in the top 100 at 18 years and two months. Infantino had taken charge of many important tennis projects in his professional life, but he had huge expectations for del Potro. One of the first things he did was tackle the forehand. Then, the serve. He got inside the court to show Juan Martín where he wanted him to hit the ball. He threw the balls himself with his hand and made corrections at the same time. Del Potro showed a fabulous capacity for retention and did not need to hear the concepts again.

"We worked on many things, but especially the forehand grip, which was very much gone," said Infantino. "It was corrected, but the change was gradual. I suggested moving it to a slightly more normal position. We also worked on the serve and it improved. He threw the ball too high and he did not push enough with his legs. He was not as effective as player should be of his height and did not have variety. It was very important that he improve his legwork, because that was what allowed him to move around the court quicker and take command of rallies, beyond his spectacular timing that often allowed him to play with little movement."

But the one who really developed the great change with del Potro's game was Franco Davin. The coach, who had also attended Pérez Roldán's tennis program in Tandil and coached Gaston Gaudio and Guillermo Coria, took on a new challenge in February of 2008 after the Australian Open when del Potro defaulted his second round match against David Ferrer due to a lumbar vertebra fissure. In addition to changing his hairstyle (he stopped wearing long hair), the Tandilian used the recovery time to begin to accommodate the philosophy of a new forehand.

"Juan's forehand was bad," said Davin, who did not accept that a tennis player who was so tall used a closed grip, which still did not allow him to always play on the baseline against the best players. Del Potro, according to Davin, had a phenomenal two-handed backhanded but in order to hit the forehand, he was delayed a few steps.

"That was when he had trouble with the better players on tour," said Davin. "A guy of that physical size couldn't play from behind the baseline. When he would do that, he would be too open handled and it hurt him. But since he is intelligent, I found out he adapted very well. When he started to practice serves he would tell me, 'No, I don't serve over on that side, because if I do that then the ball comes at me in this specific way and that bothers me,' or 'If I were to use a down-the-line forehand, then the ball comes back in a way that makes me run too much and puts me on the defensive.'"

Davin had del Potro play more on top of the baseline and did a lot of damage with his forehand there. With the difficulty of having lumbar discomfort and not being able to compete, Davin squeezed in a period of rest for the Argentine to review tactical and technical questions. The Argentine Tennis Club, in the neighborhood of Palermo, was the scene of these sensitive lessons.

"Juan is very smart and he can tell when you're really teaching him or just scolding him and doing something that is not useful to him," said Davin. "If he sees that something works for him and feels good, he accepts it. Obviously, the process takes time. Juan played a couple of pretty bad matches with his forehand. It was not an overnight improvement. Besides, he had a patchy attitude. The whole weight of being a big guy was embarrassing. It is difficult to be so tall and so young. It's the same in everyday life. Like if you go dancing and you meet a girl and you want to go slow dancing and the girl will stay on your knee. Boys suffer these things. I grabbed Juan when he was 18 years old. He was a baby."

It was during this season that Juan Martin learned to calibrate all of his new shots, raised his percentage points won with his return and became a more aggressive player. It immediately paid off for the boy, who won four consecutive titles on the ATP Tour over the summer.

"You can change almost everything at any time if what you are doing is for something productive," said Davin. "Before, when Juan was taken to the forehand, he had to rely on just returning and started the point with a disadvantage. If he caught his opponent with his strong backhand, he hit crosscourt immediately and he was very difficult to break. Instead, he began to improve a little more on the court, which was not easy because for so long he did not hit with a lot of speed. The important thing was that he wouldn't be frustrated if the changes in his game took a while to show. Juan really wanted to improve."

The forehand of del Potro did not go unnoticed in any match on the circuit. It is a hammer blow that paralyzes and fascinates spectators, who are often left speechless.

"When you've seen del Potro's forehand on your television screen, or even better, in person, you do not forget it," journalist Christopher Clarey of the *New York Times* wrote. His statement was not exaggerated. The wrath of del Potro is the most violent that has been seen in racket sports.

"It's like Godzilla knocking you out of a helicopter," said another United States newspaper, the *Wall Street Journal*.

In 2013, the season where del Potro won four 500-level ATP Tour events, the live coverage of tennis led Marcelo Albamonte, an international coach and specialist in applied sports mathematics, to analyze the winning shots of the strongest players on the circuit. The results of the study, for which he applied the Pythagorean theorem, showed that del Potro had the fastest forehand in the sport.

Albamonte began the study from the start of the tour on hard surfaces in the United States and analyzed the different speeds through internet records and a scales system. For example, Rafael Nadal hit his groundstrokes with topspin, therefore the parabola of his shots is bigger. Albamonte, the coordinator of the Universities Program of the Argentine Tennis Federation and the South American Tennis Confederation, included Novak Djokovic, Roger Federer, Tomas Berdych, Milos Raonic, Tommy Haas and Nikolay Davydenko in his analysis. He used the baseline as the start and measured the meters the ball traveled in between being hit by the players. Del Potro's speed was 110 miles per hour. If he maintained that average, the ball would travel 161 feet. Taking into account the size of a tennis court (78 feet long), a shot usually travels an average distance of 70 feet. After del Potro, Raonic hit the next fastest recorded forehand at

91 miles per hour. They were below Nadal (86 mph), Djokovic (82 mph) and Federer (80 mph).

Albamonte, who has developed reports for coaches like Davin (del Potro, Grigor Dmitrov and Fabio Fognini), Francisco Yunis (Carlos Berlocq) and Gustavo Tavernini (Federico Delbonis) created a detailed analysis of the effects of the players' strokes.

"If we take all of his strokes, except for the serve, Juan Martín's forehand can be one of the most decisive blows in the history of tennis," he wrote of del Potro. "His forehand is so consistent because it wins him so many points. He uses it to take control of the game and force his opponent's error. But why is it more consistent than others with similar power? Because del Potro hits his forehand almost flat and his timing is unique. Other players can hit it flat only from top to bottom and can only do it rarely. Juan Martín can do it almost always and effectively."

Del Potro's forehand travels at a high speed after hitting the court because it doesn't slow down as it travels through the air. For his opponents, it is generally difficult to lift such a heavy ball.

"They have more bad news, because if they hit it too short or lift it too high, Juan Martín returns to attacking with his forehand and definitively wins the point," Albamonte wrote.

When drawing comparisons between the most powerful groundstrokes that have been seen on the ATP Tour, Fernando González, the Chilean Olympic medalist and former world No. 5 comes to mind.

"My forehand, it may have been a bit looser than Juan Martín's, which seems a bit tighter," said Gonzalez. "He plays with a lot of power and one would not like to be on the other side of the court playing against him. I see our groundstrokes differently. Juan's is not as technical, although the important thing is what it generates. I used a little more body, but he is bigger and has more leverage than I had. The forehand is the great shot of tennis. It can be used to dominate and also to create angles."

Agustin Calleri, the world No. 16 in 2003 who also had very strong groundstrokes, said that del Potro's forehand is superior to Gónzalez's.

"Technically, del Potro's forehand always was good since he became a professional," he said. "Being so tall and having long arms, he has great leverage. It is the best forehand in the game. When he was a kid you could already see that his forehand was going to be his weapon, as long as he could polish his movement. González had a great forehand but Juan Martín's is better because he takes advantage of his length and has more range. In addition, he bends his legs well and that is fundamental."

Few in Argentina are more qualified to analyze groundstrokes than José Luis Clerc. The world No. 4 in 1981 inflicted damage to his opponents with his groundstrokes. For him, the key to del Potro's ferocious forehand comes with his weight.

"Juan Martín realized that his forehand is the shot that hurts others, the one that you have to hit a higher percentage of if you want to dominate your opponent and win games and he does it very well," said Clerc.

"His ball is fast and heavy, it is a hammer blow," said Tony Pena, an ATP coach and former long-time tennis analyst for ESPN in South America. "It is essential how much weight you put on your hips at the moment of contact. He also bends very well and he achieves the speed on his shots by breaking his wrist and showing the front of his rackets. Everything follows, obviously, with the great arm support he has."

"Everyone did their thing, but the forehand was changed by Franco Davin," continued Pena. "And it was Juan Martín himself who found himself in a different position when he lost his two-handed backhand after his surgeries. He found himself without a weapon and had to strengthen his other shots. It's like when a person suffers the loss of one leg and with their will, strengthens the other so that they are able to jump even higher than before. Juan's groundstrokes are the most violent on the circuit. It's only comparable to Fernando González, who did not have the same style."

According to Pena, where del Potro's groundstrokes are best fired is from the inside of the court.

"Juan improved his backhand with a slice to hold on since his forehand was not its best," he said. "His comfort zone is when he can hit a shot inside-out. He is also very good during rallies, because he is almost always attentive to being able to change the ball's direction. Power is his maximum virtue because he had a loose arm and released his wrist to finish the shot, which gave him more topspin and an angle. That is the last touch. Once, Martiniano Orazi (del Potro's physical trainer) told me that Juan won the 2009 U.S. Open weighing 225 pounds. That is to say that when the ball hits his racket strings, it is as if he was a truck with a trailer without breaks. It's awesome."

Bjorn Borg's two-handed backhand, the Jimmy Connors return, the Pete Sampras serve, the volleys of John McEnroe and Stefan Edberg, the passing shots of Guillermo Vilas - the history of the art of shot-making in tennis show that the great players are identified by their weapons. With del Potro, the missile that is his forehand is his legacy in the history of tennis.

5

Roger Federer....
From Idol To Friend

At the 2008 Olympic Games in Beijing, a shy 13-year-old boy with glasses approached the swimmer Michael Phelps, then a monster star in the world of sports, and asked to take a picture with him.

The swimming superstar from Baltimore agreed and smiled in a snapshot that the boy treasured. Eight years later, on Saturday, August 13, 2016 in scorching Rio de Janeiro, the Olympics Games was in full tilt. The swimming competition was held in the first week and the Barra Aquatic Stadium was filled by a happy but melancholy crowd there to witness some of the final swim strokes of the amazing career of Phelps. In the final of the 100-meter butterfly, all eyes were on the second lane, where Phelps had just accomplished another personal feat by winning his 23rd Olympic gold medal of his career and his fifth in Rio. But two lanes to his right, a young man ten years younger than him advanced like a battleship. Unperturbed, Joseph Schooling took the lead from the first five strokes, and there was no sign that he was going to abandon it. It was quite the opposite.

The boy, a champion in Singapore who was already competing in the elite divisions, had a year earlier won a bronze medal at the World Championships in Kazan, Russia. Now an Olympic debutant, he held the moment with a temperance that amazed the public. He completed the first length in front, and did not show any signs of weakness. He touched the wall before anyone else, and the clocks indicated that he just set a new Olympic record at 50.39 seconds. Behind him, Phelps, the South African Chad Le Clos and the Hungarian Laszlo Cseh arrived exactly at the same time, but 75 hundredths behind the winner.

The race was the final individual race in the amazing career of Phelps. As soon as the race was over, he immediately congratulated the Singaporean swimmer, who was clapping his hands in the water. Given his breakout performance at 21 years old, Schooling asked Phelps what everyone wanted to know at that time: if he is going to continue competing for four more years until the Tokyo Olympics in 2020.

"No way," said Phelps.

Schooling had just completed one of the most difficult, painful and at the same time coveted missions for an athlete: to defeat their idol. No other achievement generates such conflicting feelings in the spirit of an athlete as defeating the athlete who inspired you the most. That photograph from eight years earlier, in which that Singaporean boy barely managed to smile being intimidated by being in the presence of his hero, began to spread around the world.

On a hot afternoon on Friday, June 5, 2009, Juan Martín del Potro felt an unfamiliar sensation in tennis. On the other side of the set on Stade Phillipe Chatrier stood Roger Federer, who perhaps for the first time did not know if he would be able to beat the Argentine. A few days earlier, the Swede Robin Soderling had made the planets collide by handing the seemingly unbeatable Rafael Nadal his first ever loss at Roland Garros. From that moment on, as if everything followed script, the world understood that it was the opportunity, perhaps the only one, for the Swiss to finally win Roland Garros for the first time. It seems as though it was the sport of tennis that was making an opening itself up to allow for the revered Federer to finally have this chance to win this elusive title in Paris.

Entering the semifinal with Federer, del Potro defeated with sweeping rhythm the Frenchman Michael Llodra, the Serbian Viktor Troicki, the Russian Igor Andreev, the Frenchman Jo-Wilfried Tsonga and the Spaniard Tommy Robredo all with equal force. It was not difficult to guess the strategy of the Swiss maestro. Federer's low slice backhand would make it difficult for del Potro to attack and would give him problems. But, after three sets of powerful and solid tennis, del Potro did not seem to be bothered but what he proposed as his greatest challenge. From the beginning, del Potro gave the impression that the fate of the match was in his hands. But from the moment that story began to play out in a tight match Federer was able to convert in the important moments. He took the last two sets to win the match 3-6, 7-6(2), 2-6, 6-1, 6-4 in three hours and 29 minutes. It was also a great frustration, because both he and Federer and each of the 14,000 members of the crowd—one of them being Guillermo Vilas—felt that for the first time he was in a perfect position to beat his idol. He was crushed and annoyed and the fog that enveloped him after the loss lasted for weeks.

When two days later Federer achieved his destiny beating Soderling in the final, del Potro was already thousands of miles away. Inside, he felt that something big had escaped him. For the sixth consecutive time, he bowed to his hero Federer. But this time, the taste was bitter. Martiniano Orazi, his physical trainer at the time, detailed perfectly the evolution of del Potro's game and attitude when playing against Federer.

"In the Madrid Masters in 2008, on a hard surface, was the match where Juan lost to Roger (in the quarterfinals 6-3, 6-3) where he showed everything he needed to improve, from the fitness to the technical," said Orazi, who still treasures the notebooks with the observations of that day in the Spanish capital. It is that match that marked a before and after for the Argentine's team, the time they noticed, very clearly, what they should correct.

"Juan was winning many matches with very good rhythm," said Orazi. "In that tournament in Madrid, he had beaten Nalbandian in the round of 16, but Roger targeted all of his weak spots."

When he practiced retrieving drop shots, Juan felt uncomfortable. It was not only because he was late getting to the ball but the reason he was.

"With Franco Davin, he worked a lot on his speed and body positioning on court," Orazi said. "The focus was how to move foward for a drop since without feeling clumsy since he was so tall. That was one of the things he felt insecure about. Another shortcoming that Federer showed us was when he set Juan back with his slice. Juan bent at his torso, with his back, instead of bending at his legs and using his quads and butt. Federer also took away a lot of Juan's time. He played fast and did not let Juan lean, or stay in position on the court. There, he was often out of place. Beating Roger, his ultimate idol, was unattainable."

Journalists knew that del Potro had a poster of Federer on his wall as a youngster and having this reverence for the Swiss legend made for a difficult mental task.

Leaning over the low bouncing shots with his torso, when he was supposed to bend his knees, was a real problem for del Potro and it resulted in lots of pain.

"We discovered that's why his back was so stressed," said Orazi. "In previous years, he had problems in his spine precisely because he did not move well. We told him that he had to bend down to a point where he touched the floor with his left knee when he hit his two-handed backhand."

While training for the 2009 season, they insisted del Potro correct his technique. Months later, when he defeated Nadal in the quarterfinals of the Miami Masters, the tennis player saw a photo of him hitting a backhand during the match and immediately sent it to his coaches. "The photo showed his back knee down low while hitting his two-handed backhand," said Orazi. "Effectively, it had improved."

During the period that covered the first six matches between del Potro and Federer, from Wimbledon in 2007 to Roland Garros in 2009, the Argentine cursed and lamented because, in the matches before they would play, Roger won playing badly and by making mistakes.

"Many times Juan yelled at himself and wondered how it could be that Roger was playing badly and still beat him," said Davin. "But from the moment that Juan started winning tournaments and moving up the rankings, I warned him that Federer, Nadal, Murray and Djokovic were going to play badly against many players, but not against him because they knew that he was dangerous."

Federer, seven years older than del Potro, tried to match up against him during the warm-up. He hit a few balls from the back court and then immediately went up to net to volley, as if the Argentine could not keep up with his pace. Indirectly, he hurried to start the match.

"Those things Federer did against Juan, he did not do against players with whom he knew he could not lose unless something strange happened and he played very badly," said Orazi. "Already in the warm-up, Federer marked his footsteps on the court making more noise than usual. 'Pa, pa, pa' were the sounds of his shoes playing faster in the rally. He did this to make Juan feel uncomfortable from the beginning. In addition, once the match began, he immediately began celebrating when a point went in his favor. Those players are very astute and Roger smelled that Juan could be a great difficulty for him."

Another situation that, curiously, began to repeat came before matches in the locker room and that was starting to gain the attention of the del Potro camp, was that Roger was very talkative and the Argentine lost some focus and concentration. What was the end goal? According to Davin and Orazi, it was to intimidate him by trying to impose his figure, his legend, upon him so that del Potro would become somewhat unnerved, despite the good relationship between del Potro and Davin with Federer.

"We saw that every time Federer played against Juan, usually in important situations, he came into the locker room when there were not many people there, he talked, he played cards with us, he made jokes with the group," said Davin. "At first, it did not catch my attention, but then I started to notice that it relaxed Juan and took him out of the focus of wanting to win. That happened, generally, after practice, when we were eating or doing something before entering the match. I saw that Juan was talking to him and losing that internal fire. They talked about watches, because they both share the same sponsor, they talked about rackets, Argentina, Switzerland, or soccer, which Roger is a big fan of. In fact, at the Basel tournament we went to see his favorite team (FC Basel) and he told us that he had given a talk to the players and that was very nervous because the players were all his age. Well, in short, it was like having a nice chat with a friend, but then Juan did not enter with the match with the knife between his teeth. Federer had a clear idea of how he had to play and what strategy to use at any given time, but Juan still needed to have a bit more anger, in a good way. If you are hanging out with your idol, it's hard to beat him."

When Davin and Orazi realized that Federer's routine continued, they met with del Potro and asked him to change his attitude and said that he should no longer sit down and talk with Federer before matches.

"We told him, 'Juan, forget this, you have to beat him," said Davin. "We asked Juan not to pay attention to him, to respectfully get up and go somewhere else."

Juan Martín was far from taking advantage of all of the lessons left by the sadly unforgettable Madrid match of 2008 when they next played at the 2009 Australian Open. Juan's game was in great shape having won the lead-in title in Auckland, but Roger swept him in the quarterfinals 6-3, 6-0, 6-0 in just one hour and 20 minutes.

"I didn't expect a result like this. This is not usual," Federer said after the match in Melbourne. But at the Madrid Masters 1000 that same year, this time on red clay, Federer again won in straight sets (6-3, 6-4) in the semifinals.

About a month later, they would play in the semifinals of Roland Garros, and later that summer, in the historic final of the U.S. Open, which the Argentine won 3-6, 7-6(5), 4-6, 7-6(4), 6-2.

"At the 2009 U.S. Open, Roger tried to get close to him beforehand and Juan did not pay attention to him, but respectfully," said Orazi. "We have all the admiration for Roger but we had to keep a distance." A few hours later, the Argentine would win his first major singles title.

"Federer is a guy who we would always use as reference, because he is perfect in everything," said Davin. "He doesn't give you a game and plays perfectly and shows you clearly where you're having a flaw. For Juan, the type of game he had, Federer was always difficult to play. From the first serve he would put him in an uncomfortable position. He also played shots below del Potro's knees. He varied the heights and the effects of his shots. He did not play any two points the same. For us, it was a good physical and technical test for Juan."

In time, Federer built a sincere sympathy for del Potro, despite the frustrating defeat in the U.S. Open final. For the Swiss, he felt a lot of anger losing that night because the Argentine did not have a good start to the match and was giving out the feeling that the occasion had overtaken him. Nevertheless, he ended up winning the match.

"We knew that Roger was very frustrated after losing that final," said Davin. "He was playing well and Juan was very nervous. It seemed that Roger was going to beat him but Juan ended up fighting."

The jersey of the Boca Juniors team, signed by the players, as well as an Argentine team jersey signed by Diego Maradona, are gifts that Juan Martín gave Federer that the Swiss treasures with great affection. Even more, Federer always defended the causes of the Argentinian. In 2010, when del Potro was in the middle of his long injury recovery after his surgery, Federer was always standing up for him.

"Wrist injuries are complicated and uncomfortable," Federer said to the news agency DPA, while refusing to talk about his personal conversations with del Potro during his absence. "I heard that these type of injuries can last from three to six months. It isn't good for your mind to always be feeling pain for a long time. There's nothing fun about it. He is big, physically. Before, those type of tennis players were serve and volleyers but it's not the case with him. He has a big physical game. He's still growing and constructing his body. He's had so much success and therefore he has a lot of pressure on him."

Before the start of the Australian Open in 2011, the first Grand Slam tournament for del Potro after the operation on his right wrist, Federer didn't doubt that one of the most talked about storylines of the event would be the return of the Gentle Giant Juan Martín del Potro.

"Everything that Roger says about me is good," said del Potro in Melbourne. "We have a great friendship. I crossed paths with him a while ago and I felt goose bumps in the stomach when I went to say hello, because he is a great player and a great person. When I had a problem in my hand, he worried about me and called me. I haven't seen him for a year and it was really nice to talk for a while. He told me to be patient, that after one year it isn't easy, especially at the beginning. He knows about it, I know it, and any other player who have suffered any type of injury."

The link between the two was so strong that it was also consolidated commercially where the two played against each other in an exhibition series in Argentina in 2012. The matches in Tigre, in the north part of Argentina, and in Buenos Aires marked the first time that Federer had visited the country.

"Juan Martín is an amazing player," said Federer to a small assembled group of Argentine journalists in the No. 3 press room at Roland Garros on May 30, 2012, to discuss and promote the exhibition series. When Federer arrived for this specific meeting with the press, it was just after he had beaten the Romanian Adrian Ungur to become the all-time men's Grand Slam match victory leader with 234 wins, one more win than the legendary Jimmy Connors. As a gentleman, Federer waited for all the journalists to be accommodated in the room, and even spoke a few words in Spanish and then continued in English.

"He really improved after his time in the juniors," Federer said to the Argentine press. "He would only use around 60 percent of his abilities. I don't know why he would do that when he was big and strong. But one day he woke up and started to play like a bigger player. From there on he started becoming a different player. We played a lot of times, at Wimbledon first and afterwards in Madrid, I don't remember which was first exactly. He was very smart. I remember when I beat him at Wimbledon and he told me how honored it was for him to play against me. Later, when he beat me in the U.S. Open final in five sets I was like 'This is how he repays me?' He is really nice. I get along really well with him. We've played many times together and especially this year but our best match ever was the one in New York, where we both played our best, and even though it was a tough loss for me, it was a great victory for him."

In that 2012 season, del Potro and Federer played each other eight times. Many of them were very emotional. One of the spiciest encounters was in the quarterfinals of the French Open. They played on the second court, the Suzanne Lenglen court, and del Potro let a great opportunity slip though his fingers. He lead two sets to love but lost 3-6, 6-7(4), 6-2, 6-0, 6-3. He had Federer on the ropes but let him come back.

"My serve let me down," del Potro said after the match. Apart from that, he had issues with his left knee, playing with a support wrap on it the entire tournament.

A few months later in August they met again in the semifinals in the Olympic Games in London and played one of their most epic matches with the Swiss winning 3-6, 7-6(5), 19-17 in four hours and 26 minutes. It was the longest three-set men's match in the history of tennis and the longest in Olympic tennis history.

"It's hard to say it was a good match," del Potro said after losing the epic played on the Centre Court at Wimbledon. "I feel like I was really close, but just wasn't enough. Sports is like this, sometimes it's nice and sometimes not."

"In time, Juan started to have a pattern of game against Roger and that helped him out," said Davin. "With the serve, especially, he would win lots of points. Also, we had a strategy: Juan had to try to set up his forehand, dominate and move the ball around. If he managed that, his chances grew."

After constantly searching for ways to improve his chances against Federer, del Potro had a breakthrough on Sunday October 28th, 2012. After six losses during the season against Federer, Juan Martín finally beat him 6-4, 6-7(5), 7-6(3) in the final of the ATP event in Basel, Switzerland, the hometown of Federer no less.

"After losing so many times during the years against him, this win means a lot," he said. "Roger told me that he was happy for me. He's the best in history and a great person."

Winning the trophy in Basel held extraordinary value for del Potro. Federer was No. 1 in the world and the loss was a factor in him losing the top ranking. Federer was also a five-time champion of his hometown event and was looking to win his 77th career ATP title that would have tied him with John McEnroe on the all-time list of singles titles. It was his 62nd match victory of the year and his 13th career title, overtaking Martin Jaite, who he had equaled the week before by winning the title in Vienna. Only Vilas, with 62 titles, and Jose Luis Clerc, with 25 titles, had more ATP singles titles than del Potro among players from Argentina.

The experience for Federer in Argentina was very intense. It included, among other protocols and commercial obligations, a match of "tennis soccer" in the Boca stadium, a visit to Cristina Kirchner, in that time the president of Argentina, a breakfast with businessmen and a dinner that raised money for 1,800 school scholarships for kids in Tigre. Federer's schedule was jam packed from the second he arrived in Argentina. Federer's visit to Argentina had as much hysteria and euphoria as the Rolling Stones or Paul McCartney during their first visits to the country. The fever of "Rogermania" was showcased during a press conference in the lobby of the Intercontinental Hotel in Nordelta with the presence of approximately 400 journalists, as well as a good amount of curious infiltrators.

"I consider Roger a friend, I don't know if he also considers me one," said del Potro in that massive conference, as he eyed the guy sitting next to him. The Swiss than patted his shoulder, making everyone smile and laugh. "He is a good person inside and outside of the court. He helps me and advises me even if he doesn't have to," Juan Martín added.

Federer insisted that del Potro could contend for the No. 1 ranking, but the host took the compliment and turned it into a joke: "Roger says that being No. 1 is simple, but it's simple for him! I'm going to ask him to tell me some of his secrets. If he wants, I'll hire him for my entire life, but I don't think I'll be able to play like him." Countered Federer, "As a player I will be good, but as a coach I can assure you I'd be horrible."

In the first of the two agreed exhibition matches on December 12, del Potro won by 3-6, 6-3 and 6-4. In the second match a day later, Federer won by 6-4 and 7-6(1). The matches included a one-set opening act exhibition between Vilas and Clerc in stadiums for more than 20,000 fans.

The first of the two matches started with a 75-minute delay because a section of the seating started to give in. After some moments of fear and disorganization, approximately 150 people that were supposed to be in this section had to be evicted. The players, who were about to go on the court when this shameful incident happened, had to go back to the locker room.

Davin remembered an anecdote about the confusion: "After seeing an enormous amount of people the first day, I decided to enter the court a little bit later. I took a little extra time on purpose while Juan was already on his way to the court, but then the tribune problem happened, so I went back to the locker room, and when I go in, Roger didn't even have a chance to leave so he was there alone, sitting down. I swear I thought 'This guy is going to want to leave, he won't play.' There was the risk of the tribunal falling down. There were way too many people... So, I tell him, 'Is everything alright?' and he said 'Everything is fine, the match is being delayed a little' as if nothing. The truth is I don't know if he found out what was the situation was outside."

Federer was impressed and touched by his visit to Argentina: "Thank you, Argentina. I am leaving your beautiful country. I couldn't stop giving thanks for making my stay so memorable. The atmosphere in the stands was one of the best I've ever lived in all my career" were his goodbye words. The two exhibitions featured some of the most passionate ovations Federer ever received in his life. During those suffocating days in Buenos Aires, the relationship between the two players was strengthened even more. When Federer and his manager Tony Godsick, who also traveled to Argentina, launched a representation business called Team 8 in November of 2013, they picked the Argentinian as one of their exclusive clients. Moreover, Godsick, a former manager at the powerful International Management Group and the husband of the top former pro Mary Joe Fernandez, found similarities between del Potro and Federer, in their bond with fans, businesses and promoters.

Federer and del Potro continued to face each other, but with less regularity due to the long absences of del Potro during his injuries and the six months Federer was absent from the circuit in 2016, the miracle year that marked the return of the Argentinian. The ups and downs between the two remained intact. In November of 2016, after the Olympic Games in Rio, and before the Davis Cup Final between Argentina and Croatia, Federer gave a report in the *La Nación* newspaper on del Potro.

"What happened to Delpo was impressive and he has done really well," said Federer. "When I saw him at the beginning of this year I noticed that something had changed in his game. He changed his backhand, that he would hit more with an effective slice. It's interesting to see how he adapted his game after the surgery."

Federer also made reference to his friend after winning the Davis Cup title for Argentina in Zagreb: "He had a great year, I congratulate Juan Martín. I celebrated for you. It was an epic victory, the one at the Davis Cup and the Olympic Games was just astonishing. We played two beautiful exhibition matches in Argentina and hopefully some day we could do it again. That was one of my most amazing trips."

Said del Potro, "Roger has always been a mirror, because not only do we share sponsors, but also the same manager. He is a role model as a No. 1 person and player. I remember that as a little kid I had his racket and his clothes. We shared lots of stuff and the best thing is to have a relationship with the best tennis player in history and for him to be a person close to me."

He also amplifies, with an open heart: "Roger is the example of being No. 1 for all athletes inside and outside the court. I don't think there will be someone else like him for a long time. Depending on which side you look at it from, I can be very fortunate for playing my entire career next to him, learning and playing finals, losing and winning, and if I look at it from another angle I could think that if he was older or younger, other players and me could have won more. But on the day I retire, I will look back and be sure to be thankful that I shared some many moments with him."

6

Prison Break Escape To Victory

There were not a lot of people at the pool at the Marriott Northeast in Mason, Ohio on a weekday in August during the Cincinnati Masters tournament. The only noise was that of traffic from nearby Interstate 71. Juan Martín del Potro was trying to relax at the deserted pool, half of his battered body was in the water as he drank something with ice. Winning the title in Washington, D.C. and reaching the final at the Canadian Masters 1000 in Montreal consumed all his energy. His summer season was very productive but exhausting.

"I want to go back to Buenos Aires," del Potro, the No. 6 player in the world, said with frustration. "I want to go see my friends, be in Tandil for a while."

Franco Davin and Martiniano Orazi, who shared in del Potro's relaxation by the pool, looked at each other worried. It was just an instant pause after he notified Cincinnati tournament officials that he would not play in the event. The U.S. Open was only 10 days away and the temperature was suffocating, 40 degrees warmer than that of Buenos Aires.

"No, Juan, no. We have to stay," said Davin, del Potro's coach. "Over there it's so cold and you already made an enormous effort to adapt to the heat over here. It would be a huge mistake to go back and start again."

"I have the same opinion," said Orazi, the physical trainer. "With another abrupt change of temperature you could get really sick."

It was hard to convince him to stay, but throwing more arguments to him, Davin and Orazi succeeded. The geographic distance was always a disadvantage for the Latin American tennis players in terms of the circuit. A French guy can lose in the morning at a tournament and be sleeping in his bed at home at night time. But not for an Argentinian, for example. Del Potro suffered lots of times being a long distance away from his home. More than once he discussed with his team the possibility of making a home base in Miami, Italy or Spain during a season stretch, but he never did that, except in certain exceptions.

"We made a study in the amount of hours it takes and the advantages of living in Argentina," said Davin. "My recommendation was to choose another place. But he wanted to stay."

In that week, not flying back to Argentina from Ohio and then to go back to New York a few days later, was a great step forward.

Del Potro, Davin and Orazi left Mason and traveled to Miami. They turned the machinery off during three days and then started again. They alternated tennis practice and physical workouts at the University of Miami in Coral Gables and not at Crandon Park in Key Biscayne because it wasn't available.

"Juan was cussing a lot, because in August in Miami, it's like being in the Sahara desert in the summer," said Davin. "It's horrible at any time of the day. You go to train at 8 am and it's the same as going at 2 pm. In that moment, he was doing good in tennis and did not have to do a lot of other stuff, but in the physical part we had to work him hard a few days."

"He was exploding it, setting the ball on fire from all sides," said Orazi.

In fact, not going back to Argentina was a huge success. Del Potro was really well adapted to the heat and humidity. He was in a positive frame of mind and had renewed energy.

The Intercontinental Barclay Hotel on Lexington Avenue, between the 48th and 49th streets in Manhattan, as usual, was where del Potro and his team stayed while at the U.S. Open. One of the major worries of Davin was trying to keep Juan Martín isolated and away from comments from the public and the press that he was a real contender for the title. In that tournament, the last Grand Slam of the year, the Italian Ugo Colombini had already been added to del Potro's group as his manager. They would all move in blocks, like inside a bubble, trying to not let anything infiltrate them.

"We always try to maintain a low profile," said Davin, also the coach of Gaston Gaudio when he won Roland Garros in 2004. "The good thing about all of us thinking really alike was that we wouldn't allow for anything strange to happen that could distract Juan. It's because the people, lots of times without bad intentions, would say distracting things to him."

Del Potro was reticent to watching TV series and sometimes his free time would become tedious. He adored New York City, but it was clear that during the U.S. Open he wouldn't go out to walk or to visit tourist sites. Aware of this situation, Davin, a fan of the "Prison Break" series about a fictional prison called Fox River, bought the first season and gave it to Juan Martín. The strategy, after a slow start, transformed into a healthy addiction for del Potro. He started watching episode after episode, without stopping.

"We would reach the hotel after training or playing and Juan would tell me: 'Look I only have one or two more episodes left.' So I would leave running through 5th Avenue to try to buy the other seasons. After that, I started worrying that he would stay awake till very late because those series are so addicting that you want to see them all in a single day. That helped him not think that much about the tournament. Looking at the series decompressed him. It took pressure off him."

The series also helped generate new conversation topics among his group. "You go week after week having breakfast, lunch and dinner together, that there comes a time where you have nothing to talk about," said Davin. "What am I going to tell him? I brushed my teeth with a new toothpaste? You have no topic. So that series would give us a new topic to talk about."

A year before in 2008 in the Los Angeles airport, Davin saw one of the show's main actors Wade Williams and shared with del Potro and Orazi his surprise at crossing paths a couple of meters to someone he was fascinated with. But since his travel buddies did not watch the series at the time, they were not impressed. After being absorbed by the series the following year, del Potro then remembered Davin speaking of his encounter. "You were right. It was the guy that acts as the prison's manager."

Little by little, del Potro's rivals at the U.S. Open went down like playing cards. In the first round, Juan Monaco, ranked No. 41 in the ATP and a native of Tandil like del Potro, was his first victim of the tournament.

"He's playing incredible," said Monaco to the Argentine media after losing 6-3, 6-3, 6-1. "He is going to win the tournament."

In the second round, it was the lefty Austrian Jurgen Melzer, ranked No. 38, by 7-6(6), 6-3, 6-3. In his third challenge, another Austrian, the undisciplined Daniel Koellerer, ranked No. 62, by a 6-1, 3-6, 6-3, 6-3 score. In the Argentine era of the Copa Petrobras Challengers in 2005, Koellerer, who was later banned from tennis for life for match-fixing, had beaten a 17-year-old del Potro.

In the fourth round, del Potro dispatched the former world No. 1 Juan Carlos Ferrero 6-3, 6-3, 6-3 and in the quarterfinals, the one to suffer was Marin Cilic, ranked No. 17, a buddy of del Potro since they were juniors. But beating the Croatian was no easy task as he arrived on fire after eliminating in three sets the No. 2-ranked Andy Murray and the strong wind that swirled on the court affected del Potro on his serve. After losing the first set 6-4, del Potro won the next three sets with authority 6-3, 6-2 and 6-1.

"That match was a key," del Potro said later. "The weather was horrible and I missed a lot of balls. Then, all of a sudden I won a big point and people started cheering for me. I did a mental check and everything started to get better."

Although he never expressed it publicly, not even to del Potro, but to Davin, he always had a bitter taste in his mouth about the semifinal at Roland Garros in 2009, where del Potro seemed to settle to lose to Federer in the semifinals.

"I never talked to it with anybody, not even Juan," he said. "There are matches where one just says, 'Alright, it's good.' That match with Federer could have been won easily (the Argentinian lost 3-6, 7-6(2), 2-6, 6-1, 6-4). He felt the pressure that the entire world wanted Federer to win so that he could have, once and for all, win the title he lacked at Roland Garros. He was going to be seen as the bad guy in the movie. Even more, he would have had the responsibility to win a very complicated final, because Robin Soderling (who beat Rafael Nadal in the fourth round) was a difficult opponent."

Nevertheless, a few months later on hard courts in New York, the sensation was totally opposite. "I saw that he had the look of a champion," said Davin.

Juan Martín and his team had diverse routines in the Big Apple. One of them was gastronomic. The night before matches, they would have dinner, no matter what, in a restaurant curiously called San Martin, a block away from the hotel on 49th Street. The place, with Spanish and Italian dishes, offered homemade food. Orazi always considered trying new restaurants to break up the monotony and it was decided they would go to new restaurants on the nights after matches. Even if the San Martin restaurant was full, the owner would always make them a spot. The owner even put up a photo of del Potro on the restaurant's wall. As an entry dish, they would serve different jams and cheeses. As a main dish, del Potro would eat chicken with mashed potatoes. Usually the table consisted of three people, but in New York during the U.S. Open they added Colombini as well as Davin's father Jose Maria and his friend Fabian Heller.

In some of those relaxed dinners, Davin would make jokes to del Potro about a small detail only he could repair: the color of the clothes del Potro wore on the court. In the U.S. Open the year before, Davin had tormented him about the red and white colors he wore that were the colors of River Plate, the biggest rival of his beloved Boca Juniors team. In 2009, the clothes worn by Juan Martín were black with yellow wrist bands, which approached the blue and yellow colors for the Boca Juniors.

A constant "battle" emerged between the physical trainer and del Potro regarding sweets and drinks. The tennis player always needed to eat a dessert; he loved chocolate mousse. At one time he would even drink three sodas in one meal. That's what also provoked an exchange of opinions between Davin and Orazi, since Orazi wanted to completely remove these foods from his diet but Davin understood the process should take time.

"Little by little Juan started to understand that so many sweets and sodas wouldn't be healthy," said Davin. "We reduced it to just one coke per dinner. It was very hard to reduce it to none directly. Martin wanted to do that and Juan wanted to strangle us. I defied him and said 'You want to eat it? Alright. Eat it, but then don't complain.' So he wouldn't eat it. Or I would tell him to ask for a dessert but that we would eat it between the three of us, so he would only eat a spoonful to remove the anxiety of wanting the chocolate. In sports, having this anxiety and wanting chocolate is frequent. Juan put a lot of focus onto this, because it was hard for him to let it go."

With time, the situation got better. In fact, they would create goals and prizes after reaching an objective. Del Potro really loved fast food so they made a deal: He would only eat it when he was in the airports.

"We would wait to take a plane and he was capable of walking 10 kilometers just to find a McDonald's," said Davin. "We would tell him: 'There aren't any here, Juan.' And he would respond, 'Yes there are,' and would take a map out to find it."

It was all about habits and rituals with the group during tournaments and nothing could be altered, especially when traveling from Manhattan to Queens and vice versa, that depending on the time of day, could take between 30 minutes or more than an hour. Davin would have a small iPod where music from Rod Stewart, U2, Bruce Springsteen, The Rolling Stones and others would be played. In those moments, the small device wouldn't work via Bluetooth in the car, but only via a cable. In one of the many transfers, before the driver would start the engine, they would ask if the car had a cable hook-up to connect to Davin's iPod. If it did not, they would get out and find another car that could play the music. After that funny moment, every time they asked for a transport vehicle they would clarify that the car must be able to play their music.

Another routine for del Potro and his team that could not be changed during the 2009 U.S. Open was linked to racket stringers. In the official stringers room of the tournament, Juan Martín's weapons, with a weigh of 347 grams without the strings, would only be touched by Luis Pianelli. Native to the city of Arroy Seco in Santa Fe, he graduated as a lawyer in 1997, but his great vocation was tennis and stringing. That's how he started working at more than 15 Grand Slams and for the Argentine Davis Cup. During those days in September of 2009, Davin would take his rackets to Pianelli and when he received them he would already know what to do perfectly; work with synthetic strings strung at 63 pounds of tension. However, del Potro kept advancing in the tournament and Pianelli, however, was not assigned to work the entire tournament and would be leaving back to Buenos Aires. It created a bit of an uncomfortable situation as it might upset del Potro to know that his stringer would not be there in the latter rounds of the tournament.

"When I told Franco that I had to go back to Argentina, he told me: 'Alright, I won't say anything and you neither. Perhaps he will not notice. If we happen to go by your room and he asks for you, I'll tell him you went to eat or something.' So that's what we did," said Pianelli.

Months later, del Potro and Pianelli met up in a commercial event at the Argentinian Tennis Club in the neighborhood of Palermo and del Potro came up to him smiling and said, "What are you doing, traitor?" After the U.S. Open final, Davin confessed his little secret about the stringer.

The stringing duties for the rest of the event was handled by Scott Schneider, a young 26-year-old from Las Vegas, who managed to receive the confidence of Pianelli. In 2005, Schneider won a contest organized by Wilson that was televised in all of the United States, where they were searching for a man that would string a racket in the fastest time possible. Scott took 11 minutes and 14 seconds; he won a 42-inch TV, 1,000 dollars and a Fender guitar. The business gave him an opportunity to be part of a professional stringing team and that's where he met Pianelli.

Despite world No. 1 Roger Federer going for a sixth straight U.S. Open title–and having won at Roland Garros and Wimbledon earlier in the year – del Potro was being called a dark horse candidate to win the title. "You don't have to motivate a player when he's close to a Grand Slam final," said Orazi.

At that point, del Potro was a volcano. He did not feel intimidated crossing paths with Rafael Nadal in the semifinals (that same year he beat him in the quarterfinals in Miami and in Canada.) The only Grand Slam that Nadal had not won at the time was the U.S. Open and he was anxious to change that. But regardless of an abdominal bother, the Spaniard suffered a beating seldom seen in his career in big tournaments: del Potro beat him 6-2, 6-2, 6-2 in two hours and 20 minutes. Del Potro implemented a concert of whipping drives, hurting serves and coldness to save five break points in the surprising one-sided upset of the No. 3 seed. Bad weather forced the match to be played on Sunday, September 13 which made the final match against Federer was held Monday, September 14.

As a coach, Davin would have preferred to talk strategy with del Potro the night before the match with Federer, but that tactic never really helped him out. "There are times where the player is just too tired and that the last thing he wants to do is talk about the next match," Davin said. So, his plan was to talk about the strategy during his preparatory practice session before the match. On that Monday, the practice took place on a court closest to Arthur Ashe Stadium. Davin took advantage of the pauses and breaks in the practice session to get close to him and refresh him in match strategy.

After having a rough time against Federer so many times, Juan Martín already knew what he had to do. "I had the experience from the final match with Gaudio, where he was very nervous and stressed by the context of the match, having to play against another Argentinian (Guillermo Coria) that also he did not have a good relationship with," said Davin. "I remember that John McEnroe entered in the locker room and told him about the nerves that soldiers fighting in Vietnam faced to try to calm him down, but nothing would remove him of that stressed state. Juan Martín, instead, was very calm. For him, the tournament was already fine, already closed. So, what I mostly had to focus on as coach was trying to make him not settle for just being the runner-up."

Del Potro was the No. 6 seed and had never beaten Federer in six previous matches. The night before the match with Federer was endless. He started to chat on line with his friends in Argentina, but while the night kept on going, they left him; of course, all teenagers, they had to go to school the next day or to work. He fell asleep at around 2:30 am, but at 7:30 he woke up with no appetite. They gave him his breakfast but he only looked at it; he couldn't eat anything, not even a piece of toast. The anxiety made his stomach hurt, his head and his body. It was normal.

At that time, Juan Martín doubted his capacity to reach the fifth set. "It was understandable for him to think that since he is a tall and heavy person," said Davin. "He had a certain insecurity about his body. But he came from two weeks of playing in Washington and Montreal, playing 10 matches in three weeks and even moving from one country to another."

That doubt did not enter the minds of the team.

"Trust that you are able to accomplish it. Review the match mentally where you beat Nadal with such ease and hold onto that," the coach told his pupil before he entered Arthur Ashe Stadium, the biggest tennis stadium in the world, to play the final against Federer. Until then, Federer found it easy to dominate the Argentinian by throwing a variety of serves and slices, from below the knees, and make him feel uncomfortable. That strategy during their previous match at the French Open from three months before worked well against del Potro. But Juan Martín had learned that when Federer would position himself to hit a backhand slice, he had to open up and let him have the down the line shot and try to dominate with his forehand.

He interpreted the script with precision. In addition to ripping his groundstrokes and his serve (it reached 138 mph), the Argentinian had intelligence and a cold pulse to handle the most delicate situations, like during the tiebreakers or when he didn't get discouraged after losing the third set after committing two double faults.

"After the third set I started feeling a little fatigued and I knew it was going to be impossible to turn the game around if I didn't concentrate, calm down and to run a little more. I tried to get over that bad moment and started fighting. That's how I accomplished it: fighting," del Potro said later.

Said Orazi, "Juan started the game very nervous and it seemed as Roger was going to trample him, but Juan started fighting against him in an incredible way and he won. Roger was very angry after losing that final. In the fifth set, Juan ate him."

Del Potro invented his work of art in front of Argentine legend Guillermo Vilas, himself a U.S. Open champion in 1977 at a different location at Forest Hills, who sat among the privileged in the U.S. Open's President's Box. The extraordinary triumph of Juan Martín by 3-6, 7-6(5), 4-6, 7-6(4), 6-2 in four hours and six minutes symbolized a lot more than just the first major title for the big and talented tennis player. Just like the old black and white video of a kid with curly hair named Diego Maradona who said, "My first dream is to play in the World Cup," there are newspaper clippings in Tandil where Juan Martín refers to the U.S. Open as his favorite tournament. The *New York Times,* in particular, also pointed out this interesting perspective. Chris Clarey of the *New York Times* described this as "an original thought for an Argentine whose Grand Slam allegiances traditionally drift across the Atlantic to the French Open and its red clay surface."

"Men's tennis now has another shot add to its great hits list, but del Potro's huge serve and two-handed backhand are also effective. The racket looks small in his hands," wrote Clarey, who also quoted Vilas on his countryman's triumph, "He played a great match; he will win many more."

Del Potro obtained his first Grand Slam singles title in the first opportunity he had, just like Federer when he conquered Wimbledon in 2003 at 21 years of age. "It's always a great effort to reach the final of a Grand Slam and even more satisfaction is winning in your first experience," said Federer. "To Juan Martín, we have to give him all the credit, because it's not something easy to achieve, specially playing against someone like me, who has a lot of experience."

At 28 years old, Roger had not lost a match in the U.S. Open since 2003 when he was defeated in the fourth round by another Argentinian, David Nalbandian, who was ranked No. 13 in the world at the time. Since then, Federer had been devastating in five straight editions of the U.S. Open, beating different opponents in the final each time (Lleyton Hewitt in 2004, Andre

Agassi in 2005, Andy Roddick in 2006, Novak Djokovic in 2007 and Andy Murray in 2008) and was not extended into a fifth set.

Since the exact moment del Potro stood up off the blue cement, where he fell almost in slow motion after the last point, his life changed. He wanted to win not only because of the $1,850,000 in prize money ($1,600,000 for the champion plus a bonus of $250,000 for finishing third in the U.S. Open Series, the North American points tour leading into tournament) but because of the world recognition and immortality within the sport that it would provide.

When he entered the locker room the first thing he did was call his family. He heard shouts, celebrations and tears. He sharpened his ear and heard his mom, Patricia, crying of joy. He had a lump in his throat, his eyes got watery; he couldn't talk anymore. He hung up.

After the endless journalist commitments, in Spanish and in English, through the bowels of Arthur Ashe Stadium, del Potro and his team finally escaped to the hotel. As soon as he turned his computer on, he read an email from a friend that said: "Your dream came true. Champion of the U.S. Open 2009, Juan Martín del Potro." He got goose bumps; started to tear up again, but this time alone, in his room. After a warm shower, he celebrated, after midnight at the restaurant Smith & Wollensky.

"It was Monday, we were so tired and it was so late that we didn't know if would find an open place," said Davin. "We found it on 49th Street and 3rd Avenue. We celebrated alongside the Argentinian journalists who had covered the contest; we ate meat and French fries, drank beer, sodas and obviously celebrated with champagne. We were crazy."

Now being Tuesday after midnight, Juan Martín and his team went to a club where there was a party promoted by the singer and actor Justin Timberlake. Between so many famous people, there was the basketball player LeBron James (in that period on the Cleveland Cavaliers) who went up to del Potro and congratulated him for his title against Federer. They also met up with the actors Ben Stiller, Adam Sandler and Mickey

Rourke. Davin insisted to Orazi to get close and ask for a picture; the physical therapist was shy, but he did it. They asked, but Rourke denied them.

"He didn't want to do it because there was a massive internet paranoia on who you take picture with," said Davin. "In fact, Timberlake did not want to take picture with anyone. We found him with Juan when we went to the restroom, we asked for one and he actually accepted. It was with a digital camera but I don't have the picture as a bit later, I had the camera stolen."

Another funny moment was experienced by Orazi, when the popular Italian soccer player Christian Vieri, full of paparazzi during that week in the New York streets along with the model Melissa Satta, instructed him to strengthen del Potro more. "He found out that I was Juan's physical trainer," he said. "And he told me, 'You need to work him more here, there, so he runs more.' How dare he! He told me this a few hours after Juan killed himself running to win the U.S. Open."

As soon as Juan Martín placed his head on the pillow in his room, the phone rang; they were looking for him in the lobby. It was 7 in the morning and the party started, or better yet, continued. Being the champion of the U.S. Open required new obligations, including going to different TV shows. The man from Tandil got into the car, with his eyes semi closed, and started a media tour that had as a final destination the Empire State Building for a photo shoot. That wasn't all. After lunch, John McEnroe waited for him in a five-story shop on 57th Street and 5th Avenue to do a public interview for fans and patrons. That last trip was with the company of Davin; Orazi would wait in the hotel with the suitcases ready to go to the John F. Kennedy Airport.

Before boarding American Airlines Flight 955, announced for a 10:30 pm departure, something started to malfunction. It was Orazi's body. He started to have a cold sweat and started to have palpitations. "I was afraid that I would be suffering a cardiac problem, my body was trembling, I was dizzy," he said. When del Potro and Davin returned to the hotel with the only intention of picking up their bags and continuing their trip to the international airport, they found themselves with a deep concern. At first they took it as a little joke.

"We always made jokes to Martin, because right away he would get worried about his health, we would tell him he was hypochondriac," Davin said. "But then, already on our way, we were on the highway and at the time in the afternoon/night with all the cars leaving Manhattan, we couldn't even advance and Orazi kept saying that he was feeling bad, that his chest hurt. It was impossible to leave the highway and that made him more nervous. We finally reached the airport; so we told him: 'If we tell the airline check-in people, they won't let you travel.' But Marti insisted in calling the airport emergency people. They put him on a bed and plugged him in everywhere. In the end he didn't have anything: it's because he saw the final match with so much tension that his defenses fell and was left pale."

Said Orazi, "They did an electrocardiogram, while Juan and Franco where laughing and taking pictures. I was afraid of having a heart attack on the airplane. I'm serious! It had been seven weeks since we last saw our families and all the emotions just swelled up."

While del Potro left behind the big stage of New York City and the final Grand Slam tournament of the year, what awaited him in Argentina would be a mixture of good and bad.

"When Gaston (Gaudio) reached the final at Roland Garros, we were having breakfast alone on the day of the final and he told me, 'I am happier that the tournament is ending than to play the final,'" Davin said. "Everyone lives that situation, each in their own way. Gaston had extra stress by playing against a player from the same country. He started the tournament by being No. 44 in the world and did not expect that much. With Juan, it was different, because he had won in Washington, he was in the top 10, but he had Nadal and Federer in his way. But when you were leaving Ezeiza Airport in Buenos Aires to go to a tournament, nobody bothered you. But now, when you come back three weeks later, thousands of people are waiting. Who is ready for that? It's very difficult."

Would a 21-year-old del Potro be ready for the new world that he would inherit with his massive victory? He was, indeed, immature in some ways of the world and he was not entirely comfortable with that new change in his public profile.

"Not even he imagined that there would be as strong of a reaction to his victory as there was," said Orazi. "What he accomplished at such an early age was fantastic. That a South American had conquered the U.S. Open at his age is worth three times more for a European. A few days after coming back, I was relaxed, eating barbecue with some friends, we turned the TV on and there was Juan giving interviews. I would turn the TV on and he would appear, and each time I'd see him skinnier. At a psychological level, with all that craziness after victory, it's to go back to normal routines."

After a few days of break, the team started working again in Palermo. Juan Martín arrived fatigued and with a fever. It was a unique moment to engage in all of the celebratory activities but the wheel had to keep turning. Since the moment he would park his car for practice until he walked approximately 40 meters to the gym, he could take 45 minutes by the amount of picture and autograph requests. Just a month earlier, he was just one of the regular people and wasn't bothered. Once at the gym, between his work outs with weights, running machines and steel bars, he would again be interrupted again and again. Always with admiration and good intention, but the interruptions made it impossible for the team to focus and finish his training routine. Despite not having the ideal preparation, del Potro, Davin and Orazi traveled to Tokyo for the next tournament. They left the effervescence and isolated themselves from the craziness it produced. On October 6 in the Japanese capital, del Potro faced the Frenchman Edouard Roger Vasselin, who had come from the qualifying tournament and was ranked No. 189 in the world. In his first match since he won the U.S. Open in an epic battle against Federer, del Potro lost 6-4, 6-4. Evidently, something had changed. Now nothing would be the same.

7

A Long Nightmare

T he Kooyong Lawn Tennis Club is a spiritual place for tennis. Located in the suburbs in Melbourne, around seven kilometers southeast of downtown, it was the site of the Australian Open between 1972 and 1987 until they moved it over to the National Tennis Center in Flinders Park, the current and modern Melbourne Park.

It was on the grass there at Kooyong Stadium where Guillermo Vilas won, against all odds with his inexperience on this surface, the Masters tournament in December 1974. There, after beating the Romanian Ilie Nastase in five sets in the final, the lefty made a famous comment in the award ceremony: "I thought grass was for cows, now I think that some of it should kept for tennis." The quote caused for laughs from the crowd.

Kooyong was a talisman for Vilas, the man who popularized tennis in Argentina, because it was there that he also won two of his four major singles titles: the Australian Open in 1978 and 1979. Starting 1988, Kooyong became the site of popular exhibition tournament that led into the Australian Open.

Juan Martín del Potro didn't have many inconveniences in defeating Ivan Ljubicic by a comfortable 6-3, 6-3 margin during the morning of January 13, 2010 at the Kooyong Classic. The match, on a hard blue surface, the same as the Australian Open since 2008, lasted one hour and 10 minutes, so del Potro decided with his coach Franco Davin and his physical trainer Martiniano Orazi to schedule a practice for the afternoon. He just finished a magical season that included him winning his first major title at the U.S. Open, being the first tennis player to beat Roger Federer and Rafael Nadal at the same major, and playing in the singles final of the Masters Cup in London, where he lost to the Russian Nikolay Davydenko. He posted an 11-9 record against players in the top 10 and was ranked No. 4 in the world.

"My right hand was hurting a little," del Potro said, with some concern, to Davin and Orazi while they were having lunch after the match in Kooyong.

Regardless of the warning, they did not cancel the practice they had planned for the afternoon. After a brief break, del Potro got ready to practice. His next opponent at Kooyong would be Frenchman Jo-Wilfried Tsonga, but, after a few minutes of hitting, he stopped. His right wrist was bothering him a lot. Taking into account that the Australian Open would start in a few days, they understood that the most intelligent thing to do would be to pull out of his exhibition event. Davin told the organizers and that's what happened. Without losing time, Juan Martín went to get a magnetic resonance in the medical department at the Australian Open and the results showed it might be an inflation of the tendons.

"Luckily, it's nothing serious," said del Potro, a bit crestfallen like he still suspected something was wrong.

"Franco (Davin) called me from Australia to put me up to date," said Diego Rivas, del Potro's kinesiologist at that time. "I noticed him a little worried, because it was all of a sudden. We coordinated that when he would come back to Buenos Aires, we would do more tests."

They told Juan to rest a bit, but he only had two days before his first round against the American Michael Russell at the Australian Open. Less than 24 hours later, returning to Melbourne Park, del Potro practiced with the Australian player Nick Lindahl, and though he did not have any pain, he was uncomfortable with the support bandages he had on his wrist. By that time, an alarm went off in his environment. Even his friend Martin Palermo, the goal scorer of Boca Juniors soccer team, had called him from Tandil, where he was in the middle of pre-season training.

"It hurts especially when I'm playing from the baseline," del Potro said. "When I serve it doesn't hurt me a lot, but it's still an annoying pain. I don't know how long I can stand it. I need God to help me out a little too."

The same pain in his right wrist, his most useful hand, had also disturbed him in 2009 during the tournaments in Miami and Shanghai, but not with this intensity.

"Those pains in 2009 were just mild that cleared up fast," said Rivas, who worked with del Potro since he was 15 years old. "Sometimes when a player starts competing at a higher level, like Juan Martín had done, it's normal to feel new pains. He did have back pains before. The really tall players are more prone to suffer some type of injuries like these."

Said Davin, "There are always all sorts of pain in the body, but that was the first time that Juan said to me seriously that his hand was hurting."

He beat Russell (at the time ranked No. 90 in the world) without feeling any type of discomfort. "I was glad because I felt good," del Potro said after the match. In the second round, he had an emotional and draining victory over the American James Blake (ranked No. 45) by a 6-4, 6-7(3), 5-7, 6-3, 10-8 score in four hours and 17 minutes.

"I swear that after I hit a forehand winner during the match it made me remember the final match against Federer in New York," del Potro said. "It was the hardest second-round match I could have had."

"Del Potro has sacred fire," said Tito Vazquez, the captain of Argentina's Davis Cup team at the time, who was in Australia for scouting. "For the Argentinians, it's a blessing to have him."

Regardless of what del Potro would do in Australia, in Argentina they were already analyzing his case. Daniel del Potro was involved. Also Gonzalo Gomez, a doctor who specialized in sports trauma. "The doctors from over there and from my country told me that if I keep playing with the injury I have, I wouldn't run any major risks," del Potro said. "I hope they aren't wrong."

In the third round, he beat the German Florian Mayer (ranked No. 60) 6-3, 0-6, 6-4, 7-5. His collapse in the second set was produced, mainly, because of sweat. It was almost 98 degrees Fahrenheit out with heavy humidity which caused for his bandage on his right hand to loosen up and distract him.

"I haven't cried much since the U.S. Open," said del Potro after he was eliminated in the fourth round by the Croatian Marin Cilic (ranked No. 14) by a 5-7, 6-4, 7-5, 5-7, 6-3 scoreline. The tennis player had reached Melbourne as a Grand Slam tournament champion, with the wish to enjoy such a distinction and, without a doubt, suffered more than what he enjoyed as the uneasiness about his wrist grew day after day.

"I did not enjoy it as much as I wanted, because I had to be with the trainers a lot inside the dressing room," the Argentinian said before leaving Australia.

Without losing any time, del Potro arrived at Buenos Aires on January 25 and that same day the doctor, Alejandro Rolon, gave him a magnetic resonance. On February 11th they repeated the study to confirm the result. "Pain on the dorsal edge of the ulna. Edema of estiloides. Synovitis in the intersection of the fibrocartilage" were some medical terms used. Since no signs of rupture were found, they recommended kinesiology exercises to see how he would respond. Naturally, sports activity would be interrupted and the tennis circuit would have to wait. However, the pain did not go away. More tests were done and the uncertainty escalated. So, the team made the decision to visit a doctor who specialized in hands. After analyzing different alternatives, they reached out to Gabriel Clembosky, an orthopedist and hand surgeon from the University of Rosario, in the province of Santa Fe, who later specialized in centers in Kentucky and Indiana in the United States.

"His wrist was hurting too much and we couldn't find a clear and concrete answer," said Orazi. "Everyone offered a different solution. Clembosky gave us security and peace of mind."

"I was certain that Juan Martín had an injury in the ulnar tendon on the right wrist," said Clembosky. "But they saw other doctors who said the problem was something different. One day his father called me and told me, 'Gabriel, what do you think? What do we do? Because we have to make a decision and there are options found by other doctors.' I told him, 'Look, Daniel, if I were Juan Martín I would go see the best in the world about that wrist.' That person, to me, was Richard Berger of the Mayo Clinic in Rochester, Minnesota. I called a really important friend of mine in Spain, the doctor Marc Garcia-Elias, who was certified in bio mechanics, to ask him what he would think of Berger looking at Juan Martín. 'Gabi, send him, he's the best,' he told me. So, in that enormous moment of pressure, I gave my opinion to Daniel. He accepted it and asked me to put him in touch with Berger."

Clembosky, who knew Berger very well, immediately contacted his colleague by email and coordinated a visit. "Berger immediately was at his disposal," Clembosky said. "He's smart and knew it couldn't wait till next week. It had to be now. If he made him wait, Juan Martín would have gone to another doctor."

Berger said that he would expect del Potro to arrive immediately and that he would be waiting. Clembosky, del Potro, Davin and the doctor Gomez all traveled to Rochester. Del Potro's tournament schedule was put on hold.

The origin of the Mayo Clinic has romantic roots. William Worral Mayo, born in Salford, England, migrated to the

United States during his youth to work as a doctor, veterinarian, surveyor and even editing a newspaper. He married Louise Wright and the couple settled in Rochester, Minnesota with two children: William James Mayo, born in 1861, and Charles Horace Mayo, born in 1865. The father of the family was dedicated in his job at the time of examining the recruits who would fight in the American Civil War. In 1883, a tornado obliterated Rochester, leaving around 40 people dead and more than 200 injured. The Franciscana sisters offered to build a hospital with the condition that the doctor would be W.W. Mayo and his kids, who also graduated in medicine. And thus, it happened. The Mayos started to invite other doctors to participate in their practices and, in time, after many transformations, this small project that started out helping victims of a natural disaster turned into a leading center of medicine, science and education. More than 3,300 professionals work in the current headquarters, the same one in Minnesota as well as in Florida and Arizona. They receive patients from all over the world, and even Ernest Hemingway was once hospitalized in Rochester in 1960, a year before his death, to submit himself to treatment for depression. The legend says that during some months of convalescence, the writer was registered with the last name of his doctor to try to keep hidden.

Berger, a recognized orthopedic surgeon with degrees from the University of Iowa and Midland Lutheran of Nebraska, received the tennis player in his office. He examined him, but what was bothering del Potro wasn't in a certain place. Sometimes it would be on one side of the wrist and at other times another and that was complicating the situation. Berger explained that he was observing an inflammation. He did not perceive a rupture and said that he should rest for another three weeks. The team went back to Argentina with a plan for "conservative" treatment, with kinesiology, medication and physiotherapy.

But there weren't any changes. The pains that got better one day would then come back the next day. The uncertainty turned to desperation and confusion.

"Of course I'm saying it from my own shoes, but at that moment I saw him depressed, needing to find a way out of a desperate situation," said Clembosky. "He wouldn't even lift his head up to talk, dragging his words and not expressing himself. He was very sad, I saw him at his worst."

Said Rivas, "Juan was anxious, worried, with all these emotional doubts. He didn't know if he was going to be able to play again. He was distressed."

Surgery was looking more likely to be del Potro's destiny. The less invasive treatments did not lessen the pain. However, it was a very difficult decision. When a tennis player has surgery done on the wrist, the risk is huge. It's like when a soccer player gets a knee done, but probably worse. Berger made del Potro travel again to Rochester, but this time he told him to bring his racket, since he wanted to do another test. He injected an anesthetic into his wrist and took him to a tennis court and told him to play. Del Potro played... and he didn't feel any pain. Berger had effectively found the precise area where the ligament was damaged. A sense of relief came to del Potro as well as Davin and Orazi, who were there with him. Of course that feeling was short-lived because del Potro had to enter the operation room, something that they wanted to avoid no matter what.

Berger explained patiently how the operation was going to be done, what were the risks and how much time the rehabilitation could take. The American didn't have any problems repeating every concept. It was Monday and Berger operated on Tuesdays. They had to decide.

"It was there or waiting another week," said Davin. "We had the chance to stay around there, in Miami or where ever, and I knew Juan thought that too, as if saying 'Lets stretch this out one more week.' But in one more week, instead of returning to Rochester, we would go back to Buenos Aires. Also, in sports there's so much pressure coming from everywhere... For Juan, his sponsors, who were following the situation very closely and wondering what would happen. It wasn't easy. We had to give an answer."

Berger had a very unique habit for his patients, which was to draw a picture of the patient's affected area that would be operated on using a mechanic retractable pen with different colors on it.

He would push his finger down on the pen to use a different color," said Davin. "The red was for one thing, then the black and green... He would be scribbling and would say this is tac, tac tac. We would keep the drawing so we could look at it later but would need to have it explained more since the terms of the areas were so confusing ... sheath, tubes, tendons, stuff that go through here and there that we didn't know existed."

It was already almost four in the afternoon and the time was closing in. The day before his working day for surgeries, Berger would leave early from the Mayo Clinic, no more than six in the afternoon. Also, he had food routines and breaks that were un-alterable; similar, inclusive, to the ones athletes would do before their matches. After hearing all the details, Juan Martín asked to talk alone with Berger. Davin and Orazi left the room and closed the door. Then 20 minutes later, the door opened again. "You have until 8 pm to answer," said Berger. "Think about it, Juan. If you say yes, everything is ready. At 6 am they wake you up and give you a list of stuff to eat for breakfast. If you say no, that's alright."

"Juan was trembling, like paper," said Davin. "He wasn't crying, but he knew it was a very important decision that he had to take, that he didn't have time and was only 21 years old. It was really hard."

The anxious evaluation of the situation continued in the hotel room at the clinic. The room was very wide, family style with separate rooms with a door in the middle of the salon. On one side, Juan Martín was talking to his parents on the phone, on the other, Davin and Orazi were biting their nails, nervous as they tried to think through the situation.

"We were convinced that he had to get the operation done," said Davin. "I think it was, without a doubt, the worst of the surgeries because he did not know Berger. It would destroy your soul because he would think that his career could end. Any word we say could be wrong. We couldn't even try to humor the room."

"Alright, I'm going to do it," were the only six words that came out of del Potro's mouth. He then went back to the bed and lay down.

Davin continued with the protocol. He called the person in charge of the transport and the organizer of the operating room. Berger received the message.

"I think the doctor left the hospital knowing that Juan was going to say yes," said Davin. What he never knew was what Juan told him while they were alone. But he had a theory. "He probably wanted to say, between quotation marks, a little bit of pressure. He was at the hands of that man. Juan is very observant and all the times we went to visit him I noticed that he was searching for his confidence. Juan has no middle ground. He would trust or he wouldn't."

The night, apart from being cold, was endless. The trio only walked 50 meters outside of the hotel to have dinner. On their way back, Juan Martín took forever to close his eyes. In the mind of the tennis player, there was only room for nightmares and bad thoughts. The next day, Tuesday May 4, all the preparation during the pre-operation was overwhelming. Berger had a peculiar routine of writing his signature with a black pen in the place on the patient where he would operate. The nurses shaved his right hand, helped him to change into the proper clothes, gave him five pills to take. He had a religious stamp for good luck that his mom gave him but it got lost in all the clinic halls on his way to the operation room.

"We were in the waiting room, drinking coffee, walking on the walls," Orazi said of the dramatic time of the surgery. Said Davin, "They gave us a number and we followed him through a TV screen that was indicating what part of the operation he was on. It was longer than expected. I was talking with Daniel, the dad, and was telling him that he entered later, to keep him calmer. Once the surgery ended, we could see him. He started to wake up, but was dizzy. We took him out of the room on a wheel chair and since he was still kind of groggy, he sat down and got dizzy again. We had to go back and lay him down again."

"When he got better, we hugged each other and went back to the hotel," said Orazi.

The worse, in theory, had passed. Del Potro stayed a few more hours in Rochester, waiting for the final explanation from Berger and the details of the exercises that he would have to do from now on in Argentina.

"It's not a happy moment for me in my life. But I am used to fighting against adversity and I have all the will power to more forward," del Potro said.

The time to recover would be dragged on but it also depended on a lot of factors that were not immediately apparent. A month later, del Potro and Davin returned to Rochester. Usually they would fly to the International airport of Minneapolis-St. Paul via Dallas or Miami and then rent a car and drive approximately one and a half hours to reach the Mayo Clinic. After removing the stitches, del Potro returned to Buenos Aires and, crowded with anxiety, took up a racket for the first time on Monday, August 2. The information on del Potro and his condition was very secretive. During some nights they would see him practicing inconspicuously in a neighborhood club in Saavedra, where Davin managed an academy along with coaches Luis Lobo and Tim Azar. Generally, they would go at night, at 9 or 10 pm; also the sports psychologist would go, Pablo Pecora, and they would reserve the last four courts even though they would only use one.

"We don't know when he will return," said Ugo Colombini, del Potro's manager, to ESPN Radio. "We hope he heals 100 percent and then will see."

"Everything that he has done to be No. 4 in the world, he has to redo" was a cold bucket of reality that Davin said to the newspaper *La Nación*. "Obviously, Juan wants to come back as soon as possible. We who are with him want the same. He sees TV and everyone playing, but we must be careful, even with all his desire we don't want to get excited with a fast return."

"That period was hard," said Orazi. "His right arm, that was pure muscle, was now pure bone after the surgery. It had shrunk. There was a lot of long work ahead for the team. He had to gain that weight back."

The Tower of Tandil longed for, from his heart, to reappear for the U.S. Open in September. However, his common sense indicated that he wouldn't be able to defend the title.

"To start at a Grand Slam would be crazy," Orazi said. "It was hard for him to accept it, but it would have been dangerous for his future."

Juan Martín continued without giving any information out to the public, encouraging suspicions. "It was more that they talked about him behind his back than reality," said Davin. "But I think Juan was wrong in the communication, like a lot of times that it happened to him. When the false rumors started, instead of going out to clarify them, he would close himself and that would make people say anything. Internally, we knew that there was nothing weird. But for Juan, of course, it was going to be hard to come back. Getting back physically was going to be hard because he was big and heavy and he had gained a lot of weight. For that we did want it to stay hidden."

"The path was very clear. There were no double messages," said Rivas. "There was a waiting period before the surgery that was logical. There was always anxiety, but we had to try to make the player understand that time to recover from surgery had to be respected and to not look back."

The impatience was the worse counselor for del Potro during those months. He went from contending for the No. 1 ranking in the world to being inactive. This drastic change disturbed him, like it would happen to anybody. But on Thursday, September 23rd, on his 22nd birthday, del Potro smiled again. He took a Lufthansa flight, with a connecting flight in Frankfurt, on his way to Bangkok, to re-enter the ATP circuit at the ATP 250 tournament in the capital city of Thailand.

"He's not at his 100 percent, but there was no point for him training like a caged cat," said Rivas, the kinesiologist of the Argentine Davis Cup team under four different captaincies.

"I've never been this long standing still," said del Potro before getting on his flight. "My hand is very good and that's important. All this time it was hard for me to think positive thoughts, but my family and friends were always by my side."

Effectively, Juan Martín was out of rhythm and did not have accuracy in his shots. With a new ranking of No. 36, he lost in the first round against the Belgian Olivier Rochus (by that time ranked No. 78) by 7-6(7) and 6-4. The result, either way, wasn't of much importance. The positive thing was that he accomplished breaking an obstacle and competing after eight endless and tormenting months.

"I'm happy to be back," del Potro said in Thailand. "The most important thing is that my wrist is perfect."

Del Potro stayed in Thailand a few days to practice before traveling to Tokyo to play in the event in the Japanese capital. A 6-3, 6-0 first-round loss to Feliciano Lopez of Spain (ranked No. 23) resulted in Japan. From there, del Potro had planned to play till the end of the year in Vienna, Basel and the event at Bercy in Paris, but, instead, decided to train instead.

"I decided to close my 2010 season to train harder in the next two months and start 2011 on a strong note," he said on Twitter.

"People have to know that for a long time I'm going to be out of rhythm, way off my best tennis," he told ESPN.

During the dark period, Juan Martín, apart from being accompanied by his friends and family in Tandil, received numerous messages from his colleagues. Federer and Nadal called him and sent him emails. Even the Scot Andy Murray, whom he had a few short circuits with on the tour, reached out. "Now that we've both grown up we don't fight anymore," del Potro smiled.

On November 22, del Potro's pre-season started as he geared up for the 2011 campaign. Berger solved his problem and Juan Martín adopted him as his official doctor. Their relationship was very friendly and fluid.

Three months after confronting each other in the Japanese capital, del Potro and Feliciano Lopez crossed paths again, but in the first round of the ATP event in Sydney, the opening event of the Argentine's season. His ranking had dropped to No. 259 but he managed a physical battle of three hours and 20 minutes and won 6-7(5), 7-6(9) 7-6(3). It was too much for a first match, but it helped him confirm that he was very healthy and that his right wrist would respond. Then he fell in the second round against Florian Mayer and at the Australian Open, he also lost in the second round to Marcos Baghdatis. He returned to Argentina, rested, practiced and then traveled to the United States where he could truly feel full.

He traveled to San Jose, but got a virus infection. But even in his poor condition he competed and reached the semifinals where he lost to Fernando Verdasco. "He left the court and started to vomit," said Orazi. "What he endured that day was incredible,"

The tour continued in Memphis where he fell in the semifinals to Andy Roddick, then ranked No. 8 in the world. It was in Delray Beach, Florida where his happiness was complete. On February 27, during a suffocating day, Juan Martín won the tournament without losing any sets during the week. He clinched the triumph with a 6-4, 6-4 win in the final against Janko Tipsarevic, a member of the Serbian team that was the current champion of the Davis Cup. It was 531 days that del Potro had to suffer before winning another trophy; the last one was at the U.S. Open. It was one, two, three, four, five and even six kisses that del Potro gave to his right wrist after he won the singles final. He went running to give Davin and Orazi a hug, who at that time were more than just his trainers. On that day, del Potro finished breaking his chains. After seeing everything "all black," mostly at the early stages of his period of injury when there was not a clear answer to his problem, he finally felt that he truly did come back. He finally felt like he beat the monster that was eating his happiness.

A few days later, walking through the woods of Palermo during a long weekend, the tennis player confessed, "What happened to me was a reflection of life, everything can change in a second. In 2009, my life changed when I won the U.S. Open, but a few months later my life changed again with the hand injury. I went from being No. 1 in the world to not being anything. Everything went by so fast..."

Tennis is one of the most physical sports. The weathering that tennis players endure, season after season, from January non-stop until December, results in a huge increase in player injuries. With players hitting one-handed backhands, the pattern of injury is more frequent in the elbow. With two-handed backhands, the hips and the wrist (precisely the posterior ulnar tendon) were the ones that started to suffer.

After starting the 2011 season doing small but firm steps with a ranking of No. 485, he finished the year with two titles (Delray Beach and Estoril), helping Argentina to a runner-up showing in the Davis Cup against Spain in Sevilla and a No. 11 year-end ranking. In 2012, he kept moving upward. But in August, after winning the bronze medal at the Olympic Games in London, a small pain in his left wrist manifested for the first time. Del Potro started hitting a slice backhand so his left hand won't require more work. With del Potro's two-handed backhand, by the way he adjusts his grip and hits through the ball, it placed enormous stress on the accompanying left wrist and opened it up to deterioration by the extreme repetitive movements.

"It's a technical topic," said Clembosky. "It's the two-handed backhand, standing in front of the ball and not on the side. There's no way the avoid it. I don't know it. The tennis players that do it move their hand to a maximum position of ulnar deviation that has energy and very important precision;

sometimes nothing happens, but other times yes. If they bandage themselves too much they can't move."

"The left hand we had it as backup. It's the left.... I don't know. Juan had power on his right but then the left started to become a nightmare," said Davin. "Berger, not understanding much about tennis, started to give us questions why he would hit or how with the handle, or why he wouldn't play with one hand, or if he's doing something wrong technically."

No one, inside his team wanted to think that del Potro was facing an obstacle like the one that happened with his right hand. However, week after week the tennis player started to feel little but constant stings that bothered him. Despite that, he ended 2012 with a ranking of No. 7, qualifying for the Masters in London (he lost in the semifinals to Djokovic), winning four titles (Marseille, Estoril, Vienna and Basel) and posting a 65-17 match record.

In March of 2013 the official diagnosis of del Potro's lingering wrist problems came through: a grade 1 sprain of ligaments in the left wrist. His contact with Berger increased, by email, Skype and personally. Between them, a cordial come-and-go relationship was produced, moreover, del Potro and Davin ended up going lots of times to eat at the specialist's house, something that's not really seen between patients and doctors of this size. He continued some therapy and started to take pain relievers. He would also hit his backhand slice more often. Regardless of that, he made a huge effort to compete and his level was still high. He closed the year as the No. 5 ranked player, winning four ATP 500 titles (Rotterdam, Washington, Tokyo and Basel), playing in the Masters Cup in London for a fourth time in his career, obtaining the most amount of points in a season (5,255) since his fantastic 2009 (6,785) and for the first time in the same year managing victories against Djokovic, Nadal, Murray, Federer and David Ferrer.

He couldn't have started his 2014 year any better: he won the opening event of the year in Sydney beating Australia's Bernard Tomic in the final 6-3, 6-1. After that there was the

Australian Open, where he wasn't defending many points since in 2013 he lost in the third round. The No. 3 ranking was closer than ever. But, in an astonishment to the tennis world at the time, he lost in the second round against Roberto Bautista Agut of Spain in five sets. He returned frustrated to Buenos Aires; something was wrong and it wasn't exactly tennis.

On January 27, despite his early loss in Australia, he moved to equal his highest career ranking of No. 4, a place where he stood for three weeks in 2010 before his injury. A day later, he traveled to Rochester so that Berger could see him; the discomfort in his left wrist was getting more repetitive. The American surgeon recommended 20 days of rest and treatment. Del Potro re-appeared in Rotterdam, with the illusion to defend the title, but lost in the quarterfinals to the Latvian Ernests Gulbis. His worries got worse. The wrist was fragile; his mind, worse. The Argentinian next traveled to Dubai and there everything became even worse. Del Potro had to abandon his match with the Indian Somdev Devvarman after losing the first set 7-6(3).

"I tried everything, but I can't be the player I want to be," del Potro said, depressed and with his eyes wet with tears. "I'm going to announce tonight or tomorrow what I have and what would be my future plans."

He knew what was to come. Unlike 2010, when he lost a lot of time looking for an exact diagnostic, now they knew it. They were sure they wanted to give Berger the responsibility again for the operation.

After endless sessions of kinesiology to try and avoid, at all costs, the more invasive step of surgery, he traveled to Indian Wells and signed up to play singles and doubles. He played in doubles with Cilic, but they lost in the first round to Daniel Nestor and Nenad Zimonjic. After the match, he withdrew from the singles event. "Participating in doubles helped me understand that I'm still not ready," he said.

He traveled to Miami, tried to distract himself by watching the polo games in Palm Beach, where his friends the Pieres brothers were competing, but when he was close to playing in Key Biscayne, his fans got another knock on the chin. "I still feel pain and I'm not in condition to compete. I'm sad," he said as he erased himself off the list of participants of the Masters 1000.

"I was very sorry to see Juan like this, playing with pain," said Davin. "He would do everything he could, therapy, taking anti-inflammatory. I would ask myself for how long he would put up with this suffering?"

There was definitely no other option than the operation, the second one in four years. It was a curse.

On March 24, it was snowing in Rochester. Del Potro, Davin and Ramiro Alberti, a childhood friend of the tennis player, moved the curtains in the room where he was assigned at the Mayo Clinic and the panorama was really desolate. During the surgery, that lasted approximately two hours, it was discovered that the damage in the ligaments were worse than originally believed.

"Taking into account the damage, it's amazing that he could even play," said Berger.

Delpo received total anesthesia and had a stamp with the image of Father Francisco that accompanied him. It was sent specially by an emissary after finding out his health problem.

Berger explained to Davin what he had done during the surgery. When the tennis player, at that time ranked No. 8 on the ATP computer, woke up the surgeon transmitted calm and assurance to him. He received numerous support messages on social media from tennis players around the world: Pico Monaco, Stan Wawrinka, Ferrer, Radek Stepanek, Kim Clijsters, Jose Perlas and others. Also Greg Norman, the White Shark Australian legend of golf, wished him a quick recovery on Twitter.

To del Potro, they put in something that's technically called an anchorage in the pyramidal bone: a type of harpoon tip with special strings that come out that can provide stability. Six weeks later, after the operation, del Potro, who wore a splint to keep the wrist stationary, returned to the Mayo Clinic so

Berger could analyze him. With a better mood and accompanied by his friends, the tennis player took advantage of his trip to the United States to move over to Las Vegas to see the boxer Marcos El Chino Maidana against the undefeated champion Floyd Mayweather. Del Potro arrived the night before the fight at the MGM and visited to Argentinian boxer in his suite. He woke him up from his nap. ESPN.com played their encounter.

(Del Potro) How are you champ? It's a pleasure to meet you, I've come to wish you good luck...

(Maidana) Thanks, Juan Martín. How are you?

(DP) Well.... you see, recovering from the wrist injury, I had an operation done and still have a couple months to go. I came from Miami and I wasn't going to miss your fight. But yes, sorry that I woke you up.

(M) No, there's no problem, I was resting a bit, thanks for coming...

(DP) The thing is I know what it's like to wait for a match, it bothers me when curious people come and now the curious one is me, but what do you want, when I heard you were going to fight I asked if they could buy some ringside seats, I couldn't miss this. The funny thing was that they told me that Mayweather invited me to see the trainings. You think I was going to go see him! I'm Argentinian. How are you, Chino?

(M) Good, very relaxed. I don't know what problem Mayweather had with his gloves, but it doesn't matter. I'm going to hit him either way...

Hours later in the Grand Garden Arena in the MGM, Mayweather stayed as the welterweight champion winning the decision by a majority of points.

The tennis player, likewise, lived an uncomfortable moment when at the end of the fight an Argentinian spectator insulted him and recriminated him for not participating in the Davis Cup. Del Potro looked at him seriously, annoyed, but didn't react.

The rehabilitating process of his hand was slow but he remained active. Juan Martín achieved more movement each day in his exercises that were proposed by the kinesiologist Adriana Forti, who had previous experience already with tennis players like Paola Suarez, Svetlana Kuznetsova and Yaroslava Shvedova.

On May 29, del Potro finally returned to a tennis court: he moved around, hit some groundstrokes and volleys, but with a support wrap on his wrist. In the final days of July, the player posted on his Facebook account a video of him hitting softly a backhand for the first time since his hand surgery. The moment was filmed on a hard court in Rochester along with Berger looking on, applauding after the tennis player hit the practice shots.

Some tournaments, like the Malaysia Open, started to promote the image of del Potro in advance of their tournament. That didn't mean that the Argentinian was going to play there, on the contrary. It was part of a commercial strategy. The desire to return to the tournaments provoked lots of anxiety for Juan, who only followed the sport by watching a few tournaments on TV. It wasn't recommended that he increase in rate of recuperation, but to stay in moderation.

"In August or September," is what he said about his plans to return to the tour. Everybody, logically, asked the same thing and it became irritating for him. The question "When are you coming back Juan?" that del Potro would hear every day on the street or in the club where he would train started to annoy him. There was no exact date. He took advantage to test some prototype tennis rackets that they gave him.

Orazi was faced with the enormous challenge of getting del Potro's physique back into playing shape and returning him to the strength that he had before the injury. It was primordial to not get exposed to new difficulties after the body weakened by the surgery and the subsequent inactivity. They focused on taking care of his spine, because to demand more of one arm than another, or a bad posture, could trigger other muscular problems.

The recovery went slower than expected. Although there were no recoils for del Potro, a few times his wrist would still give him some small problems. All the pieces of the tennis player, including a cardiologist specialized in sports medicine, Roberto Peidro, gathered together to analyze how to proceed with his rehab. Each gave their own opinion. And, after a thorough debate, they knew that the healthiest thing would be to reprogram the calendar, forget about 2014, perform a strong pre-season and start 2015 from scratch.

"I prefer to have patience, be prudent and prepare for next year," del Potro said in October. He rented a huge house located at the beach of Carilo facing the sea. He moved there with his work team with the intention to isolate himself from the noise and fury of the city of Buenos Aires and perform a solid physical base that would permit him to, by the end of the year, return to peak physical condition.

The morning alarm clock rang at 7.30 am and the noise rebounded in the entire residence of luminous windows to start the day. Under the supervision of Orazi, del Potro endured many types of exercises in the sand with a wide array of workout devices. He also had access to the red clay courts at the Carilo Tennis Club.

"It was hard to be once again on the operating room, but the trip until that day was worse, especially in Dubai (the last tournament he played), when I knew that this could not continue," said del Potro to *La Nación* during the two-day training session in Carilo. "We went to Rochester, had a meeting with the doctor, who suggested the operation, and I think that day, I don't know if it was because I was very anguished or sad, I thought about it less than in 2010. I told him 'Do it, do it now.' The next day I got up at 6 am, I went in the operating room and he proceeded. I knew that leaving that room would follow my recovery and I should look forward. This process was longer than the one on his right hand, because when they opened me up, they found something worse, but I wasn't so scared or with that much uncertainty."

During those pre-season days in front of the ocean, del Potro revealed how thankful he was to Berger. "In him we found a simple guy, professional, and I had an advantage that he became fond of me," he said. "We became good friends. That's a great advantage, because it's hard for a doctor in the United States to give you his cell phone number. They are closed up and attend to lots of people... I started to meet his sons, his wife, visited his house. When he would check up on me, because of flight issues I couldn't go and come back in the same day to Miami, so I had to sleep over there, and we would always have dinner together, we would talk a lot. He operated on me, but also would take care of me and give me the mental clarity that I needed."

The last previous match for del Potro had been on February 25, 2014 in Dubai. Thus, when on January 7, 2015, after leaving the tournament in Brisbane, he spread the word that he would return to the tour and that he wanted to play in Sydney and at the Australian Open. This was happy news for Argentina tennis. But not everything would be promising.

Del Potro played in Sydney (where he received a special invitation) and beat the Ukrainian Sergiy Stakhovsky and the Italian Fabio Fognini but lost in the quarterfinals against the Kazakh Mikhail Kukushkin. The pain in his left wrist returned. Actually, it never left, but now it started to hurt like at the beginning of the nightmare. Two days before his scheduled return to the Grand Slam stage, del Potro was forced to withdraw.

"Del Potro is one of the players with the worst luck," said Rafael Nadal in Australia. "I went to greet him, gave him a hug, I asked him how he was doing and he said he was doing alright. That's why I was surprised when they left the tournament."

Said Novak Djokovic, "It's a big shame. He's a great player and a great guy. When you have pain, the short term solution is cortisone or injections that could have you play a day or two, but for long term it doesn't help. I hope he is positive in these moments and to be persistent in his intention to come back to the circuit."

By then, del Potro analyzed himself and his game and considered that as a potential solution to the problem to try and alter his technique and to hit his backhand with one hand. "If he can't hit a two-hand backhand I would try with one," said Nadal. The Bulgarian Grigor Dimitrov also gave his opinion: "I saw him the other day and I told him that he should start hitting his backhand with one hand. I don't know if he'll try it, but I insisted that he should do it." But at the age of 26, this was something impracticable.

"I don't think it'll cross his mind even for a second," said Marcelo Negro Gomez, del Potro's childhood coach at the Independence Club of Tandil. "He's too old to change. At the age of 16, 17 or 18 yeah he would try it."

It was a traumatic time for del Potro. After the first operation, the tennis player did exactly what he was told with all the protocols. They took care of him so he wouldn't have to do anything to risk injuring his wrist, including not letting him carry heavy bags. He did a very strong pre-season and was able to compete again, but then suffered an injury again.

From Melbourne, they traveled to Los Angeles and from there, once again to Rochester. On January 20, del Potro returned to an operating room so they could even out a bone that rubbed against another on his left wrist. The X-rays only showed a ligament injury, that was repaired, but that didn't mean there weren't any other internal injuries. "It was hard, hard, hard," said Orazi.

Berger told del Potro that he expected him to play in about a month or so. During the first days of February, Berger took the cast off del Potro and he started his rehabilitation... once again. Meanwhile, he continued with his recovery exercises in Miami. He shared on Facebook a video where he was making a backhand gesture inside a pool with a squash racket.

"The wrist is very complex and to fine tune it in rehab is not easy," said Rivas. "The wrist has bones, ligaments, tendons, and for all that to start working normal again is not simple."

In harmony with the Daniel Orsanic, Argentina's Davis Cup captain and the Argentine Tennis Association, del Potro attended the team's Davis Cup series with Brazil at Tecnopolis to support the team. He was there cheering for Leonardo Mayer, who won an historic match against Joao Souza 7-6(4), 7-6(5), 5-7, 5-7, 15-13 in six hours and 42 minutes, the longest Davis Cup singles match ever. After the epic Argentine victory, del Potro traveled to Indian Wells where he tried to play only in the doubles with Marin Cilic. However, the Croatian begged off due to injury, so del Potro had no choice but to try his wrist in the next tournament in Miami. "He had no rhythm, but he couldn't stand not playing anymore," said Orazi. "He was tired of just practicing." Ranked No. 616, del Potro lost in the first round in Miami to the Canadian Vasek Pospisil.

Totally demoralized, del Potro and his team returned to Argentina. They started to seek new doctor's opinions for what was ailing his left wrist. It was not because they stopped trusting Berger but just to add more opinions and by having more specialists involved to try to find a solution. They got in touch with Clembosky again, the same hand specialist who was very efficient with his diagnosis of the damage in the right wrist and who recommended Berger. The verdict was that del Potro would have to get another operation. It wasn't a bad joke. On June 15, del Potro communicated that in a few days he would get a left wrist operation, a third surgery in 15 months. He did it through a video message of 14 minutes and 55 seconds where he spoke of his condition, with an upset tone of voice, crystal eyes and demolished words.

"At first it was tendinitis, today it's worse. The tendon is damaged," he said. "They recommend another surgery. With all the frustration that it means to me, I've decided to put my body again in an operation room and hopefully there will be a definite solution. From there I want to be happy, with or without the racket... I won't give up... I left Miami feeling horrible. I don't deserve to enter another tournament with my wrist hurting...

I don't want to abandon tennis, don't want to hate the sport. I prefer to take time off and to leave it aside for a while."

He denied being depressed or having thoughts of retirement, but he did recognize quite honestly that he was struggling mentally to cope with his condition and accept his circumstances.

"It was a dreadful period of time," said Davin. "It ended up being worse than the first because even though they knew the diagnosis, Juan's hand still hurt. It was very frustrating. Juan had family, lots of friends and all of us who supported him, but tennis is solitary and there are stuff that only the player suffers. He suffered a lot, but he always had a grip on his situation."

Back in Buenos Aires, after his last operation at the Mayo Clinic, del Potro gained weight and went to the gym, but without the company of his team. On July 24, through Facebook, the tennis player announced that he was cutting his ties with Davin and Orazi, with whom he reached the peak of his career.

"I only have words of gratitude for all the years that we've worked together and I wish them the best," he wrote. "Also a special gratitude for their respective families for the warm support apart from tennis."

The motives about the disbandment were various - fatigue, uncertainty, stagnation, lack of motivation. The trainer and physical teacher needed to keep working and they didn't know when they would be able to again. Del Potro didn't have any certainties about his future. Davin had been accompanying del Potro in his various trips to Rochester, including the last few, when the relationship started to break. Davin had told del Potro that he had made a life decision to settle in Miami along with his family, something that at first didn't seem like an obstacle to continue working with del Potro.

"With Juan we had a very strong relationship, because it wasn't just as his coach, but as friends, family," Davin said to *La Nación* in February of 2016 after a long silence about the situation. "We had many experiences, good and bad. Juan obviously didn't like it when I told him I wanted to go to Miami.

The intention wasn't to stop working together, but maybe just me going to Buenos Aires at different times. He still needed a little more time to recover. We talked a little about that, but he wanted someone to be with him longer and I couldn't do that, because I was adapting to a new country with my family. Also, it's not like I left him when he got his first injury, on the contrary. We were together a long time."

"I am more determined than ever to come back," said del Potro after the announcement of the break from his team. "A new career starts for me. The hardest parts of my career are behind me."

The surgeries that Juan Martín suffered in his wrist were amazing episodes of bad luck. Each was a severe obstacle that prevented him from taking a leap forward in tennis. The severity of the injuries, the numerous trips to see and talk to doctors to get a proper diagnosis and the speculations on whether, in fact, doctors properly treated the injuries added to the stress of this time. However on one particular day, that was not unlike any other, started with a special optimism. Something or someone from above have him gave him an inspiration that del Potro himself could not explain.

"What a pleasure it is to see you again!" wrote del Potro on social media on September 30, 2015. The legend posted a photo with his note that showed him holding a racket on the tennis courts at Crandon Park in Key Biscayne. It was six months after his last match, precisely in that same spot on Key Biscayne and del Potro had returned to once again grip a tennis racket. The worst had passed. The best was about to come.

8

The Great Emotional Change

The elite athlete usually thinks that they are the sun and that the rest of the people are planets and are obligated to rotate around him. The individual sports like tennis, golf or boxing, to quote the ones with highest resonance, are linked a lot more to methodical personalities, those who are competitive and, lots of times, who are the most solitary. The tennis players, the golfers and the boxers don't depend on a team performance, but they only depend on themselves; on the court, the green or the ring. For example, there's just the athlete, his body and mind. But, different psychological studies show that athletes in team sports are more extroverted, anxious and dependent.

"That characteristic that high-level athletes have, a lot of times, separates them from real life," said fitness coach Horacio Anselmi, who worked not only in tennis, but also in combat sports, rugby and swimming sports among others. "How many times do you hear people on the street talk about a top athlete and say 'That person is complicated.' It's not that they are complicated. It's that they are at the top of their profession. They are like that. Take them or leave them. They aren't there to socialize. They're there to beat everyone else. They are people who try to impose their will against others, every day, every week. And it's hard."

Anselmi was part of the Argentine Davis Cup team contingent in Zagreb for the Davis Cup final in 2016 and warned del Potro to take advantage of running freely through the woods when in Palermo because he was going to reach a moment where he wouldn't be able to do it by the siege of people wanting to be with him and talk to him due to his fame.

"Juan looked at me and laughed," he remembered. "That's part of the stuff he has to put up with for being good. People have no clue how much it bothers them to be harassed. They have no idea. Also, the guys with that characteristic are cut by the same scissors. They are all similar. They are organized, neat, obsessive, meticulous, slightly introverts. That's why they don't like big crowds of people. They prefer to be in a corner. If they see a big crowd, they escape. Sometimes that personality generates a more complicated social life, because it has to be all for them and can be very egocentric. Those who are surrounded by these elite athletes have a big ego, but in difference to them, when we are on the street no one is chasing us, we don't have those problems."

A teenager who was "skinny, curved, long hair, nice but also reserved, and not so sure about his body since he hasn't grown in the last few years" is how physical therapist Martiniano Orazi described what he came across when he first met and started to work with del Potro around halfway through 2008. From the start, after setting the guidelines for their working relationship, there was a strong empathy that they had for each other.

With years of strong experiences from the circuit and good team chemistry, Orazi and coach Franco Davin became an emotional backrest for del Potro. This level of comfort that del Potro had with his team gave him an absorbent attitude with them. He held their opinions in high regard. The three were together more than they were with their respective families.

"The life of a tennis player has lots of stuff that the people don't know and that's why it's sometimes unfair what is said," said Davin. "Juan Martín, in that way, is really conservative. He doesn't want to say anything. I believe that's also what brings more problems to him. He would always keep to himself and not say anything. Everyone would understand if he spoke up for what he wanted, especially if it was a complicated matter. He was very complicated for me, because if he wouldn't talk, I didn't know what to do for him. Logically, I would have wanted to do what he needed."

Del Potro endured many physical insecurities that directly affected the rest of the team. These naturally influenced Juan Martín's temperament. "He was also asthmatic and very allergic and he still is, but it got better over time," said Orazi. "He would take his medication. The change of temperature would really bother him. He was a little insecure about his respiratory capacity, his resistance and how he would finish demanding matches. He had lots of retirements in matches. He almost had a record for that."

Del Potro hauled more than 10 retirements in less than two years: three in 2006 (Acapulco, Mumbai and Bratislava), six in 2007 (Australia, Las Vegas, Estoril, Rome, Tokyo; Stockholm) and one in 2008 (Australia). It was too many.

Over the long haul, the allergies were a real obstacle for del Potro. It was a limitation that wasn't easy to resolve. "It was complicated to medicate him because of the risks," said Davin. "We had to ask for authorization of therapeutic use from the WADA (the World Anti-Doping Agency) and an asthma attack doesn't wait on you. You were somewhere and maybe he would have an attack at five in the afternoon and over there in Canada (where the organization is located) it was already closed to try and communicate with them. It was horrible because Juan couldn't take anything, so we had a few problems. It would start to manifest and close his chest up. It was really bad. He was really scared. The attacks wouldn't happen while he was playing, but any other moment, and the temperature changes would kill him. April and September were the worst months. He was also scared of the doping stuff, because on top of that there were lots of cases in Argentina and obviously he didn't want to be one of those. But sometimes the doctor attending to him would have to tell him, 'Juan, this isn't simple.' Now it's more normal, because there were lots of asthma cases. But it was a long time where he suffered."

There were other times when he would want to stay alone when he had a little bit of vertigo. He wasn't kidding when he said he wouldn't get on a roller coaster, not even if he was sedated.

Regardless of the daily drama, the small group of the player, coach and physio lived with each other at all times when they were on tour. Their routine continued when they rented a house a few blocks from the All England Lawn Tennis and Croquet Club during Wimbledon.

"It was like the house from the show 'Big Brother' because we had to go shopping, cook and clean," said Orazi. "Everybody had their own room. For each chore we had games or would do a dare, to not get bored, since we were there for a long time and in the neighborhood of Wimbledon at night there's nothing, just foxes. We would have fun by any means, listening to music, watching a movie, but sometimes time just wouldn't advance."

Said Diego Rivas, del Potro's long-time kinesiologist, "Juan Martín proved to have a winning mentality of a great champion. He relies on his team and depends on them to shield and protect him."

With health and body working without interruptions, del Potro lived in an overwhelming whirlpool, that lots of times didn't let him see his surroundings. At some moment, the system itself, wrong advice, certain misgivings and some bad decisions made him distant and isolated in his own world.

"What we do, it's difficult to have one's feet on the ground and realize that all the time. It's like you are on autopilot, everything goes by so fast," Juan Martín once said.

But the blows that life gave him in what could be called the third part of his career - after the three left wrist surgeries - opened his eyes in many aspects, tempered his personality, made him assess some issues that previously went unnoticed before his eyes and ears. Apart from the first operation on the right wrist in 2010, and the repeated visits to the operating room between 2014 and 2015 due to the damage of the other hand, led him to bottom. Therefore, when he got back from his injury hell, he didn't do it the same way. He released his feelings like never before. He became an extremely emotional player.

"When the stuff that has happened to me, happens to you, your life goes by another side, not by a racket or what you could do in a game. Luckily I was able to play tennis again. That's what I always loved," said del Potro. "Now I see stuff from another point of view. When someone is in this crazy type of life, it's hard to stop, think and analyze. But I had a terrible experience that made me stop my career and it allowed me to see who is beside me supporting me and who really valued me as a person. This stuff made me more sensible."

During the moments with great uncertainty and anguish, del Potro's social media accounts were filled with messages of support. But there was one in particular that moved him. It was the story of Claudio Idio, an Argentinian who settled in La Paz, Bolivia, who was making a living as a hairdresser despite losing two fingers on his right hand. Del Potro himself said what had happened during June of 2015, when he didn't know what was going to happen to his career.

"My wrist problem was at its worst moments, when I lost easily in Miami and a group of fans made an encouragement video for me, but there was one person in particular that when I saw him, it reached the bottom of my heart," said del Potro. "I was in the car with a friend and in a parking lot in the United States who told me, 'Stop I want to show you something your fans did for you.' I was waiting for my turn to go to the operating room when they told me everything was ready. I see the video where this man, who lost lots of fingers, telling me that even like that he works, that he didn't give up, wouldn't give up, he had a job, he was happy and wanted me to also not retire. I started to cry. I broke down. This message was the one to finally convince me to go get my operation done and try to play tennis again."

After an enormous recovery in 2016, del Potro would never be the same. He was completely free. He dazzled even his worst detractors. The psychologist Patricia Wightman affirmed that the Olympic Games in Rio de Janeiro changed his spirit positively.

"He wouldn't be the same person after that experience," she said. "It was too glorious what he did at the Olympic Games. He took his body out of the swamp. From there on he was going to avoid people, places and situations that made him feel stuck. In his moment, and to my judgment, he had too much pressure that led him to have injuries. The physical problems caused by all these pressures are a complicated subject. So, to start to understand his recovery, he would aim for his mental aspect. I live off working with athletes and I see there is a connection there."

According to Wightman, del Potro's physical problems were linked to his mind: "I don't know what type of doctor he visited, surely a really good one, but all of a sudden he's healed? Or in reality did he just find the correct path to confront his fears? He found how to let go and fly. He loved tennis and you can tell. He feels unchained and doesn't want something or anyone to tie him up again. Did his injury teach him a lesson? Yes, it did help out. To get away from tennis, that was making him suffer? Was he needing a break? We could find various answers. From here on, is his wrist totally cured or can the symptoms come back and bring pain? We don't know. What I do know is that there was a reason inside Juan Martín's head to fall into that suffering and then there was something that smoothed his soul."

The mind is the engine of tennis players. Among the top 100 players on the ATP circuit, the majority of the players train with the same intensity and have equally high quality technical skills. However, what truly marks the difference is the mental strength.

Ivan Tcherkaski works as a sports psychologist with histories with rugby players, motorists, pro golfers as well as tennis players such as Gisela Dulko from Argentina and Flavia Pennetta from Italy. With Pennetta, precisely, he had an overwhelming anecdote that linked her with the power of psychology: "I accompanied Flavia in 2015 because she was analyzing the possibility of retiring, but was in doubt. She wouldn't decide until before reaching the U.S. Open in New York. In a changing room in Cincinnati she ended up deciding. It would be her last U.S. Open. 'I won't tell anyone. Just let it come naturally,' she told us. After winning the U.S. Open she announced it in front of everyone! It's because she was free, happy, didn't have to give explanations to anyone and I see the same string with Delpo. You can tell he's made friends with his profession again... He came to believe that he had lost what he loved. However, life gave him another chance and he took a more relaxed approach the next time. Now he's more mature. He is not a 19-year-old kid anymore."

When assessing the weight of the emotional part of his dramatic return to tennis, Diego Rodriguez, the one largely responsible for repairing del Potro's battered body, found a valuable sense.

"Tennis is an emotional duel," he said. "The tennis players are all very good. Also, medicine has advanced so much, the nutrition and in the physical care that everyone does is kind of the same. But then, of course, an aspect is missing. That's the concept of emotions. If you are working and provoking certain positive emotions, it's going to be easier than in some moment of frustration and anguish. You grasp to those arguments from an emotional point of view to overcome them. Juan Martín had them. He found his real self. He recovered something that was almost lost."

"I suffered so much that now I don't complain about anything," said del Potro in February of 2016, during the first tournament he played in Delray Beach, Florida. And, beyond some isolated nuisances in that 2016 season of dreams, you could see him enjoying every moment inside the court as well as with the fans, the officials and even his opponents.

"I'm getting older and the hits I've taken in these last few years changed my life," said del Potro. "At the beginning of my injury with my left wrist, I thought it would only be a short layoff and that it would even help to relax a little. But then the inactivity was prolonged until it seemed as if I was never going to be able to play again. What before seemed automatic and natural, today seems different and now I enjoy it more and do not take it for granted."

There were lots of years where del Potro was conscious of what was said about him, the comments of the readers in the articles in the newspapers and their versions online, social media and everywhere. It's possible that some members of his group are still doing that, of course. Inclusively, one afternoon, Rafael Groppo, del Potro's local manager, visited the *La Nación* newspaper to speak with the editors of the sports section to try to understand how the comment system worked on the web and how he could try to limit the methods of participation of the readers. The important thing is that Juan Martín managed to get rid of a great amount of that peripheral baggage that he was carrying on his shoulders.

"Juan Martín did not carry the Davis Cup trophy on his back, he carried the people of Argentina on his back," said Marcelo Gómez, his coach without a filter. "I think he cared about what the taxi driver, the teacher or the architect said. It hurt what people said on the street and on social media when he was criticized. The trophy itself was not an obsession; I never saw it that way. Yes, he wanted to win the Davis Cup, but his favorite tournament since he was a child was the U.S. Open. He always had pressures and lived that way. All his life he played well and everyone went to see him. He played in any club and everyone wanted him to lose. Why? Because the environment is like that, envious. Or do you think that everyone was happy that he recovered? Sorry, man, but no. This guy is a genius playing tennis. But after the moments of great triumphs it was loaded with ridiculous pressure for what would come. It happened after winning the U.S. Open. But he matured a lot after that."

The world changed for del Potro. He was baffled in the depths of the seas but was brave and battled with determination and minimum of amount of oxygen in his tank to reach the surface. He recovered his energy and caught his breath and moved ahead. He managed to smile and came back to life.

9

Agus, The Other Angel

Juan Martín del Potro extended his Easter week vacation a couple of hours more than usual. He spent a few days at the farm, on the outskirts of Tandil, along with his friends. It was half way through April of 2014 and the tennis player, a month removed from his first surgery on his left wrist, had to soon travel to the Mayo Clinic in Rochester, Minnesota to be examined by the surgeon Richard Berger.

Arenales 100, in the mountain city, is an asphalted street that seemed very quiet even in its busy times, and where the cars park on both sides of the street without hysteria. The street featured low houses with small gardens at the front, sidewalks of classic tiles and trees with little shade. It was a middle class neighborhood, a few streets away from the popular Monte Calvario, where a 22-meter monument of Christ on the cross and the Via Crucis stations are usually visited by people from all over the country during the year.

Returning back home, del Potro, who couldn't drive because of his splint in the wrist while the ligament repairs start to consolidate, asked a friend who was driving his truck to take a sidetrack and to go to Agustin Acosta's home. The little eight-year-old boy, whose case shuttered the town for a few months, was waiting, patiently, in his small living room.

"I'm waiting for a famous person," said Agus to his family who were waiting with him.

With a few days old beard, and wearing a blue sweater, jeans and shoes, Juan Martín asked for permission and tilted down his head so it wouldn't hit the door while going through it. He was a bit shy with his greeting and sat down on a chair next to Agustin's. He got a little closer and put his hand on his right shoulder.

"Hello Agus, look at the gift I brought you," said del Potro to the boy and unfolded on the table one of his t-shirts, autographed.

Agustin, a little restrained, made a grin of happiness. He was meeting one of his idols.

The life of Mariano Acosta and Claudia Ferreyra had become a constant battlefield since November of 2013. It was also like this for Marianela and Franco, their oldest kids. Everything started during a morning and without notice. Agustin, the most spoiled child in the home, was at school, the state number 34 of Tandil, when he started to feel ill and suffer dizziness. The school authorities called his mom, Claudia, to pick him up from school.

"I brought him home and he started to move around a lot in bed," said Claudia, with tears in her eyes in the same living room where del Potro talked with her son and where a photo of the meeting is now displayed. "His dad would tell him to rest. 'I'm feeling OK now. Let's go play ball in the backyard,' he said, and he went to play. Then he started to play on the computer. Agus loved sports. He was a soccer fan and that afternoon he wanted to go back to school because he had physical education class. But since he felt bad and I was going to work, I left him at my mom's house at five. But, an hour later, my mom called me urgently saying that he was ill again. When I go, I see him in a somnolent state, on the couch with a groan. I picked him up, with the idea of taking him to my husband's shop (a small regional food shop), but on the way I started to notice that it wasn't just a normal illness. I went to the Children's Hospital. We went in at 6:20 pm, they told me it was dehydration, but it was nine pm and he wouldn't get better... We couldn't wake him up. They did a tomography and found a small stain at the root of the brain. It could be a tumor, a cyst or a false image of the scan, they told us..."

That day in the Children's Hospital, there were doctors from the Mother and Child Hospital from Mar del Plata. Agustin had really low blood pressure and wasn't in a healthy condition to travel to the Garrahan Hospital, the national leader in pediatrics in Buenos Aires. They transported him by ambulance the approximate 180 kilometers to Mar del Plata. There, you could say, the nightmare began.

"We arrived at noon, he entered the operation room at four in the afternoon and at 10 pm the doctors informed us that... it was a tumor," said Claudia. "They needed to remove a piece to see what treatment to follow, but it was in a very delicate area and was a life-risking surgery."

"You don't know what to do. Your world comes apart," said the dad, Mariano. They did the operation and took a sample of the tumor. He was in a 10-day pharmacological coma. They still waited for the biopsy results. Meanwhile, in Tandil, the news started spreading mouth to mouth. One day they started collecting money to help the family out economically, in the stands of the Ramon Santamarina, the city team that was fighting to ascend to the National B - the second category of Argentine soccer - a flag appeared with the legendary: "Have Strength Agus." The boy was a fervent fan of the club with the black and yellow t-shirt.

On December 4, 2013, Ramon Santamarina, the favorite team of the Acosta family, played in the world stadium in Mar del Plata for the Argentine Cup. A day before, in the same city, Mariano and Claudia knew the results of the scans. There was no going back. It was a real hit. The tumor had spread. The only thing left was to try and make his life as comfortable as possible with love and some medication.

In Tandil, the situation didn't pass unnoticed. It fact, it was the contrary. The city people got involved, gave support and prayed. Since the day that Agustin got ill at school, his father locked his store and didn't re-open for a couple of months. All the hams and cheeses were spoiled. The neighbors, with touching solidarity, took over, among other stuff, to pay the taxes. The owner of the shop stopped charging rent. The municipality also collaborated with the family. The local news followed the story with respect. A client let them borrow an apartment in Mar del Plata for Mariano and Claudia, in its busiest season, so they wouldn't spend money during this long treatment. The corticoids doses and the endless sessions of chemotherapy had changed his aspect a bit, but they didn't remove his mischief or love of sports.

"It was hard for everyone," said Claudia. "For his friends, seeing Agus with his face swollen was hard. It was hard to be strong beside him. We had to go to the backyard to cry, unload and re-enter the house. But he was withstanding it. He never cried. Only once he asked what he had, and when we explained, he said: 'Alright, let's do these rays and kill this trash.' He was eight years old and was talking like an adult."

Before that visit, the Acosta family never had any contact with del Potro. The closest thing, Claudia recalled, was to have seen him at a distance when Juan Martín won the U.S. Open in 2009 and then went strolling in a car through Tandil. "I was at work, downtown, and I went to the corner to cheer for him," she said.

A fan of Boca Juniors and Santamarina, Agustin loved soccer. Not so much tennis, but he would follow by del Potro's matches on TV.

"The rest of tennis he wouldn't watch, but yes Delpo," said Mariano. "There was a special connection, I don't know why."

Mariano took advantage of every opportunity he had to take his son to a Santamarina game, pushing him in a wheelchair to the Municipal Stadium of General San Martin. In those months of 2014 there was a great buzz around Santamarina because they had great chances of ascending in league play. Many team members adopted Agustin with affection and used him as a good luck charm. Every time they would see him in the stadium they would cheer for him.

At that moment, del Potro was also worried, despite the differences with Agustin, but about his own health. The pain in his left hand was disturbing and he couldn't find any less invasive treatment. That didn't prevent this story of this boy from reaching him and touching him. Those who know him more intimately say that behind his veil, del Potro is a deeply sensitive when it comes to hard-life situations like this. The death of his sister in a car crash, when both were little, for Juan Martín logically left a huge scar on his soul. A believer of God, del Potro cultivated spiritually that is totally independent of realization of donations or presences in solidary events. It's something inside that goes beyond actions.

"Juan gets really touched by kids and their stories of fighting," said Orazi. "Generally the fans would ask a lot of stuff and yes I would sometimes tell him that something is happening to some kid with a problem, he would help him. He has a very special sensitive spot for kids in general."

"When one person goes through such difficult times, his empathy and concern grows," said Pablo Pecora, a graduate of psychology and, the time, director of the Argentine Tennis Association Department of Psychology. "In each brain there's a print of pain from each event that relates to some story from your past and when you relieve it in a way, it affects you even more. In the case of Juan Martín, his sensitivity with hard situations doesn't have anything to do with any kind of public relations image he wants to make. It's the contrary. It's the most real thing. If he wanted to show it, he would call the journalist when he does these good will acts. However, he does it with low profile. Also, it has to do with his own personality. He's introverted. It has to do with that. His memories activate and he tries to help by any way, even if it's just staying with the affected person for a while."

Pecora, whose resume included working seven years with David Nalbandian and five with Gaston Gaudio, explained that it's complex to measure how these traumas from the past affect the evolution of an elite athlete. "To some, it powers them, even if it sounds crazy saying it, but it's the truth," he said. "To others, it harms them. To others, despite the pain, it helps them mature in personal aspects that end up helping them in the sport. It's as if those life traumas made them mature by force. Juan Martín, for example, is a mature guy inside the court, has an incredible focus. And it has a lot to do with his childhood construction, his development."

Del Potro's visit with Agustin at his house lasted 40 minutes. Natalia, a friend of Claudia's, recorded the magical moment by video and it went viral on Facebook. There were a lot of conversation topics; the friendship between del Potro and soccer star Martin Palermo, another idol of Agustin; the matches that where approaching in Santamarina; the kinesiology exercises.

"He went right beside Agus to talk and they isolated themselves from all the other voices," said Claudia. "Every now and then someone would ask Juan Martín when will he return, he responded, but then would look right back again to Agus. 'I still have a few months before playing, a few months,' was what del Potro said to an aunt of the boy. He still had uncertainty about his return to the tour."

Mariano told Juan that Agus had a problem where he couldn't move his hand anymore. "He is doing rehab," Claudia told her son. "And then Juan Martín told him, 'You're doing just like me, getting better through recovery.' Agus' right hand would fall, two or three times we would move it and when Juan took a picture with him, he hugged him subtly and grabbed his arm to hold his hand. There were details that at that moment we didn't notice, but after, re-watching the video, we saw. I don't know if the visit changed Juan Martín, but there was a special connection between them."

Despite the enormous difficulties he was suffering, Agustin confronted what happened to him with an overwhelming spirit. He wouldn't lose faith. Even more, during the exchange of soccer opinions, del Potro mentioned Lionel Messi and Barcelona. Agustin, who was a fan of the English team Chelsea, influenced by his older brother, responded sternly in disapproval. It was clear that Agustin was not a fan of the Barcelona team. Everyone started to laugh. The kid was very entertaining.

When walking through the street, already with the chemotherapy treatments ongoing, people passed him, looked at him and smiled, but not with sorrow, but with endearment. "That boy has been someone special in another life," said a friend of his father who practiced alternative energy healing. "He transmits a special energy. Contagious. He wasn't some extra person."

By then, some of the Santamarina soccer players who became fond of and identified a lot with the history of Agustin would come to the house to visit the boy and play soccer matches on PlayStation. But, Claudia said that the meeting with del Potro was extra special.

"Something that he told me later was, 'Hey, mom, am I famous? Because Delpo came to see me?'" Claudia said. "I said that was not the case, but the whole world likes you. That's why they come to see you. He didn't want to take off the shirt that Juan Martín gave him. It was huge on him, like a skirt, but he would always wear it to his chemotherapy sessions."

Before saying goodbye, del Potro and Agustin agreed to go together at the Bombonera to see a Boca match. The tennis player promised him that, when he returns from the United States, in a few weeks, he would take him along with Palermo. "Alright, it's good," said Agus in agreement. Juan Martín gave him a hug and left the Acosta house. Claudia accompanied him to the street. Some of del Potro's friends waited for him in the truck, parked a couple of meters outside.

"How is the situation from here on out?" del Potro asked Claudia. He was told the bad diagnosis.

"Damn… It can't be," said del Potro, shaking his head in sorrow.

"We are going to continue until the very end, because we can't stop fighting, but we know he has no hope," Claudia told del Potro. Juan Martín told Claudia not to hesitate to call if they needed anything and offered any help he could provide.

A few days later, del Potro traveled to the United States and on May 1st, after returning to Buenos Aires after visiting with doctor Berger, he didn't forget the promise he made to Agustin. The two of them, in their respective part of the world, each celebrated the historic league promotion achieved by Santamarina on April 29th after the team beat Juventud Unida 3-1 in Gualeguaychu. Later, Boca would play in their stadium on Sunday, May 11th against Lanus and del Potro wanted to give the boy that chance to be with him at a game. Agustin, however, was in a more delicate state.

The previous Friday before the Boca match, Agustin was with his parents in the shop that they had opened. Mariano, trying to not cry, asked his son why he wasn't happy, since he would soon be with del Potro in the Bombonera.

"No, dad, I won't travel on Sunday," Agustin said. "I won't make it. It's a long trip."

"That destroyed me," said Claudia. "He had already figured it out."

That Saturday at 4 am, the small boy started to suffer respiratory problems so they urgently took him to the Children's Hospital of Debilio Blanco Villegas. On Wednesday, May 14th, after a touching fight, Agustin's small light turned off.

Torn apart, Natalia, the same friend of Claudia's who had contacted Juan Martín's father Daniel to tell him about Agustin, texted the father again to tell him the sad news. When Juan Martín found out, he was paralyzed with grief and sadness.

By being famous, del Potro was at various times involved in many complex and difficult situations, but none like this one that touched him so deeply. According to many, Agus was a special beacon and he continued to shine sending messages until his last moment....and perhaps even beyond that.

Agustin and his dad used to walk on the street a lot, just to stroll around, a way to distract themselves or to buy stuff. During one of those days out, the boy said he wanted a cat. But not any normal cat like a white or black one. It had to be a tiger striped cat, with a certain amount of black dots in his body. Of course, the doctors told the parents to stay away from pets, because of the possibility to acquire some type of bacteria. Even with that in mind, Mariano started to search for an animal with those characteristics that his son had asked for. He searched all the vets and pet shops. He never found one like Agus wanted. The day the boy passed, Mariano returned home and went to the kitchen to drink a glass of water. He looked up and observed his backyard and saw, out of nowhere, a cat with the characteristics that Agustin had described.

"I started to cry," Mariano said. "I went outside. I said 'Agus.' And got closer. The cat stayed. I picked him up and took him inside the house. My wife, who did not know about that talk we had, thought I went crazy."

"He started to scream. 'It's Agus! It's Agus!'" said Claudia. "This man went all crazy on me, I thought, after seeing the cat. I didn't know anything. Then, Fede, the younger cousin, said the same thing, because he had also told him. It was the cat that Agustin had asked for. Me, that I have a phobia for cats, went to the backyard, he would go around my feet and sit next to me and stay there, looking at me. He stayed for a week. One day he disappeared, and he didn't ever come back."

Del Potro kept suffering through his left wrist problems. He started to hit very gently with his two-handed backhand in practice and returned to Rochester again to see Berger. In October, he announced that he would not return to the circuit for the rest of the year. He wasn't in condition. The 2015 year brought the tennis player two new surgeries and much more doubt.

"Agus demonstrated a great energy until his final days and because of that, beyond knowing the severity of his illness, we believed until the last moments that he would be saved," said Claudia. "In time, with what had happened, when he saw that Juan Martín was doubting if he was going to be able to play again or not, he thought that if an eight-year-old boy who fought off such an enormous illness, having so many limitations, why wouldn't he be able to do it? I don't know if the angel of Agus helped Juan Martín a little, but there was something that made him say 'I need to get back.' With my husband, he left us a sensation of being a sensible guy and someone who has his own story. That kiss he throws to the sky when he finishes his matches. He suffered through a lot and he knows what losing means. He lived it."

"Intimately that visit left us something more," said Mariano. "Today, we don't just want Delpo to win matches. We get very excited seeing him play. I get very excited each time they mention his name. How much did he help Agus with his visit? Lots and lots. He made him feel good. It was an engine for him to continue, at least, with an emotional spirit, with the will to continue fighting, to continue."

Time passed. Del Potro managed to surpass his most difficult obstacles of his career and return, with health and success, to play tennis.

"The beautiful thing about those visits (like the one he did to Agustin Acosta), even though the moments aren't the best, but because they come spontaneously and someone can make another person happy with so little," del Potro said. "It's a memory that marks me as a person. Since I was also little, I would get excited with meeting my idols, so now if someone puts me in his spot, I get full of pride and I get excited each time I could do it."

The ex-No. 3 player in the world rowed with wind against his tide to come out afloat. With courage, family support and friends, he managed. By the streets of Tandil they think that, also, there was an angel helping him, who pushed him to go on even if all seemed lost. Whoever wants to believe...

10

Davis Cup:
From Trauma To Freedom

Room No. 1453 at the Minsk Hotel in Belarus was a place of mystery in April of 2004. It was in this city, when part of the Soviet Union in the early 1960s, where Lee Harvey Oswald lived for a short time before he became one of the most infamous people in the world by killing U.S. President John F. Kennedy. However at this time, a group of men were plotting a much different undertaking.

Gustavo Luza, the captain of the Argentine Davis Cup team, faced a challenge of beating Belarus in the event's quarterfinals on a surface so fast it would motivate a complaint from the Argentine Tennis Association, who felt playing on such a slick surface was detracting from the game. There was tension in the air, but this is often the case in a Davis Cup environment, no matter what two teams are competing. This time Luza had to confront the difficulties and do what he could with what he had. The main problem was how to beat the two strong Belarusian players, Max Mirnyi and Vladimir Voltchkov, in their favorite home conditions on a fast indoor court. It was a tall task.

Luza was enduring despite receiving a series of disappointments leading into this match with Belarus. Just two days before the matches were to begin, he gained some relief when Guillermo Cañas, his top player for the week who just arrived in Minsk after a series of long flights and connections, finally responded positively to a right knee test that had him worried if he would be able to compete. Prior to that, the bad news for the Argentine team came in like an unending nightmare: the successive desertions of David Nalbandian with a right ankle injury, Juan Ignacio Chela with scheduling problems, and Guillermo Coria, who was plagued with a sciatic nerve problem that caused him to abandon the final of the Masters Series event in Key Biscayne. So Luza had to build the team with Cañas, Agustin Calleri, Lucas Arnold Ker and a young Juan Monaco.

The skeptical journalist who chronicled those Davis Cup days mentioned an unknown name at the time in his reporting. "The Argentine team started practice with Arnold, Monaco and a young Juan Martín del Potro, who joined the team as a practice partner," wrote the correspondent in the *La Nación* newspaper. That "young Juan Martín," without knowing, started to take in his first breaths of the unique Davis Cup atmosphere that in the years to come would provide many more suffocating moments.

Juan Martín was only 15 years old and was blissful in all of the new opportunities that were accorded to him. He didn't worry about what was going on around him and, like most teenagers, did mostly what he pleased, like helping himself to a chocolate or an ice cream each time he walked by a refrigerator. He enjoyed the comforts of being part of the Argentine Davis Cup contingent in Belarus.

"I remember a boy of 15 years old, very fresh, very relaxed, like that one who is quiet, enjoying being there, where I started to work with him for the first time," said Daniel Orsanic, who worked with Luza as part of the Argentine Davis Cup team in Minsk. "It was a very difficult series, because it was hard to assemble four players. I remember that Cañas went at the last moment and was a bit injured. And the match conditions didn't really favor us. Mirnyi and Voltchkov were huge favorites playing on the fast court with fast balls. We never were able to adapt."

In the practices, Juan Martín showed his potential as a world-class powerful player, but also what he needed to work on to still develop.

"I remember that I practiced very little because that surface was very fast and it was very hard for me," said del Potro years later. "I couldn't return the ball to the boys. And I also remember that I was with Orsa (Daniel Orsanic) as a helper and that's when I met him. In every series of the Davis Cup you live new experiences, nice stuff and stuff not so nice, but you always learn something."

But nothing would help counter the power of the Belarusians, who from the first day slammed the door on any small hopes that Argentina had of victory. Voltchkov and Mirnyi beat Calleri and of Cañas, respectfully, in singles on the first day and on Saturday, they beat Kerr and Calleri and clinched the best-of-five series without even losing a set. On Sunday, they formally concluded the matter by a 5-0 margin with Pico Monaco, in his Davis Cup debut, wining the only set for his team during the series in a three-set loss to Voltchkov.

Luza remembered those hard days in Minsk and the reasons he, dictated by his intuition, added a young del Potro to the squad.

"When I was captain I believed that taking juniors to the Davis Cup series was an important part of their formation as players," said Luza. "For the Belarus match, to take del Potro, it was his first trip to a Davis Cup, his first contact. It really was a difficult experience for him because he was part of a complicated locker room and team. For starters, we couldn't form the team and then they beat us easily. We never could adapt to the speed of the surface. He had a debut in the Davis Cup with a very silent locker room. I called him because he was an important part of the future of the team and also because he had a great serve that helped us practice, despite being so young. At the time, I received lots of criticism for taking him and now he has one of the best serves in the world, so I didn't really choose that incorrectly. There are better ways to start your Davis Cup career. He was a junior, very young, slept a lot, we had to drag him around and one day he got mad because we didn't let him go out dancing with the rest of the team because he was too young."

This is how the difficult and sometimes painful road of del Potro would start in the competition that for Argentina, from the times of Guillermo Vilas and Jose Luis Clerc, would become an impossible obsession.

Three years later, del Potro, then 18 years old, fell on the court in excitement and exhaustion after Jürgen Melzer of Austria hit his final shot into the net. The Intersport Arena in Linz, Austria was the scene of del Potro's best victory of his career – at least up until that moment. It took a few hours for del Potro to clearly understand what he had just done: his victory in the fourth match of the series made him a hero. In his Davis Cup match debut, he ended up providing the clinching point for Argentina. The win established much more than just the win for his team, but also a victory against his own doubts, to be able to win a five-set match against a much more experienced opponent playing on his home court. Juan Martín cried and let himself be hugged by his captain Alberto Mancini and by the entire team who had a mix of joy and admiration for this daring and talented kid.

"I am the happiest person in the world," del Potro said to the press after he could articulate his feelings without any tears in the immediate post-match emotion. "This is incredible, a dream. It's my greatest moment in life. I have no more words to give thanks to, just the entire team for trusting me and supporting me. I thought about them because it was beautiful to represent the team and having a team behind you that supports you in everything. I also thought about my family, friends and my work group. This is beautiful and it helps me take stock of my game. I hope that in Argentina people will enjoy this as well."

The other points in the 4-1 victory were contributed by Cañas and Jose Acasuso. Argentina only lost the doubles point where Acasuso and Sebastian Prieto couldn't beat Melzer and Julian Knowle.

That Sunday, February 11 of 2007 marked the official start of del Potro's Davis Cup career. In the cold of Linz, this character appeared with a granite stubbornness that was so indispensable and resulted in a monumental victory in Davis Cup for Argentina.

"Del Potro is in his takeoff era and we want to continue to improve and move up," said his trainer Eduardo Infantino in a column for *La Nación*. "He is consolidating his game, as seen in his results, but I am more interested for him to get firm in the technique, his physical body, his tactic, his mental toughness and his attitude. He will get stronger week by week. He has to get his volley better as well as his mobility. But now I feel a great deal of satisfaction."

The spectacular debut of the young Argentinian was properly accorded on the official Davis Cup website as they wrote, "Linz was a witness of the birth of an 18-year-old star." Del Potro was progressing as a player and his physical condition was evolving to get closer to what the professional circuit demanded.

The team's Davis Cup aspirations ended in the next round against Sweden a few months later in Gothenburg. The return of David Nalbandian to the team wasn't enough to overcome the Swedish standouts Robin Soderling and Thomas Johansson as well as the doubles star Jonas Bjorkman, who clinched the series in the Saturday doubles with Johansson on the fast court at the Gothenburg Convention Center.

But del Potro represented himself well again, losing admirably to the fast-rising Soderling, who two years later handed Rafael Nadal his first ever loss at Roland Garros. The first two sets were resolved in tie-breakers but the man from

Tandil lost 7-6(4), 7-6(4), 6-4. On the final day, del Potro beat the Davis Cup debutant Robert Lindstedt in a festival of aces: 17 for the Swede and 16 for the Argentinian.

The start of his fulfilled destiny awaited in 2008 with strong results, but with a bitter taste as well. While the innumerable conflicts started to bubble that prevented him enjoying the honor of playing Davis Cup, he was also starting to enjoy resounding victories. Part of the conflict with the Davis Cup that caused him anxiety was balancing his personal ambitions on the ATP Tour with the dream that he carried with him since he first started holding a racket – to help Argentina win the Davis Cup.

"In that year I was just starting to play," del Potro said. "I was very young, I was going my first steps in the first level of tennis, going into the top ten, starting to live the beautiful thing that it is being on the top of pro tennis."

Physical problems caused him to withdraw in the middle of his match against David Ferrer in the second round of the 2008 Australian Open and commanded him to be off the tour for two months. This left him out of the calls of captain Mancini for the next two successful Davis Cup matches against Great Britain and Sweden – both 4-1 victories in Buenos Aires. But the second part of the season for del Potro showed that he was ready to take on the world's best. It was the time of his initial eruption on the ATP Tour and when the world of tennis started asking who that del Potro guy was. He won four consecutive ATP singles titles (Stuttgart, Kitzbuhel, Los Angeles and Washington, two in clay and two on hard court). He won 23 matches in a row before losing to Andy Murray in the U.S. Open quarterfinals. He moved again into the national spotlight in Argentina in the Davis Cup semifinals against Russia, once again in Buenos Aires. Del Potro was overwhelming as he erased Igor Andreev and Nikolay Davydenko without losing a set as Argentina were the victors by a 3-2 margin. That day of euphoria when he beat without a sweat Davydenko in the fifth and decisive match of the series was memorable because of the joke or the exaggeration, depending on how one wants to see it, in referring to Spain, the opponent they would now face in the Davis Cup final at the end of the year: "We are going to remove Nadal's underwear from his ass!"

As del Potro became the hero of the team with his two victories, it fired a light of conflict with Nalbandian, who lost two opportunities to clinch the win in the doubles and again in the reverse singles. Personal clashes and inner conflicts started to manifest for del Potro in Davis Cup, eventually troubling him so much that it would get to the point of him giving up on Davis Cup for an extended period. With an expected victory against Spain in the final forthcoming, what would transpire would be one of the darkest chapters in the history of Argentine tennis.

In those two months that stretched between the semifinal and the final at the Polideportivo Islas Malvinas in Mar del Plata fermented the conflicts that exploded like from inside a pressure cooker in November between the walls of the locker room and the Costa Galana hotel, the refuge of the team and captain Mancini. The negativity was so great that it even outshined the gift that Argentina received in the form of the announcement that Rafael Nadal would not be able to participate in the final for Spain due to tendonitis in his right knee that kept him off the court for months. With Nalbandian hungry for crowning himself in the Davis Cup and del Potro in full ascent, it seemed impossible for this opportunity to escape for Argentina.

The team climate was highlighted by the growing clashes with Nalbandian, and there was much disagreement over the prize money distribution, the chosen court surface and where the final should have been played in Argentina. Nalbandian insisted that the final should be played in Cordoba, his hometown, where he had a started a sponsorship with a local bank.

"Juan Martín's father, at no moment, said that he should be paid differently than the other players," said Franco Davin, then the coach of del Potro. "He confronted Nalbandian and told him that he wanted the prize money to be the same for everyone."

Rumors, the real ones and the ones fed by a myth, permeated. The anger between Nalbandian and del Potro got to a point of no return. In a group meeting in the Costa Galana shot a direct clash between the two key figures.

"And you, idiot? You're not going to talk? Or is your little daddy going to keep doing it for you?" Nalbandian said to del Potro, who stayed quiet. He was too young, without his molded personality to say something back to his face to a player like Nalbandian. In an environment almost unbreathable, the moments the group shared in full were a problem: during the time they would eat, del Potro and Nalbandian attempted to sit far away from each other.

The fury of Nalbandian continued with the choice that del Potro made to play the Masters Cup in Shanghai, with all the physical wear because of the game and traveling to China, just before the Davis Cup final. But del Potro, at 20 years of age, had managed to qualify for the first time for that exclusive year-end tournament where the cream of the tennis crop assembled. His youth emboldened him to believe that he was capable physically and mentally of playing both events that were held just a week apart on different corners of the planet. He didn't want to lose anything. It was logical.

But he couldn't do as much and this didn't take long to be exposed. After an encouraging start with Nalbandian sweeping Ferrer, one should expect that Argentina would take a 2-0 lead with del Potro next facing the inferior Feliciano Lopez. Spain came with limited expectations, but it was still Spain, by then two-time Davis Cup champions (in 2000 and 2004) who were always intimidating with their legendary Armada, complete with gladiators who refused to give up. The Spanish lefty took advantage of a tired del Potro, also hampered with a bad thigh, and to the disappointment of the excited local crowd, opened the doors for the Argentine collapse by tying the first day with a 4-6, 7-6(2), 7-6(4), 6-3 victory. The hole became deeper on Saturday with the defeat of the doubles team as Nalbandian and Calleri fell by a 5-7, 7-5, 7-6, 6-3 score against Fernando Verdasco and

Lopez. On Sunday, the atmosphere was tense as all knew that del Potro wasn't in condition to face his match against Verdasco. Jose Acasuso fought valiantly but lost 6-3, 6-7(3), 4-6, 6-3, 6-1 that gave Spain the 3-1 victory. The debacle of a team that had everything to win but wasted the chance because of its own shortcomings and miseries left that 23 of November 2008 as the most painful date for Argentine tennis in its history.

"What happened at that moment with the Davis Cup was what had happened to lots of elite athletes in the country: leaders that weren't ready to handle some players," said Davin. "When a new amazing player appears, they lose it. I was the captain for that Cup and no one asked me what plan I had. So, as they could choose correctly, they could also choose wrongly. If a guy goes to the Davis Cup and takes his entire team, or goes to the Olympic Games and rents a house close to the club instead of being close to the Olympic Village, like we did in London (for the Olympic Games of 2012), it was because I wanted to win. And the federation or the captain have to try and support that guy. In some moment they didn't value him. Juan is a guy who never asked, for example, how much he was going to win for prize money in the Davis Cup. At one point he said 'I play for free, I don't care, I want to win the Davis Cup.'"

The tremendous crisis unleashed by the defeat to Spain was felt for many years and demanded radical changes on how Davis Cup in Argentina would be organized. A basic change, and the one that was most intriguing after the remote leadership style of Mancini, was resolved with an unthinkable play by the Argentine Tennis Association. On December 16th of that year they chose Modesto Vazquez to take the helm of that heeled ship. Tito, who was going to have Ricardo Rivera as his assistant, had already passed through a tunnel of disagreements between 1986 and 1988 when he had his first experience as Davis Cup captain while also dealing with two polar opposite personalities, Martin Jaite and Horacio De la Peña. But his later activities moved him away from the top players and the ATP Tour, to the point that his appointment was met with a lot of dissenting voices.

"If del Potro crosses him on the street, he wouldn't recognize him... It's been a long time since he played the circuit," said Javier Frana, the former world No. 14 in doubles and an Argentine TV commentator. "Usually they search for someone who knows the current players. I hope that the players can understand each other with him and that everything will go well."

It would be great news for del Potro, because Tito, from his first moments as captain, let people know his sympathy and admiration for the man from Tandil, whom he protected at every moment. And despite his debut as a captain in February of 2009 in Buenos Aires against The Netherlands, del Potro was not available to play. About a month before the match against the Dutch, he announced his intention to only play on hard court surfaces in this time of the year.

"I'm playing on hard courts and Davis Cup is on clay so it would be hard for me," he said, adding that they could count on him when they otherwise need him. It seemed he had recovered his optimism after the dark days in Mar del Plata. "We are stronger. We learned from that series against Spain and we have a really good team."

But the team won easily enough without him, registering a 5-0 shutout with team members Juan Ignacio Chela, Juan Monaco, Martin Vassallo Arguello and Luca Arnold Ker.

"I took over as the captain in a complicated moment after the debacle in Mar del Plata," said Vazquez.

So much so that in the first series of 2009 he didn't have players who wanted to participate: not Cañas, nor Calleri, or Acasuso, not even del Potro, no one.

"The only one who supposedly wanted to play for the flag was Nalbandian, who actually told me on the day of the series, as if to give me a signal," said Vazquez. "After winning that series against the Netherlands, the moment arrived to start designing the future. I had a good relationship with Franco Davin since he started his career as a coach when I worked with the Argentine Tennis Association. I went to England to talk with him and with Juan Martín, with the idea of incorporating him to the Davis Cup. We were going to play against the Czech Republic in Ostrava. We went with Rivera to Roland Garros and we found out a little about the Czechs and the situation on how they beat France in the first round. We found out that there was a place in Paris that had the same type of court that the Czechs used. When I got to Wimbledon... obviously Juan Martín had suffered the previous Davis Cup a lot, I knew him very little. The first time I saw him was when Eduardo Infantino took him to Wimbledon (in 2007 when del Potro beat the Italian Davide Sanguinetti and lost in the second round against Roger Federer). I was working with the British Federation and he told me, 'Come see this kid I have, he plays really good.' It was Juan Martín. I thought he seemed as he was still in development and it was logical for him to be a little off sync in some movements. When I met up with them, in the house they were renting, we talked a little about the Davis Cup. To me, he was the most important figure and I wanted to meet him, to start a relationship and for him to play. Yes, without any doubts, he was very affected by the traumatic experience that he went through in Mar del Plata. There was bad publicity leading into the final, when he said he would play in the year-end Masters tournament in China and the image that was created in Argentina was that he was against the country by playing there before the Davis Cup final. It was forged with total ignorance for what it is to a 20-year-old boy, going to the tournament featuring the top eight players in the world, regardless of the time difference between China and Argentina. If they would have let him sleep when he returned and treated him the way he deserved, the result could have been the other way. They created a very negative image of him. So much so that when I became captain of the Davis Cup, the entire world, including the Federation leadership, told me that Juan Martín didn't want to play. There was even doubt if Davin wanted to leave being part of the effort to dedicate himself only to the circuit."

Based on his rapid rise up the rankings, del Potro was not criticized for missing the first round match to start the season. The 2009 season marked his real explosion on the tour, even before its final crowning in New York in the memorable final against Federer. Only doubts in his mind prevented him from lifting the trophy at Roland Garros, stopped in the semifinals against the Swiss legend. However, del Potro started to prove that he belonged in the elite level of the game and that his future was opening up to him. At the middle of his rise was his spectacular performance in Ostrava against the Czech Republic in the quarterfinals which surprised no one. With Nalbandian out of action because of a hip problem that required surgery and causing him to miss the rest of the year, the "Tower of Tandil" was the clear leader of the team. His performance was demolishing, one of his most memorable Davis Cup performances. Free from inhibitions, playing in a difficult away-from-home environment, he first overwhelmed Ivo Minar and then Tomas Berdych, both in straight sets. However, those two points needed a third one that never arrived. Even though a great performance from Monaco, having Berdych up against the ropes in the opening match, leading two sets to one, Argentina lost 3-2 with Radek Stepanek beating Monaco in straight sets in the decisive fifth match.

"We went to the Czech Republic with very good preparation," said Vazquez. "We trained in Paris for three days (on a taraflex court, a synthetic carpet, at the Sportif Center Claude Dassault Du Val D'or in the Saint Cloud neighborhood.) Delpo shared a room with Facundo Arguello, who was his sparring partner. We felt good, even as a visiting team, when arrived to play the Czech Republic, who were a very good team. The country was really cold and rigid, with its communist remnants, where there was some distance between the native people and us. One of the circumstances that I remember vividly was how we entered the arena through a hallway screaming a chant that we had – that gave me goose bumps. We almost won the series. Monaco almost beat Berdych but what Juan Martín played against Berdych on the final day in his house, when he beat him 6-4, 6-4 and 6-4, it was mind blowing. My head exploded. I knew the guy played good, but I was never this close when watching him. From there he became very important for Argentina."

Something important happened on that Sunday night, July 12, 2009, when everything concluded. While sadness still enveloped the team because of the loss, the team climate seemed to improve. It was cold and just about everything was closed in Ostrava, but, after the intense and exhausting weekend, del Potro got close to Tito and proposed to make everyone go and to eat a final team meal.

"It was weird, but I thought it was nice," said Vazquez after the effort that was put forth, regardless of winning or losing. "There was only one place open in Ostrava, and there was the Czech team celebrating their victory. But that proposal by Juan Martín, to take the team to celebrate the last night, I thought it was really nice."

Two months later, del Potro burst to the top of the tennis world after conquering the U.S. Open. Tito wasn't that surprised, looking back at what he had lived through with him.

"When Argentina won the semifinals in 2008 against Russia, a new idol was born, that was Juan Martín," he said. "Nalbandian stopped being the main actor. I was there, working with younger kids for the association, and I remembered that the crowd did a standing ovation for him. But there was an ego problem, he didn't understand that if he accepted him (Nalbandian to Del Potro) he would have won his Davis Cup a lot sooner. And he would have also been the king any way even if he won in 2008. After his hip operation, Nalbandian wasn't the same. His career changed. For me, the architect, the key, if we were going to have chances to winning the Davis Cup, was Juan Martín."

But those chances vanished the next season when del Potro's wrist problems started; in this case his right one, that left him off the courts for almost the entire year. Del Potro's return to Davis Cup would not come until exactly two years after the great performance in Ostrava, a comfy 5-0 win against Kazakhstan in Buenos Aires in the quarterfinals. In the captain's chair was Tito Vazquez, who charged ahead during that season still stuck by the unresolved conflicts between del Potro and Nalbandian. In order to not disrupt either player, he devised a strategy of sharing training sessions with Caio Rivera.

"I had showed Juan Martín that I was going to protect him," said Vazquez. "In the third year (2011) I had David and Juan Martín on the team together, which is what the press and the public had been waiting for, to see what it would be like for them to coexist on the same team. The press continually harassed me how I would plan for this dynamic? It was hard, very hard. My relationship with Nalbandian was bad. From day one he wanted me out as captain. Caio Rivera got along well with Nalbandian and I got along well with Delpo. We did this to have harmony. It was the first time I was going to act in that situation and I had to see how it would flow. I can't go to a situation with concepts the journalists or other people gave me or that happened before I was involved with the team. I wanted to observe them and not judge on what I had heard happened before."

A normal coexistence was sought for the team. On one night, they invited the actor Ricardo Darin to eat with the team to relax the atmosphere.

"What I noticed was that David's influence on others was important," said Vazquez. "It had already happened to me the first time I had been captain. Jaite's influence on other players on the team distanced himself from de la Peña, who was the player I was able to motivate to play well. That is what Nalbandian was doing. He had shown it in France the previous year (in Lyon where Argentina lost 5-0, also in a tense atmosphere). Little by little, he was getting the guys on his side, even the ones who were making their Davis Cup debuts, like Zeballos or Mayer. I'm a straight guy. I say things face to face and won't try to win your friendship. There has to be a minimum respect between the coach or the captain and the player. I noticed that this was happening and tried to protect Juan Martín. If he likes rock and roll and Nalbandian likes salsa and David would tell him 'Come to the room at 11 pm to listen,' the other wouldn't go, not because of a lack of partnership. They have different tastes. The proposal was to go out and eat as a team; each one individually would train in their best way possible and they tried being the best they could emotionally."

Enduring that tension and maintaining the team's best chance for victory was a delicate balance that couldn't always be achieved. Many times it was overcome simply by the quality of the players. By the time Argentina visited Serbia in Belgrade on September of that year for the semifinals, the compromise of a civilized co-living was working reasonably well. Del Potro's level of play was sublime. Janko Tipsarevic could do very little to stop him on the opening day and, combined with Nalbandian's victory over Viktor Troicki and Argentina enjoyed a 2-0 advantage after the first day. After Argentina lost the Saturday doubles, it set the scene for the decisive Sunday. Del Potro, by that time, was as fierce a threat of anyone in tennis, and faced Novak Djokovic, who had just won the U.S. Open earlier in the week. But Djokovic only arrived in Belgrade just on Wednesday, after an exhausting final in New York played on Monday, none-the-less against Rafael Nadal.

Tired and battered, Djokovic faced a man in del Potro who played with a rhythm and with such precision that it was complicated confronting him even in his best state. He only lasted until the second set as Djokovic realized his physical condition or his tennis would not be enough to beat a such a fired up and relentless rival as del Potro, who triumphed 7-6(5), 3-0 retired. It was another sensational triumph for the man from Tandil.

Even with that pair of aces, the Davis Cup Final represented a little less than an impossible challenge – beating Spain in Spain in Seville on red clay with both Nadal and David Ferrer being very inspired for the Spanish team. To boot, the internal struggles of the Argentine team was far from clearing up.

"The rumors had already started that I would get replaced by Martin Jaite as Davis Cup captain the next year, despite whatever happened in the final," said Vazquez. "This made it made it complicated for me to feel well at certain moments. It was an unpleasant situation and for my personal ego. Winning that semifinal in Belgrade was a great satisfaction. Against Spain, in Seville, there was a chance for a stroke of luck to appear."

The truth is that there was nothing one can do against a rival that was practically invincible. The 6-1, 6-1, 6-2 beating that Nadal inflicted upon Monaco on the first day foreshadowed the incredible task that faced the Argentine team. To top it off, Ferrer played like never before in the second singles match beating Juan Martín 6-2, 6-7(2), 3-6, 6-4, 6-3. Nalbandian was only in shape for the doubles and, with Eduardo Schwank, registered a 6-4, 6-2, 6-3 win over Fernando Verdasco and Feliciano Lopez to give some air for Argentina. However, an intractable Rafa closed del Potro's doors in the definitive day, beating him by 1-6, 6-4, 6-1, 7-6(0). Of course, as always, the rumors started swirling during the final, one of them being that del Potro asked to not play on the last day against Nadal.

"Not at all," Vazquez said to dispel the rumor. "There was no doubt that Juan Martín would play both singles. He never wanted to erase himself from the line-up. Vazquez said that he would not withdraw del Potro from the singles line up even if he was drunk!"

After the conclusion of the series, del Potro was so exhausted that before the closing official team dinner on that final Sunday that he had to ask the team stringer Luis Pianelli to help him get his tie knotted because he couldn't even lift up his arms.

It was another Davis Cup final lost to Spain, but under quite different circumstances than three years earlier in Mar del Plata. However, the clouds of dissent and disappointment would not clear up so easily, especially surrounding the captain. In mid-December, exactly three years since he was named the

Argentina's Davis Cup captain, the AAT officially named Martin Jaite as his successor.

"I wanted to lead the team the following year," said Vazquez. "One more year, we had all matches slated to be held at home, because we played against all the favored team previously in away matches. The Davis Cup would be won, regardless of Nalbandian, who to me was just a decorative figure, and of not vital importance. In one more year we would have won the Davis Cup. We were headed for a royal flush: quarterfinals (2009), semifinals (2010) and finals (2011). We made great achievements on the third year with our two most important players (del Potro and Nalbandian) when we went to Serbia and Spain as visitors. We had a valiant loss in the final and for the coming season, we would likely play our matches at home. I think we would have won it, but I can't prove it."

The arrival of Jaite, with Mariano Zabaleta as the assistant captain, seemed to forecast more hard times with the internal relationships of the team. Jaite's previous relationship as Nalbandian's coach in the days of the Davis Cup Final in Mar del Plata in 2008 stirred negative thoughts in del Potro, who also was left hurt after the replacement of Vazquez, who always supported him and by his estimation did a good job with the team. Knowing that the situation was far from being easy, the new captain took the helm with praises and positivity.

"Juan Martín del Potro is a beast and a player who's going to fight for the top ranking in the world, I assure you," Jaite said, also acknowledging that he didn't know much about del Potro's personality because of their generation gap. "I know him very little," he continued. "When I organized on the Futures level, he worked his way quickly through that level because you could see already what he was going to do in pro tennis. I got to know him a little more when I traveled with Gaston Gaudio in 2007, but after that, almost nothing. I know everyone else a little more."

However, the 2012 season started on pessimistic terms between Jaite and del Potro.

"We won't play the Davis Cup in Germany," Franco Davin announced January 6, 2012. "Juan Martín's physical condition is most important. Playing on clay and the next day starting to compete on hard courts is a big risk."

Jaite would start his tenure as Argentina's Davis Cup captain without the best Argentine player, then the No. 11 player in the world. The absence created a new breeding ground of negative talk surrounding Argentina's Davis Cup efforts. Social media posts were critical of del Potro and his decision. Jaite hurried to put cold cloths on the heated criticisms of the top Argentine.

"You're not a traitor if you don't play Davis Cup," he said. "I don't see it like an obligation for our homeland or nothing less, no one has any obligation."

Despite del Potro's absence, the first step was taken without any major inconveniences. At the University of Bamberg, the site of Germany's first round match against Argentina, it was so cold with temperatures down to 14 below zero that going outside was a question of bravery. But in the Stechert Arena, the heat was put on by Monaco, Nalbandian and Chela who pulled together a not-surprising 4-1 win over the Germans, who while having a famous Davis Cup history with three titles in 1988, 1989 and 1993 but with great players from another era like Boris Becker and Michael Stich. In this series, the German threat was presented by Florian Mayer, Philipp Petzchner, a veteran Tommy Haas and Cedrik-Marcel Stebe. The other great German player at the moment, Philipp Kohlschreiber, dropped out the week before.

Happy with Argentina's victory, del Potro congratulated his countrymen on their victory via Twitter: "Congratulations to the boys and to the entire team for the great triumph facing Germany," he wrote. For Juan Martín, 2012 would be a pivotal year in his relationship with the Davis Cup.

At the start of April for the quarterfinals, del Potro enjoyed a home Davis Cup experience like he had never had before. An allergy in the eyes, fever and vomiting had placed his participation in doubt against Croatia in Buenos Aires but on that weekend del Potro was destined to further enhance his role as Argentina's tennis idol.

As a distant advance of what would happen between Argentina and Croatia in Zagreb in 2016, del Potro beat Ivo Karlovic on Friday and on Sunday he swept Marin Cilic, losing only four games. Del Potro was acclaimed by his home crowd like he had never experienced before. The sustained ovation from the people was part of the perfect script for del Potro on this day, that also featured a tender moment when a butterfly landed on his racket between points. Nalbandian congratulated him after the triumph against Cilic that decided the series and placed Argentina in the semifinals. Destiny appeared to be favoring Argentina as their semifinal against the Czech Republic as well as a potential final against either Spain or the United States would be on home soil in Argentina. However, the trap was just around the corner.

September marked the start of del Potro's darkest times with the Davis Cup. The story of that semifinal with Czech Republic, again played at home in Buenos Aries, was convoluted from the start. Nalbandian, again afflicted by physical problems with an abdominal tear, was not able to play and del Potro arrived at Buenos Aires from New York after an enormous effort in the quarterfinals of the U.S. Open against Djokovic. His doctor Richard Berger had prescribed 15 days of rest to take care of his left wrist, which began to bother him once again.

The first signal of trouble in the Davis Cup team camp came when del Potro chose to practice with Davin and work out in the gym away from the team, choosing to train at the Argentine Tennis Club in Palermo and not the Parque Roca in Buenos Aires. "I really want to play for the people," del Potro said to the media. Inside of the team camp, the string that held together Jaite, Zabaleta with del Potro was pulled as tight as can be. The tension manifested from circumstances such as Juan Martín not wanting to be part of the official team dinner before finally being convinced to attend.

By the middle of the week, del Potro began to practice with the team and used Diego Schwartzman as a hitting partner along with Leonardo Mayer. The distrust in the team environment continued to grow.

Miguel Khoury, the Argentine Davis Cup team doctor, said a few days before the start of the series with the Czech Republic that he was not sure if del Potro would even be able to compete due to his wrist problems.

"Del Potro playing here is an act of courage because he didn't rest, as recommended by his doctor, due to his enormous desire to play Davis Cup," said Khoury. "Doctor Berger indicated a treatment for him and also indicated some risks that could happen if he played, but Delpo said that his desire to play is greater. What Juan Martín has is a ligament inflammation in his left wrist. To play the U.S. Open, he had to receive shots so he could play."

In a little over two and half hours, del Potro got the first point for Argentina after beating Radek Stepanek 6-4, 6-4, 6-2. In the end for del Potro, it was a pyrrhic victory, or one that inflicted such a devastating toll that it almost felt like a defeat.

"I had no backhand," he said. "It's really hard to play this way. The serve helped me and the forehand too, but when you can't do damage with all your shots it becomes difficult. I am a player who tries to be aggressive with all my shots. It's frustrating that from one side I can't do it and the wear is very big, even though now that I won it's a great feeling…I took a risk because I played with a lot of pain. The less I think about that, the better."

Del Potro was relieved after the victory, but he would soon be convulsed with what was coming. From outside, until Stepanek tossed some wood into the fire regarding del Potro's condition by saying, "He caused a little stir heading into the match about his form, but he didn't seem injured. I saw him completely healthy."

That same night, del Potro let the group know that his wrist pain was too intense and that he didn't feel that he could play on Sunday against Berdych, a vital point for the series. Outside the walls of the team, the rumor of the possible absence started to spread on Saturday morning. Under pressure and with great responsibility on his shoulders, the doctor made the decision that at that moment was open to be questioned but, with time, proved to be beyond reproach. When the chatter became so intense, Jaite finally confirmed that del Potro would not play on the final Sunday and announced that Carlos Berlocq would play his debut Davis Cup match for Argentina in his place. Khoury, in a declaration of 44 seconds, explained what had happened with del Potro: "Juan Martín ended yesterday's match with great pain. Regrettably, we thought that he wasn't in any condition to play on Sunday. He is going to continue with his treatment that was previously laid out, with therapy and the immobilization of the wrist for ten days. We thought it was the best decision for his problem."

Since Monaco lost to Berdych on Friday in five sets and Berloq and Eduardo Schwank lost to Berdych and Stepanek in straight sets in the doubles, there was no margin of error on the final day. Berlocq lost convincingly, in place of del Potro, falling 6-3, 6-3, 6-4 to Berdych that clinched the victory for the Czechs. It was the first loss by Argentina at the Parque Roca in Buenos Aires since they started playing there in February of 2006. When he left the stadium, Juan Martín was accompanied by whistles mixed with screams of support.

"I understand that they had to whistle or cuss someone out because of the pain of losing in the semifinals," said del Potro later upon reflection of the moment.

Del Potro's relationship with Jaite and Zabaleta was broken, as well as his association with Davis Cup in Argentina. Over the next few conflicted months, news stories came to light about what had happened during that tortuous weekend, apart from all the tension on the team and with the relationship between del Potro and the leadership of the Association. For example, one that attributed the boos of the people to have been influenced by Hector Romani, one of the influential leaders of the AAT, who already was unhappy with del Potro. It was former AAT President Arturo Grimaldi who defended all of the accusations and questions directed towards del Potro.

"I don't agree at all with the whistles to del Potro nor do I understand why the people were outraged," Grimaldi said. "Juan Martín did his best to play, gave the first point to Argentina and later felt such pain that did not let him continue. He gave everything he had."

Everything that happened from there on out was part of a long and dark tunnel that started to travel through del Potro. There was a lack of communication with Jaite on what his plans were with regard to Davis Cup in 2013. Finally, in the last hours of the year, del Potro said he would not play in the Davis Cup in 2013, choosing to concentrate on playing on the ATP Tour.

The external interferences, the criticisms, the suspicious looks of some colleagues contributed to this decision, but del Potro also himself acknowledged that his silence contributed to the confusions and lack of communication. "Yes, there are times where keeping quiet would generate stuff or form opinions that aren't real," said del Potro. "I admit that there are times I should not keep quiet."

Del Potro's absence did nothing but wake sleeping rants. The 5-0 victory for Argentina over Germany at the Parque Roca in the opening series of the Davis Cup in 2013 fired up the tension between del Potro and his companions, who in the locker room "dedicated" the victory to del Potro, at a distance, with sarcastic songs. In the press after winning the doubles point with David Nalbandian Horacio Zeballos was asked if he had received a congratulations from Juan Martín: "From who?" he answered with sarcasm. It was an unthinkable joke that years later he would regret. "I tried to be funny and I messed up," said Zeballos in March of 2016. "I talked about it with del Potro and the relationship is alright."

The uncertainty of del Potro's status with the Davis Cup team caused for much conversation on the topic. Lucas Arnold

Ker, the stalwart doubles player for the Argentine Davis Cup team, spoke passionately of del Potro's absence from the team.

"Sometimes I get sad with the whole del Potro stuff, that he is losing an opportunity and I don't understand it," said Arnold Ker. "It sucks that he isn't here. Some say 'Federer won't play Davis Cup for Switzerland and nothing happens.' But our country is different. I would love to pass my passion for the Davis Cup to del Potro. It goes beyond the connections with your teammates. I also don't think that David (Nalbandian) is a saint. It's like the soccer team: when we are playing the World Cup and if (Lionel) Messi is in a fight with (Gonzalo) Higuain, it doesn't matter, you still gotta play and win. Del Potro doesn't realize what he is losing and the good it would do to him."

The silence from the AAT toward del Potro only made the relationship more strained. Romani, the AAT vice president, was one of most critical voices against del Potro, but would not speak with him, despite del Potro stretching and changing next to his locker at the Argentine Tennis Club.

"I have no contact with him," said Romani in September, only deepening the division. "We have no dialogue and we really don't know why he doesn't play. The reason he gave was respectable, but hard to comprehend. It's the same as if Usain Bolt doesn't want to run so he can take care of his body. Let's hope it was only for this year and that in 2014 he comes back."

Del Potro responded to these indirect questions posed to him by hardening his position that would lead in a more traumatic point: the irritating letter that, by halfway through November, he directed to Arturo Grimaldi, the president of the association, and to Jaite, where he employed unusual hard terms.

"I am tired to get invited by email or via messages while at the same time being pressured to play via the press and trying to make me look bad in public opinion. I think that is hypocritical," del Potro complained, adding that he was never consulted for his opinion about the decision on who should be the team captain or what surface the matches should be played on and, when they did do it, they never considered his opinion.

All the gaps were closed for a Davis Cup reconciliation for del Potro due to his strained relationship with the federation leadership and Jaite. It became even more distant based on the injury problems he had with his wrist.

In October, Argentine tennis was hit with the news of the death of Grimaldi, the federation president, due to cancer at the age of 63. Grimaldi was sympathetic to del Potro and his positions. He would even send text messages to del Potro's father, despite his weak health, where he would ask him to please make Juan Martín return to the Davis Cup.

In the days after his death and after all of the condolences (Juan Martín sent a letter to the Grimaldi family), del Potro made a public statement via the media about his distance with the federation. "There are times when you are bothered but what is said, especially when they are things without foundation," del Potro said. "I already made it known what I think and what my position is." He also called for a major restructuring in national tennis in Argentina, emphasizing what he observed as a lack of support for youth and the lack of a national training center for tennis. A voice that again and again insisted in defending him, just like criticizing the leadership, was from the ex-captain Tito Vazquez, who three times during the year, on social media, published letters with sharp terms.

"I know how they dirtied your name and still do it... I know about all the critics and the hypocrisy that is feeding with words and ghosts and miserable smiles that are enjoyed by the misfortune of others," he wrote in one of his postings.

Jaite's contract as Argentina's Davis Cup captain came to a close at the end of 2014, ensuring the team would return to the World Group with a win over Israel in the playoff in September in Sunrise, Florida in the United States. Shortly afterwards, efforts started to take shape with the intention of working to bring del Potro back into the Davis Cup fold.

.The "return operative" started in a meeting on November 24 in a hotel in downtown Buenos Aires where Daniel del Potro, Juan Martín's father, met with two leaders of the Argentine association, Daniel Fidalgo, the third vice president, and Diego Gutierrez, the legal secretary. Armando Cervone had already taken the spot of the deceased Grimaldi and headed the leadership team. It was a first effective substantive movement to repair the relationship with del Potro. The positive steps of reconciliation started to multiply when it was decided that Romani, the critic of del Potro, would leave his post at the association in May of 2015. The key decision made at the end of November was to install Daniel Orsanic as the new captain of Argentina's Davis Cup team. All of these were met with approval from Daniel del Potro. In subsequent meetings, it was decided that del Potro would get more involved in development with the federation and that his old coach Negro Gomez would also work officially in this area.

Orsanic started talks with the players about playing in the first round match in 2015, a home match against Brazil. The team also added three support professionals with close and friendly ties to del Potro: the Dutch physiotherapist Christiaan Swier, the stringer Luis Pianelli and the doctor Javier Maquirriain.

"After those days in Belarus I saw del Potro again lots of times on the circuit," said Orsanic. "Not in the juniors, because later I started to train Acasuso so then I didn't cross paths with him until he started playing with professionals. I always had a good relationship with him but we weren't that close. I trained other players and he was with his work team, but we would always say hello affectionately, maybe because of the memory of that series against Belarus. But I never had that much of a relationship with him beyond that. From the moment I started my work as the Davis Cup captain I think it was the same, but the relationship was enhanced for obvious reasons. From the very first moment, I wanted to be at his disposal and so the other players could also feel close, so they knew I was there to support them. With Juan Martín, it was important for him to know that despite me being the captain of the Davis Cup, I was there to support him, to count on me. That was given through time."

On February 12, 2015, what everyone waited for happened. After so many talks and some concessions, del Potro announced in Miami that he was ready to return to the Davis Cup team. He would not immediately play in the upcoming tie against Brazil due to continued recovery from his second operation on his left wrist. Two and a half years after that traumatic series against Czech Republic that sowed so many wounds, del Potro was ready to reconnect to the Davis Cup world, a place that always combined his sports dreams with an immense sensation of responsibility that prevented him to truly enjoy his career as a tennis player.

"All those times were rough," said Martiniano Orazi, del Potro's trainer during many of these years. "He did not enjoy the Davis Cup. The most painful thing was how much he really loved the event. He really loved the Davis Cup, to play with the people cheering, to play for Argentina. Sometimes in a normal tournament he didn't have that. To be told, all those stuff was very painful and it consumed him, because he always cared about his country and the Davis Cup."

The patience, knowledge and discretion from Orsanic started to build a foundation, starting with the frequent appearances of Leo Mayer, Federico Delbonis, Diego Schwartzman and Carlos Berloq. But what was needed was the definitive impulse that could only be provided by a different player of a higher level. But these were still dark times for del Potro who kept on fighting to overcome his injury and not allowing him to even have a glimpse of professional tennis. Meanwhile, the balanced work of Orsanic guided the team into the Davis Cup semifinals in 2015, where Belgium, playing at home in Brussels, was an insurmountable obstacle.

In July of 2016, on a hot day in Pesaro, Italy in the Davis Cup quarterfinals against Italy, Delbonis, Monaco and Guido Pella distracted the hours by playing card games and listening to music. In that locker room at the Circolo Tennis Baratoff, one of their companions preferred another routine: sitting 10 minutes alone, in silence, with his attention only focused on changing grips on all of his rackets. Del Potro soaked in the environment of his return to the Davis Cup that was so delayed. His return was on the doubles court, alongside Pella, where they gave Argentina a point in beating Fabio Fognini and Paolo Lorenzi in a hard five-set match lasting three hours and 50 minutes.

That long road back to Davis Cup that left him on the shores of the Adriatic Sea also found him reconciled with Monaco, his old friend with whom had patched up old differences. With Monaco they shared lots of stuff: beyond their difference of age (Juan Martín is five years younger than Pico), they went to the same school in Tandil, the San Jose, and they also schooled their games at the Independent Club. But since the fateful series with Czech Republic in 2012, the link between the two vanished. With the distancing, resentments broke up: when Monaco wasn't aforementioned by Orsanic to play with Brazil in 2015, his people doubted that that was because of del Potro was asking for it.

"My relationship with him is void," said Monaco during those days. "I know he will return to the team when he recovers because I read one of his communications and I'm happy, but I have no dialogue with him."

Not even the wedding of a mutual friend in the Tandil Valley at the end of 2015 helped to bring them closer. During the wedding they actually avoided each other. But the message Orsanic focused on from the beginning of his tenure was to build the bridges between them. A few talks during the Miami Open patched up some of the wounds and reestablished the old relationship. They blamed the media for manifesting the disagreements and set forth that they would all get along going forward.

The victory against Italy, where Juan Martín contributed with that doubles victory, was buoyed by Delbonis, who dispatched Andreas Seppi on the first day and their local idol Fognini to clinch the 3-1 win. It served as a prelude for the return of the full and healthy version of del Potro. But even during these more peaceful times, what did not disappear was the enormous weight of responsibility of Davis Cup.

In the semifinals against Great Britain in Glasgow, he assumed again his lead role in singles and registered an extraordinary victory against Andy Murray, until then the best player of the season and the one who had snatched his dream of the Olympic gold medal in the final in Rio de Janeiro just weeks before. Orsanic decided to squeeze what energy was left in del Potro in the doubles, pairing him with Mayer against the Murray brothers, Andy and Jaime, to try and finish off the victory. The risk, however, was not successful. But after Andy Murray beat Pella to tie the series, it was Mayer who propelled Argentina into the final by beating Daniel Evans in the fifth and decisive match. The victory gave del Potro a giant sensation of relief.

"The ovation that the English public gave Juan Martín was a great show of respect," said Orsanic. "The cheered him before the match against Murray started. From that day I'll remember everything Juan Martín did during that first to last point. During some part of the match, Murray just played to try and wear him out, he had him two sets to one. It's one of the greatest Davis Cup matches that we've ever seen. It's not often that a Davis Cup series starts with a match of this caliber."

In the preparation for the final clash with Croatia, the team was dominated by tension. Del Potro took advantage of a meeting in Buenos Aires to convey to his teammates the bitter experience of Mar del Plata in 2008. He told them what he had done wrong that time, what stuff not to repeat.

"In a certain sense we already feel like winners," said del Potro. "It's not easy to reach a final with no player inside the top 20. We are happy to have reached this far and by how we achieved it. The conditions weren't in our favor, but the path we built to reach this final was something to be proud of."

The story behind that weekend of November in 2016 was strong enough that his thousand details would endure for a long time. In Zagreb, like in Glasgow, Orsanic was challenged to solve who would play for him in the doubles and trusted the stamina of Juan Martín to play and thus play all three days of the contest. On that memorable final day, he became a legend with his incredible comeback against Cilic, setting the stage for Delbonis to finish the victory. The image of Delbonis falling to the ground in exultation after the last ball hit by Ivo Karlovic went long instantly became the unforgettable postcard image for Argentine tennis.

"It's a dream come true," said Orsanic. "Juan Martín is our reference. Having been able to win the Davis Cup brings enormous joy, but it is also something that a player of that skill crosses off a list. It's like it frees them. It's beyond the desire. They are achievements that transform players at level to a higher regard in their place in the sport."

"From my perspective, it's very similar to a movie," said del Potro a few days after the victory. "My matches, my return, the Olympic Games in Rio, the Davis Cup. It was all like a dreamed movie, dramatic, that ended with the best ending. Then, the way that the team started knowing each other and assembling perfectly. Each one understood what role they occupied. I never felt more or less important than my teammates. They knew what I could give, what I could teach. I knew what I could learn from them too. Each one occupied the space they were giving. With a great captain like Daniel, that would toe the line and we would all understand the message. We achieved the dream the entire country wanted. By finally achieving this dream of winning the Davis Cup, now I have everything to enjoy tennis and do what I want to do."

His Davis Cup journey lasted 4,620 days, from that Sunday, April 4 in 2004 when at the age of 15 he arrived in the cold of Minsk to practice with the team and take chocolates from the fridge.

Few knew the union of Juan Martín del Potro's personality and his tennis game like Davin. The man of Pehuajo who guided him through all the courts of the world during his best and worst years can express himself like no one else about what the Davis Cup produced in the body and soul of del Potro. Davin's opinion was like a meticulous X-ray.

"In the life of an athlete there are lots of very difficult moments and the Davis Cup was on that was very hard for him, but he lived lots of those," he said. "Girlfriend break-ups, for example. The Davis Cup was terrible and very unjustified. One thing is the pain or the depression because you can't play if you are injured and another was something unjustified. It was like they didn't want him. He always wanted to play the Davis Cup. For him, being able to make surface changes cost him a lot. Like arriving from Wimbledon and getting off an airplane and going to play on red clay with little time to adapt. Those are the things that Juan did not communicate well enough and did not take care of himself. Everything bad that came out of the Davis Cup did not allow him to enjoy his career. He was the one who had to win all of his matches and shoulder the burden of the team. There are few players in the game who hold that pressure."

On Monday, November 18, 2016, after resting a little bit by all the excitement of an unforgettable day and by a surprising anti-doping control at 5.30 am, Juan Martín del Potro appeared at 8:15 am in the lobby of the Double Tree, the hotel chosen by the Argentine delegation to shelter his dreams as a champion.

"Finally, it's over," said del Potro to the author. "I feel as if I were 20 kilos lighter. From now on I can sleep calmly..."

He joined his teammates in a van that left for the Zagreb airport. Hours later, the seemingly endless Argentine celebrations began. That weekend turned Juan Martín del Potro into a free man.

11

A World Fascinated By The Gentle Giant

In the middle of the match against Rafael Nadal at Wimbledon in 2011, Juan Martín del Potro pretended to give the ball to the ball boy who quickly entered the court, but when he got close, he retracted it. The trick was repeated, but the ball boy quickly realized that the Gentle Giant del Potro was just having some light-hearted fun. The humor made everyone laugh and loosened the tension on Centre Court at the All England Club.

Another time at the Australian Open in 2013, del Potro played Jeremy Chardy and after he missed a shot, the man from Tandil nearly smashed his racket after missing a shot. He walked toward the end of the court with an embarrassed expression, as if wondering what was going on. He walked towards an elderly line judge and unexpectedly put his arm around the shoulders of the official. It was if he wanted to share his misery with a friend. The Gentle Giant often goes from fury to a joke in just a manner of seconds. The people cheer him.

At the Davis Cup in 2012 against Croatia in Parque Roca, del Potro patiently watched a delicate butterfly fly in front of him and land on his racket. The Gentle Giant then gave the butterfly a kiss before allowing it to fly away to safety before he belted a serve.

These moments, and many others that are similar, can be found on YouTube and are celebrated by fans around the world. Most of the time on the court, del Potro maintains a serious gesture, sometimes even seeming to be mad.

During the majority of time that he's inside a court, del Potro maintains a serious demeanor, sometimes even seeming mad. He has a natural grimace on his face that matches the ferocity of his hits. However, at all times, he is on the edge of breaking that rigidity and acting like a little kid who is just having some fun. It is as if "The Terminator" would say a joke. Del Potro isn't a Terminator, but as a player he resembles one with his size and the unusual power in his game. The combination between one thing and the other makes him a lovable guy, the guy who respects the common observer while at the same time is able to make you smile.

A curious example, and there aren't many, where the Gentle Giant has "informal interactions" with his work colleagues is with the French chair umpire Pascal Maria. They have a trusting and respectful relationship and the two have been involved in a few colorful incidents on court. At the 2016 U.S. Open, del Potro rubbed Pascal's bald head in the middle of an on-court discussion and at the Davis Cup semifinals in 2015 against Britain in Glasgow, he jokingly pulled at Pascal's tie.

Of course, del Potro does not enjoy sympathy all the time. Like any exposed personality, he also has his fair share of criticism. Those who question this or that of his personality or tennis game and life, such as his playing style, an "unwelcome" defeat or any professional decision he makes. This is how it is in the world of high stakes pro sports. During a good amount of time in his career, the potential for criticism made him resistant to speaking fully with the media. Although that reluctance still hasn't disappeared completely, he enjoys the favor of the people where ever he goes, and is seen as superstar in in certain places on the planet.

There are various points where he would stop to look at the issue. You could start with one that seems minor, but it isn't: the handling of the English language. The world of tennis, especially in its portion in Argentina, knew of the tightness that existed between he and another Argentine legend David Nalbandian and the English-language journalists. The curious thing is that Nalbandian handled the English language with some ease, thanks to the fact that he had traveled the world since he was 10, playing junior tournaments. And yet, many times his answers to English-speaking journalists were very dry – "no" or "yes" and that was it. That is what happened at the U.S. Open in 2002, where Nalbandian arrived as a new star in tennis after his runner-up showing at Wimbledon. Nalbandian's press conference demeanor stupefied Liz Clarke, a writer from *The Washington Post*, who turned to Alfredo Bernardi from *La Nación* and asked "What is Nalbandian's issue with us? Why are his answers so bad? He has to understand that the important newspapers are read by marketing people from around the world and if he acts this way, it won't give off a good impression to potential sponsors."

Many years later, in an interview with that same Argentine news outlet, Nalbandian explained his posture: "With the press, I put up a shield, because if you're not taking care for yourself, you're dead."

Nalbandian's handling of the English language did not suit him well. If it had been different, taking into account the high quality of his play and results and his many titles, and his popularity among fans and sponsors would have been greater worldwide. Del Potro can express himself clear and fluid in English. At some point during his life and career he understood that using it to communicate without obstacles in the English-speaking world was vital and important for his personal brand.

"I learned it talking," del Potro said with a wink to *Brando* magazine in 2009. "I studied it as a kid in school because I knew it would be important, but then I got lazy and didn't have time. But I listened a lot. I read and tried to learn. Lots of people speak it better or worse than me, but I talk. The people know you're doing an effort to communicate."

Ugo Colombini, the Italian who for many years managed the international contracts of del Potro, said years ago that del Potro's proper handling of the English language, especially with the media, was an important factor in his popularity.

"It makes things easier," he said. "He can express his personality more, his way of being, his sensations. The people and the sponsors love that. He talks a fluid English and can communicate very well. After winning the U.S. Open, he was a great character. We were on the main TV channels of the United States and lots of people saw him. They knew his face and his profile. It's not easy to accomplish that, especially if it's someone from South America."

It's in those cases when del Potro acts just as an elite professional athlete should. He started to understand that after he won the U.S. Open in 2009 that winning that title transformed him to a higher level of regard and responsibility. He would receive wild cards and preferential treatment for the rest of his life. In the second round of the 2016 U.S. Open, for example, he faced the American Steve Johnson, who in a previous press conference had objected to del Potro receiving a wild card entry into the tournament over an American player. The majority of the forums on the "Talk Tennis at Tennis Warehouse" message boards backed up del Potro in the difficult conversation. The del Potro – Johnson match was scheduled in prime time on Arthur Ashe Stadium, more so because of the stature of del Potro than of Johnson, who was at that time the second-best American player.

Ben Rothenberg, a tennis journalist from *The New York Times,* explained how del Potro is a rare phenomenon in tennis: "He isn't one of the most known athletes in the United States, but inside tennis he is loved and extremely popular. On one hand, he is underestimated as a character for entertainment. People in general don't appreciate how good of a show he puts on, how much attention he draws with his matches and how much charisma he has. American tennis fans aren't always ones who always root for American players, but even so it was surprising to see how many people cheered for del Potro against an American. He has very faithful fans here."

The United States is fertile ground for him having won a third of his career singles titles on American soil, including the most important one at the U.S. Open. This was also the stage where in 2016 he experienced one of the most emotional moments of his recent career. While he lost in his quarterfinal match against Stan Wawrinka – who would win the event days later – the thousands of spectators who stayed until very late at night in Arthur Ashe Stadium gave him a very touching ovation that lasted 80 seconds. It was so emotional a moment that Wawrinka, far from getting mad, understood the situation and walked to the side and permitted the tribute to del Potro to continue as the fans acknowledged his journey back from so many difficulties with injuries. Many of the fans who expressed their affection to del Potro were in fact from Argentina, as the numerous flags and chants and songs that were seen and heard from all corners of the stadium.

The return of del Potro to the U.S. Open was highlighted in a feature article in *The Wall Street Journal* by Tom Perrotta called "The Most Beloved Man in Tennis." Wrote Perrotta, "He loves how the Open has changed—a roof over Arthur Ashe Stadium, a new Grandstand court, practice courts with stands—since he last played here, in 2013. He's grateful for all the fans who cheer for him and ask for autographs. And he's touched by the words of fellow players, who don't want to lose to him, but know how much tennis suffers without him." He continued, "He's no longer afraid to say that he's starting to feel like the same guy who won this title, way back in 2009.

In those same days, the official tournament website proclaimed: "Welcome Back, Delpo!" The U.S. Open, spurred by the creativity of a journalist, tagged him with the nickname that would accompany him until his last day as a tennis player: The Tower of Tandil. The idea was forged in the mind of Luis Alfredo Alvarez of ESPN and had a random origin.

Said Alvarez, "In the tournaments where we are present we have good access to the players and during the 2009 U.S. Open, when he wasn't playing on Ashe Stadium, a co-worker would interview him in the tunnel outside of the court. I never go to the press conferences since usually I am busy with the broadcast but one day we went with Javier (Frana) and we crossed paths with Juan Martín, who asked me when I would interview him on the court. 'When you lift the trophy, because by the way you're playing you're going to win the title,' I told him, and he laughed. It occurred to me to tell him that he would grow higher than the Twin Towers if he won the tournament. He won, he won and won and I started calling him 'The Tower of Tandil.' I was walking through New York, I saw a tall building like the Empire State Building, for example, and took a good picture and published it saying that I just found Juan Martín. It was like a joke that kept on growing."

When del Potro consecrated himself on that glorious Monday against Roger Federer in the U.S. Open final, Alvarez, who never lost sight of that "commitment," went down to the locker room to see the Argentinian champion. They didn't let him go in and had to appeal to the Brazilian Luiz Carvalho, by then the press man of the ATP, so that he could tell del Potro that he was there. A few minutes later, Juan Martín appeared soaked in champagne and he melted into a hug with the journalist, who then conducted the agreed interview. The nickname had gotten so strong that even *The New York Times* referred to Juan Martín as The Tower of Tandil. "He really liked it and always recognizes it," said Alvarez.

Jose Luis Clerc also has an authoritative perspective of the love that is given to Juan Martín. Playing alongside his fellow Argentine great Guillermo Vilas, he reached No. 4 in the world and won 10 titles in the United States between 1980 and

1983 and played in another four finals on American soil. Clerc, who went on to become a TV commentator, said it is quite rare for the American crowds to get behind a player like del Potro.

"What I saw with Juan Martín during the 2016 U.S. Open I had not seen with anyone," said Clerc. "The love that the public gave him was spectacular. And I'm not saying it so much about the match with Wawrinka, the one with the famous ovation, because it was full of Argentinians. I'm saying this from all the other matches, where the majority were Americans. The Americans really respect the efforts of Juan Martín. The North American tennis fan isn't as thoughtful like the French and the English, but they are passionate and love the charisma, the triumphs, the aggressiveness, the fight of incredible balls that make you jump off your seat. And Juan Martín gives you all of these."

If for any actor to reach the stage in Broadway meant reaching the peak, for an athlete it's something similar being able to present oneself in Madison Square Garden in New York City. There haven't been many Argentinians who have enjoyed the privilege and pleasure of doing his thing in the stadium on 7th Avenue in New York that is known as the world's most famous arena. Carlos Monzon, Ringo Bonavena, Guillermo Vilas, Gabriela Sabatini, Emanuel Ginobili, Pablo Prigioni, among other Argentine athletes, and not very many more. However, del Potro was added to the list in March of 2013 when he was included in a special exhibition sponsored by BNP Paribas where he played against Rafa Nadal to close the event, preceded by a match between Serena Williams and Victoria Azarenka, by then the No. 1 and No. 2 in the world. It wasn't his only experience there. His dazzling return to the tennis world in 2016 earned him a second invitation. On Monday, March 6, 2017 he was again summoned for the BNP Paribas Showdown, to play along with Venus Williams, Garbiñe Muguruza, Jack Sock, Nick Kyrgios, Kei Nishikori, Andy Roddick and Lleyton Hewitt.

On the other side of the Atlantic, del Potro also has an avid fan base. The tipping point for him in Britain came at the

2012 Olympic Games when he battled Roger Federer valiantly on Centre Court in the semifinals before losing 19-17 in the third set before recovering to beat Novak Djokovic in the bronze medal match. At Wimbledon 2013, less than a year later, those battles were fresh in the minds of the British journalists and fans. The next day after his victory against the Spaniard David Ferrer in the quarterfinals, some journalist took his last name to make him play against an old comedy character of English television, Del Boy. A few months later, when del Potro returned to the capital of United Kingdom to play in the ATP World Tour Finals, *The Sunday Times* received him with the title "Del Boy at home in London."

"I thought about that comparison because they are both very loved guys," said Barry Flatman, the author of the article. "Here the people remember those battles at Wimbledon because of two things: the way in which he fought, and the respect and education that he shows in his attitude as an athlete. This is something the British value a lot. Also, in that match against Federer he had fought so hard for so long, and to lose, that made them appreciate him. That's why they support him."

In addition to being one of the most popular captains of the Argentinian Davis Cup team, Tito Vazquez worked seven years for Britain's Lawn Tennis Association and remembered clearly the reaction that del Potro generated in the United Kingdom. "Juan Martín won lots of fans in England," he said. "He was very loved. He definitely generated a connection with the TV audience."

Several years ago, some sparks erupted between del Potro and Andy Murray that created a tense rivalry between the two. But that was left buried by the amount of sympathy generated by del Potro in Great Britain, according to Paul Newman from the newspaper *The Independent*. "People call him 'The Gentle Giant.' I also see him like this, an educated guy, very polite," he said. "I remember that a few years ago there was a controversial comment about a touch he had with Murray in Rome when he complained that his mother Judy was making too much noise from the side of the court, but that was forgotten."

Stuart Fraser, British journalist for *The Times,* said, "Del Potro looks humble and funny inside and outside of the court. The recurring image that I have in mind is of his matches, hugging his opponent from the other side of the net. He will give his all on the court and still lose, but he's always going to be very sporty with his opponent. That makes him well-liked. His comeback also shows the players that you don't have to give up. He has won the respect of almost the entire tennis world. He will provide inspiration and motivation to the players with long-term injuries."

It's something similar to what former world No. 1 Jim Courier said about del Potro: "He is seen in the United States as a happy giant. He is tall and has a fierce game, but he doesn't reach the people by scaring them. He is a good person and is one of the top players in the world. That's why he's such a fan favorite."

Away from those markets, the good feeling between del Potro and fans have produced some unexpected situations. Martiniano Orazi cannot forget a fleeting but incredible anecdote that he experienced in Japan in 2008. Del Potro's team traveled to Tokyo to participate in an event, without Franco Davin, the coach, who stayed in Buenos Aires. At the time, it was an important tournament in del Potro's rise up the rankings. He reached the final but lost it in two sets against the Czech Tomas Berdych, but his ranking moved from No. 12 to No. 9 in the world as a result. But, on the way to the hotel one day, a girl went up to Orazi and told him in perfect Spanish: "Hello, Martiniano. How is Juan with his toenails?" Orazi was completely surprised.

"For starters, who knows me in Japan?" he said. "No one knows me in Japan. And then, because they asked me about something that Juan was suffering from at that moment. He had already reached such popularity, in so little time. The excitement that Juan Martín generated in Asia and in the United

States was out of the ordinary. I've never seen it with any other player except Federer, Nadal, Murray or Djokovic."

The fact that del Potro has not reached the very top of the tennis world but has gotten really close is another factor in his strong popularity with the fans. In that sense, moving in the second tier of top players is an advantage as he does not generate antagonism with fan groups of other top players, which would produce a polarizing effect that would subtract a certain part of support. For example, perhaps Rafael Nadal would have more fans if he was not the major rival to Roger Federer - and vice versa - even though it seems that none of these things could affect the affection Federer receives among the tennis fans of the world. Having an identifiable adversary is like resigning to distribute a cake: some portions go inevitably to the plate of another.

The Hero of the Resistance

There are more angles from which to explain the attraction that del Potro exerts among the tennis public in particular and the sports world as a whole. The magnetic man from Tandil epitomizes the story of the man who returned from oblivion, who overcame all adversities and returned to show that he is still alive and fighting again. This is a storyline that historically has great effect in movies, but this time happened to someone in true flesh and blood.

The majority of the journalists who go around the world following the professional circuit, as well as current and former players and those who are responsible for running the tournaments, agree that del Potro's story is special.

"Fans in the United States love a comeback story," said Chris Widmaier, Director of Communications for the U.S. Tennis Association. "When great athletes have a bad injury and work hard, fight and are resilient and work hard to come back, fans value that and that is what del Potro personifies."

His story of resistance aroused curiosity. "During his long recuperation, we always asked about him and probed among his Argentine journalists his chances of recovery and they painted a bleak picture," said Javier Martinez, journalist of the *El Mundo* newspaper in Spain. "Once his team was dissolved, and given the information they gave me, I came to think that this latest attempt to return was only the result of absurd stubbornness. Fortunately, it has not been so. Seeing him with the silver medal around his neck at the Rio Olympics and the resilience in the Davis Cup Final was a huge joy. If he had overcome three wrist operations, how could he not fight to the limit in the match against Cilic? Delpo is a true example, one of those types that capture the essence of sport."

Martinez added that del Potro, with his comeback from injury, showed the true human nature of his character. "He gained the sympathy of the fans," he said. "They saw in him as a good-natured guy. He was a hero from the street."

"Without a doubt, he is one of the great players of the last decade," he continued. "If he did not get injured, who knows what it could have achieved from the moment he burst onto the scene. As he demonstrated with his magnificent results, he was called to intrude into the 'Big Four' (Roger Federer, Rafael Nadal, Novak Djokovic and Andy Murray and he, in fact, became ranked as high as No. 4 in the world)."

A representative "from the other side," Rene Stauffer, author of the book of *Roger Federer: Quest for Perfection*, and journalist of the Swiss newspaper *Tages Anzeiger*, has an opinion.

"Del Potro is a lovable giant," he said. "He has a great personality on and off the court. He is a great competitor and a very modest guy. There is an enormous gap in his soft personality and strong game. I think that this combination of both aspects is what makes him so popular. He is an authentic person with an amazing serve and a great forehand, and when he's on fire, it's very satisfying to see him play. Even the Swiss public have sympathy for Delpo, despite the fact that he beat Federer twice in the finals of his tournament in Basel."

Carole Bouchard, the former tennis reporter from the French newspaper *L'Equipe,* added a similar commentary: "The crowd has been connecting with his fights, his tears," she said. "The people also love when champions return, the miracles and the stories that end well. Juan Martín, also, has a very entertaining game and has been part of so many incredible matches against the best players. He is like a huge teddy bear. He has this image of a guy who is still fighting despite whatever happens. He puts his heart on display for everyone to see. I don't think anybody thought he could come back so strong. No one knew that with his left wrist injury that he could compete again at such high level. Since he talked about his retirement, his return felt like a miracle. But once he noticed he was back physically, and was mentally dedicated, there was no doubt that he could compete with anyone, as he did in the past. His tennis never needed years to return, it was about his physical condition."

Christopher Clarey of *The New York Times,* one of the most influential journalists in tennis, shares the vision of his colleagues and compares it to other major sports stories of the year. "There was no better comeback story in tennis in 2016 then when del Potro returned in the second half of the year and then playing a key role in the first Davis Cup victory for Argentina. And if it were a normal year in the sports, no one would have matched it. But 2016 was the year of Leicester City (the unthinkable winner of the Premier League in England), of the Chicago Cubs (Major League Baseball champions after 108 years) and the Cleveland Cavaliers (champions of the NBA for the first time in 52 years). So 2016 was a year of destiny for comebacks and great stories."

Apart from that, Clarey pointed out that the Argentine could have had more of an impact on the game if not for suffering so many misfortunes and injuries. "Based on his talent and charisma, del Potro should have been a more important figure in the sport," he said. "He had the game to turn the 'Big Four' into the 'Big Five' and the game to threaten anyone on any surface, even Nadal on clay due to his ability, with his height and vision that could neutralize Nadal. But modern tennis is also a test of durability. It's part of the set of abilities required and something was missing: technique, physical training, proper response to the initial pain. But Delpo kept being an important figure in the sport. He is a memorable player who plays memorable matches and leaves a good impression with his playing style... It was at the U.S. Open in 2009 where I found out the power of his shots. I thought, by then, that he was the future No. 1 and that he would win multiple Grand Slams."

Between his fellow tennis pros, it's no usual to hear compliments about del Potro that not only focus on him as a great player, but also expressions of satisfaction that he was able to return to the circuit after his injuries.

"He is an important player for the circuit and it's amazing to see him return," said Nadal in the Spanish newspaper *Marca*. "It's great news for tennis, and he is an important person for our sport in South America. The level he has isn't something he has to show off; the entire world knows that when he is fine he is one of the best in the world, without a doubt. When he was healthy for a few consecutive months, you could see the results. He has done something huge for Argentina, a country with an enormous tennis tradition."

In the disappointment of his loss to del Potro in the first round of the 2016 Olympic Games, Djokovic still acknowledged: "I am delighted for him, because he is a great guy and has suffered a lot."

But del Potro already enjoys one of the most gratifying privileges for an athlete: turning into the mentor for those of future generations. In the first round of the ATP 500 event in Acapulco, Mexico in 2017, del Potro faced the 19-year-old American Frances Tiafoe, who extended him to a tiebreaker in the third set. For Tiafoe, it was an emotional match since del Potro had been his idol for many years. Back in 2008, when del Potro was starting to make an impact on the tour, he won the title in Washington for his fourth straight tournament title. His rise up the rankings increased his popularity among the dazzled fans in Washington, D.C. who wanted to be like him. One of the many autographs that del Potro signed that week was for Tiafoe, at the time just a boy.

"Del Potro was the first to sign my ball and that meant a lot for me," said Tiafoe. "He will always be one of my greatest idols. It was a pleasure to meet him."

Daniel Orsanic can't just only describe del Potro from his position as team captain of the championship-winning Argentina Davis Cup team from 2016, but also from the ATP Tour. His descriptions projects a good image of The Tower of Tandil with regard to his attitude inside the court, towards the fans and his rivals and also on what he overcame through the years to get back to competitive tennis.

"He is a very respected player, not only by his game but also by his way of acting in the tournaments," said Orsanic. "He is respectful with the other players, with the public and the organizers. Any tournament wants him in their field. But in 2016, so many tennis fans wanted him to return and they wanted him to be healthy enough to play, regardless of what country he played for. The best example was during the U.S. Open and the match against Wawrinka. That was something historic. I was there and I saw it. It generated lots of respect and even his rivals who were fighting for the same glory were happy for his return. That goes beyond the ranking; it has to do with personality and what an athlete gives to his sport. And Juan Martín gives a lot over to tennis. It generates lots of joy to see him. Lots of people got happy honestly."

This profile of playing and presenting himself in such a respectful manner also makes del Potro attractive commercially around the world. The good image of del Potro sells. He has been utilized commercially in many aspects in the tennis world, but one of the funny ones come from the world of video games. Virtual Tennis 4, the fourth sequel of the franchise of tennis games from Sega (the Japanese company dedicated to the development of entertainment), included the Argentine player between their characters to choose in the game. Players can chose to play as legends such as Boris Becker, Jim Courier or Stefan Edberg or women like Venus Williams, Maria Sharapova or Ana Ivanovic, and modern players such Roger Federer, Novak Djokovic, the Chilean Fernando Gonzalez, Rafa Nadal, Tommy Haas and Andy Murray. The game was launched in 2011 for the most popular consoles. Del Potro is seen dressed with a sky blue shirt, black shorts, a headband and white wristbands. "Hits hard" is the description that the game makes of him when you are offered the chance to play as him.

Guillermo Ricaldoni, the Managing Director of We Are Sports, a company that provides services in sports marketing and a former director of marketing of IMG Argentina, said that there is a difference, from the point of commercial perspective, between individual athletes and those of enormous popularity in team sports, like soccer.

"Unlike these, the tennis players, golfers and Formula I racers aren't just from one country, they are shown as international superstars," Ricaldoni said. "The tennis players are from the world and that is clear with the sponsors of del Potro. His figure is very good for marketing. What is asked in this world of business is being successful in the field and having great behavior outside of it. Del Potro fulfills both requirements. He achieved great triumphs, is very respected by his colleagues, very coherent and consistent with the stuff he says. If I were a brand, I would hire him."

Ricaldoni said that the victory in the U.S. Open allowed for del Potro to conquer the corporate market and explode his brand. "Before winning in New York he had managed to win four titles in a row and he hinted that he would become a future tennis icon, but the explosion was in the U.S. Open. If in tennis the money is in Asia, and the tradition at Wimbledon and Roland Garros, the business and the exposure are at the U.S. Open. I think that two or three titles at the Australian Open doesn't have the impact of doing it like once in New York. The public adopted him and they didn't do it just because he spoke English well."

After a dark era in terms of communication, as well as the aftermath of the controversial 2008 Davis Cup Final in Mar del Plata when Argentina lost to Spain, del Potro "had to reinvent himself as a public figure," according to Ricaldoni. "He didn't feel like talking so he wouldn't do it. As Groucho Marx said, 'Better to remain silent and be thought a fool than to speak and remove all doubt.' And I think del Potro in some moment thought, 'I prefer to seem apathetic and not talk, than to do it and to send lots of people to hell.' His performance in Rio in 2016 helped him to transform himself into a more emotional player."

Symbol of a City

The beautiful city of Tandil has a population of less than 120,000 but it is there where del Potro is the pride of the city. His identification with his native place is very strong and permanently affixed. During his entire career he refused to establish his base of operations at sites that operationally would have favored him. Instead, he favored his hometown.

Miguel Angel Lunghi, the Mayor of Tandil, said that through Juan Martín the city has gained more awareness to the outside world. And curious happenings have occurred because of this association.

"People wrote to me from Spain, who I don't even know, and congratulated me on the beauty of our Municipal Palace that we have that they saw in some live transmission during the reception that we did to Juan after the Olympic Games," Lunghi said. "When journalists call him 'The Tower of Tandil' – that helps that people know about our city. We try to have all our internet pages updated and well-designed because we know there are people from all over the world going into Google to try and learn more about Tandil."

It could compare with what the great Guillermo Vilas meant in his time to his city of Mar del Plata, but even more, because the tools of information in modern times is infinitely more powerful than in the era of the great Willy.

In his luminous office of the municipality, meters from the balcony from where del Potro greeted his neighbors many times after returning from a great conquest, Lunghi explained why the player today is one of the promotional resources to the outside world.

"Lots of people enter our sites of tourism to see the architecture and hotels," Lunghi said. "A few months ago we received, along with the Negro Marcelo Gomez (the former coach of del Potro), kids from Colombia, Ecuador, Chile and Uruguay that came for six months or a year, sent by their parents, to train and to find the method of Tandil tennis. For us, it's a foreign exchange and for them, it's a learning experience. That has been promoted due to del Potro, but also from Mariano Zabaleta, Pico Monaco and Perez Roldan. In this time, the tennis schools have great attraction."

Lunghi likes to compare Juan Martín with another native son of Tandil named Rene Lavand, who is also endeared in the city. "He was an illusionist who traveled the world and who, in an accident, lost an arm and with one hand he would do miracle stuff with cards," said the Mayor. "His example and the one from Juan Martín showed that you should never have to give up, despite whatever you have. To be able to overcome oneself is marvelous."

12

"The Environment"

In the Palermo neighborhood of Buenos Aires a man who is obsessed with tennis watched a practice session of Juan Martín del Potro as a young kid would do. People also observe him as he watched the practice. He then walked inside the court, by invitation, and then started to hit balls with the Argentine star, the player he saw so many times on TV or from a seat by the court.

The man in question was the actor Ricardo Darin. He probably won't forget that morning at the Argentine Tennis Club, where he was accompanied by a colleague, Carlos Santamaria. The hitting session occurred prior to a Davis Cup series and started a friendly relationship supported by mutual admiration. In reality, the actor's admiration of del Potro is actually stronger. His support for del Potro is unconditional and therefore he gets thrust into certain situations like the one he was during a magical Sunday in November of 2016 where he would have wanted to have been in Zagreb, Croatia.

"That weekend I went crazy, I got sick," said Darin. "I was in Madrid, and I was talking to all my Argentinian friends where I could go watch him, because I was about to go to Croatia. Being in Spain I calculated that I had a great opportunity to go watch the final, but there were no direct flights and what seemed like a three-hour flight would be an eight or nine-hour flight with a layover. I was paranoid because I had to travel back a few days later. So I flipped the TV channels until finally, by luck, on Teledeporte, a European channel, they were showing the Davis Cup because it was the final. They couldn't take me out of my house. My family was teasing me, my daughter, my wife... There was no way to get me out of my apartment. I spent hours and hours standing in front of the television, because I couldn't even sit down. I ate, smoked, drank; everything together. I ended up drunk and alone, like a bad crazy guy."

When he talks about del Potro, Darin isn't Darin. He is fully involved as a fan and gets overly excited in describing in detail some moment or something that he felt while watching del Potro play in person or even just on television. Like many others, Ricardo also had a fantasy of being a tennis champion like del Potro, but he fulfilled his destiny as an actor. However, he lives his other fantasy vicariously through del Potro. He is such a fan of Argentine tennis that he even watched the 2004 final at Roland Garros between Gaston Gaudio and Guillermo Coria literally on his knees right in front of the television. His passion for the sport makes watching del Potro play irresistible.

"It is something that is difficult to find in this sport, the sensation that even if you're behind, you always have the confidence that the guy can fight until the very end," Darin said of del Potro. "The best example was the match with (Marin) Cilic in the Davis Cup Final. The Davis Cup is something very big. Fortunately, thanks to him, to Federico Delbonis and all the team members we have it in our country for the first time. But the match he played with Cilic I thought was huge in many ways, but mostly by not giving up. We have such admiration for him, not just for his tennis but because of his effort, his will and his strength. We all feel that what he needed when he went through his hardest parts of the injury was support, stimulation and that vote of confidence."

Del Potro doesn't miss out on a movie premiere of Darín when he can, but at the same time he knows that each time he goes out on the court some place in the world to play, the actor and protagonist of the Oscar-winning movie "The Secret of Her Eyes" will be in front of a television somewhere to see him and suffer with him.

"The people admire him for his tenacity, because of his tennis, by his way of being," said Darín. "Yes, he is an extraordinary player and people know that, but it has more to do with his personality, that of an easy going guy."

Darín isn't the only person close to del Potro in the world of movies. Pablo Trapero, the prestigious director, is another long-time tennis fanatic. He played tennis as a teenager, but without much aspiration. Just to "pass the time," he said of playing with friends, without great requirements of training, just for the pleasure of playing. Life took him through a different professional route that showed him satisfactions but also created obligations that didn't leave any room for those enjoyments. Even today, each time he can, he carries his bag with rackets and rehearses a classic one-hand "old school" backhand that he learned as a boy. The passion for tennis marked him in such a way that he transmitted it to his son, Mateo, who developed it a few steps further than him, playing competitively at a high level in a club.

To the famous Argentine director, his activities and his personal habits also permit him to enjoy traveling, and with it, attending tennis events, including Wimbledon and the Queen's Club event in London. He even helped del Potro kill time during a rain delay that always leaves tennis players in a situation of uncertainty. It was at Queen's during a rain delay where Trapero found himself with del Potro and his group in the player's lounge. Their talk about movies helped del Potro to relax at the moment before returning to the court.

"For me it was like being at Disney," said Trapero. What at that moment was an anecdote but later turned into something that helped del Potro greatly in his hardest moments.

The presence of Trapero in the stands when del Potro played would become something regular each time that the director could work it into his schedule. In December of 2013 he did not deprive himself of watching del Potro play an exhibition against Lleyton Hewitt in Argentina. His wife accompanied him, the actress Martina Gusman, and during this time his mind spun around an idea of producing a documentary film about del Potro.

"We talked a lot of times about doing a movie about his story, a little joking and a little serious," Trapero said. "He is very inspiring for us who follow tennis who know his history and the pain he endured and the associations and interactions he had with the public, who sometimes were a little ungrateful of him. He is a character in the sense that he doesn't have a body of a tennis player. He is huge. Yes, there are other big players, but it's harder to adapt to the game. There are lots of these storylines that are attractive. Not even mentioning the U.S. Open against Federer in his best moment, an epic match. He has played many epic matches, against Murray, Djokovic and you don't forget them. I remember one where Djokovic withdrew in the semifinals of the Davis Cup in 2011 in Belgrade. You would see Nole cry like a boy, powerless, that he couldn't play. Or the match with Cilic in the Davis Cup, two sets down, everything against him... and then a tremendous comeback. The match with Murray in Glasgow was impressive. With Wawrinka at Wimbledon. Matches with lots of emotion. Tennis could also be boring sometimes, but he has lots of matches with drama. In fact, it happened to me, seeing him play the simplest games, mostly during that stage where it was hard on him to return, where you would see him and think he got bored of playing. I never doubted about his return, but I didn't know he would return like that. That's why we joked about the movie. At that stage of someone's career, with so many injury problems, just coming back to play is enough. To keep doing what you love and what is your passion is already a gift. Now, winning the Davis Cup... We had everything against us. The good thing about the Davis Cup is that the entire team also gave what they had to give."

How does one express all of this? There are many anonymous faces around the world who exercise a fascination of del Potro that isn't hard to explain. This universe of excitement is re-created each time that del Potro steps inside a tennis court, to the fans there in person to see him play but also the millions around the world watching on television. There is another universe around del Potro and that is an inner circle.

Those who see it from the outside define it with the impersonal term "environment," which does not explain much but refers to something imprecise. Fame or admiration is not enough to get close to anyone.

This explains his closeness with characters like the soccer players Martin Palermo or Roland Schiavi, for example. Especially in the case of Palermo, the relationship was the opposite of that of Darin or with Trapero, where the flow of admiration went mostly from the tennis player towards the soccer player. A rabid fan of Boca Juniors, del Potro couldn't stop idolizing the greatest goal scorer of the team by wearing his soccer jersey.

One day in September of 2008, Palermo went in sort of as a surprise on the court at the Argentine Tennis Club to meet the 19-year-old future U.S. Open champion who was training there. Or better, to let this young kid meet the soccer star. A hug on the court, a talk first, then an exchange of phone numbers and the start of a friendship fed by something that later would unite them even more: the story of personal redemption, something that also was the highlight of the career of Palermo.

Then in February of 2012, del Potro had been invited to a celebrity tribute match for the goal scorer in the "Bombonera" and it was something almost natural, despite the fact that in those same hours the national team would be preparing for a series for the Davis Cup against Germany. *La Nación* newspaper wrote that day: "Juan Martín del Potro doesn't care what they say about him. Despite that, while the Argentinian Davis Cup team is in Germany to compete in a match where he won't play, he will be present in the farewell of his friend Martin Palermo. Delpo played in the second half and had the privilege of replacing his friend Martin and there was more: he got an assist to a goal scored by Esteban Bichi Fuertes."

Del Potro was on the field of Boca to see the team and Palermo and Palermo was at the Parque Roca to see the Davis Cup team and del Potro – this was an exchange that happened while Palermo had the xeneize shirt on. However, this personal relationship was hardened when del Potro needed the support the most. The experience of the soccer player was helpful to del Potro to find the light at the end of his injury nightmare. Some specific advice was that he referred the help of Mara Villoslada, the sports psychologist of the Boca team, who also worked with Palermo.

"He trusted my opinions, mostly during the time of his injuries," said Palermo. "From the situation that I went through I was helpful and comforting to him. In all the operations he had doubts and uncertainty. Not so much in the first one, but mostly in the ones that followed. He was with his doctor in the United States when he was diagnosed and he ended up calling me, like searching for a last opinion to help him make a decision. For him to come to me, despite having already received the doctor's opinion, Franco Davin's opinion and from his family, made me feel very responsible because it was about his future. He was very scared of not being able to play again and I told him that he had to try again, to get an operation and to go through rehab again. It was the only way to make him feel well. After he left the hospital after talking with the doctor he would call me and ask, 'What do I do?' Then in the final one he told me, 'I don't know what to do, I don't want an operation, I don't want to be standing still for so much time again.' And I would reply to him, 'You have to get another operation done. Do it, and start with the recuperation.' Or I would also tell him that if he didn't want to play tennis any more then don't get the operation. All the talks were sort of like this. I tried to be close to him, helping him and supporting him in what was his last part of his recovery, when it was hard for him. It kept on hurting. He wasn't well and it was a matter of becoming aware and to moving him forward like I did. I felt as a part of that help. But the worst moment was before that final operation. It was very hard to make him understand that he had to get another one done. He just had to think about going into the surgery room and see what happens. The moment where I mostly felt him was at that one. He felt really bad and was alone. He left, traveled, saw the doctor, left and the first thing he did was call me to ask what to do."

The relationship continued and remained strong. When Juan Martín lived in the neighborhood of Belgrano, he was neighbors with Davin. From roof to roof, the jokes traveled as well as the invitations to eat barbecue. New York, Miami and during various series of the Davis Cup had Palermo sitting in the player box, supporting his friend. And a custom that continued as the telephone call from del Potro to Palermo after a match.

"The most gratifying thing for me was that after the match ended with Cilic in the final of the Davis Cup, lying on the trainer's table, he called me," said Palermo. "That he would take his time to do it was emotional. He told me he couldn't believe it, that he was exhausted. I told him to enjoy it because it was a prize. It gave me great satisfaction. I tell him constantly, 'All this, is great, but it's not enough. You still have more.' What does he tell me? 'Yes, Yes.'"

Del Potro's story with Roland Schiavi is similar to that of Palermo. In May of 2015, del Potro, hampered with his left wrist injury, was going through one of his most uncertain times of his career. He would ask if he would be ready for Roland Garros or perhaps play in a doubles match in the Davis Cup quarterfinals against Serbia. Both ended up not happening. During those days he traveled to Lincoln, the Buenos Aires locality where Schiavi was born and lived. Living in a city of less than 30,000 inhabitants relaxed the soccer player's spirit and he invited del Potro there to spend some time with him. He spent a day on the farm and in town and signed many autographs and he posed in endless photographs with boys and girls who played in the local soccer, hockey, swimming and basketball programs. He also paid attention to anyone who gave him advice: to go see the Indio Coria, a Mapuche healer known throughout the province. He took these shows of affection with a smile.

In 2013, Schiavi was playing for the Shanghai Shenhua club in China and, when del Potro competed there in the Masters 1000 tournament in Shanghai, the defender, who wasn't a fan of tennis "except in important matches," asked for a pass to the tournament, which is where they first met. Now with an established connection and friendship, del Potro used Schiavi's farm many times as part of his rehabilitation, mostly during the second part of 2015. Schiavi, by then a coach, had accompanied him to run through the practice fields. Del Potro was happy to return these friendly gestures, including assisting in the presentation of the official biography of Schiavi in November of 2015.

The skinny guy, winner of nine Boca trophies, including the Intercontinental in 2003, also remembered those difficult moments in the life of his friend. "I was helping him a little for him to recover, but it was all him," said Schiavi. "The hard work he would do. I tried to not talk much about tennis but about other stuff. I knew the entire world was asking about that, so I tried to clear his mind. For a tennis player, the wrist is like the knee for a soccer player. It's very important. But we always tried to talk about other stuff. I also don't like when people talk to me about soccer."

Schiavi took great joy in del Potro's eventual return. "And on top that," he said, "to crown him with the Davis Cup is like a golden pin."

The environment among athletes at the Olympic Games is something very special for those qualified enough to experience it. The camaraderie that is experienced between athletes from different sports can't be compared with any other environment. The Olympic villages placate this unique coexistence. To the athletes, the experience is gratifying and inspiring in many aspects, including having the opportunity to observe daily how the fight in their respective sports and, in the modest accommodations of the village, forge special friendships. One of those occasions came from the relationship between del Potro and Sergio Hernandez, the successful Argentine basketball coach, who guided his nation's team to Olympic bronze at the 2008 Olympic Games in Beijing.

Hernandez had crossed paths with the tennis player fleetingly in some occasions where the contact didn't pass through a lovely greeting, but the first deep chat between them occurred at the London Games of 2012. One evening, Hernandez went to eat to the Olympic Village after a victory with Emanuel Ginobili. He saw del Potro and got close to him, gave him a hug and asked why he wasn't staying in the village, something that reflected an image of someone who wanted to keep their distance.

"I saw him like a kid with a new toy," Hernandez said. "And he responded that he was not in the village because Wimbledon, where tennis was being played in the Games, was far from the village and he couldn't waste that energy of moving each time he had to play, and that he had come for a medal. There I started to see him as someone different, absolutely committed to what he was doing. There are athletes who do their activity because they have an ease to it and that's it. Others have talent and also potential to their qualities, like Ginobili, (Luis) Scola, and (Andres Chapu) Nocioni. From that day I started to follow him more closely. I started to look at everything he would do, to see his recovery and everything he would suffer, because it seemed as though he wouldn't be able to return."

That first exchange revealed that there was a lot in common between the two. The friendship was secured with time, always with a sporty atmosphere around. Thanks to those talks, Hernandez described del Potro with a thoroughness that sprouted with admiration.

"We have a difference of age and activity, but we talk the same language," Hernandez said. "In London, we had very deep conversations and at the Olympic Games of Rio de Janeiro we strengthened that link. There he stayed in the village because the tennis venue was closer. He had more time to talk and I noticed that he feels a spectacular passion by what he does. One thing is to be committed with an Argentine shirt or the club one that hires you and other is to do it with what you love in life. He is committed with what he does. I started to see why he was different. You could have lots of qualities, but the chosen ones try to get one aspect better day by day, to take what you do as science, getting a hit better, incorporating a diet, a rest, a training system. Roger Federer, Novak Djokovic or Rafael Nadal, and in their times Guillermo Vilas, Bjorn Borg or Andre Agassi, apart from playing tennis well, were obsessed with what they did. They probably changed their methods of training until exploding. What made Nadal and Federer seem like they would retire to just come back and win a Grand Slam again is the best example."

Hernandez said that what he sees in del Potro is comparable with the genius who he had to work with: "He is very similar to Ginobili in lots of stuff," he said. "When you are with Juan Martín you could talk about barbecue, of the time, women... but when you talk about tennis, you talk about tennis. That is to say, he is obsessed talking about the game. He likes doing it from that deep side. Like all those geniuses, they aren't talking all the time about their activity. They aren't monothematic, but when the time comes you see that they love what they do. They don't take it as just a game; that it's something more. It's what I see similar to these guys, like Manu, Delpo, Scola. They are passionate for what they do. They take it as if it was art. They don't believe that everything is won with just punchy or with luck, or they lose because the referee damaged them. No. Their looks are on the search for perfection."

The knowledge from the world of basketball developed in Hernandez an acute look of general sports, beyond the traits that are specific to tennis, which is loaded with an inevitable individualism.

"Everyone has an ego," he said. "You have to have your individual side to stand out. In the case of the tennis player, it's exacerbated, by the solitude of the life of the individual athlete. The player has to be made by his accomplishments and failures, alone. Lots of stuff from the tennis players are weird for us, the ones from the team sports, like sharing a locker room with a rival before a great final or a match and the difficulties of the captains of the Davis Cup, for example. Juan would tell me: 'Each one of us has their own trainer, physical teacher, kinesiologist and their own routines. So, when you are in the Davis Cup you can't make a 100 percent change.' Maybe, two days before a match you could practice your serve, in the afternoon your volley and then your groundstrokes. But maybe Pico Monaco has a different routine so, the captain has to accept those habits and not impose, so that later you could play together. I understood him. But it's weird. When I receive a team for a national competition, Manu doesn't come with Gregg Popovich (the coach of the San Antonio Spurs)..."

Hernandez also talked about success, something that del Potro has battled for his entire career. "Hopefully his example will help the Argentinians understand what it's not about being a No. 1 but about already being that No. 1 for giving it all on what you do. Labeling someone as a failure for not being No. 1 is ridiculous. We saw in him a talented athlete. It was very clear that he would be top 10 and even more, at least I thought so. But all this until his injury problems. There we all put him in a different spot. Not by his heroic performance during the Olympic Games or the Davis Cup, but by his example. We all see him with different eyes. This that happened to him, his return after being absent for so long, made it so that the people who followed him in this sport started to value him even more and put him in the even greater leagues along with Sabatini, Vilas, Ginobili, Maradona, Fangio... Before, lots of people saw him like a very good tennis player and that was it."

There is another friendship that del Potro cultivated with a sports figure. The Pieres last name is one of the most famous in polo and Nicolas is one of the talented siblings of the family who competes for the Ellerstina team. Del Potro got curious about this game that combined dexterity, intelligence and a special quality - knowing how to move in a team. Little by little he turned into a follower during the Argentinian season. It started becoming a habit seeing him in the polo fields and, in particular, around the Ellerstina team. He started to cultivate a friendship with Nicolas. The Pieres then started to come to the courts and follow their new friend when he was competing in England or South Florida.

In 2015, during the darkest times for del Potro when the nightmare of the injury in the left wrist prevented him thinking of a return to pro tennis, Nicolas and his brothers, who were in the United States, were close to him. "It was there in Miami when he decided that he was going to get another operation done," said Nicolas. "He couldn't stand the pain. Each time he had to play an important match he would further hurt his hand. It was a hard time going into an operation room, but like many athletes, he had to confront it and did very well. The worst moment, surely, was that one. He stayed at my brother Facundo's house during a few weeks, where he didn't want to know much about tennis anymore; he came to visit us during our matches. He came and left from Miami to Palm Beach, that's an hour away by car."

Palm Beach is the stage for high level polo between January and April. There are various tournaments in exclusive enclaves, where those involved also proliferate the golf courses and the mansions. The Wellington area, in particular, is the equestrian center. Del Potro would socialize with his Argentine polo friends there, participating in barbecues at night and card games.

"He is a fanatic truco player and lots of times we played cards," said Nicolas. "He spent a lot of time with us in Florida, not so much in England because when he plays Wimbledon he's more concentrated. There we would go visit him at the house he rented, but it was only for a few days."

Pieres is also impressed by the courage of del Potro to overcome so many difficulties: "His returns were shocking. The medal in the Olympic Games, the Davis Cup, beating the best... and more in a sport like tennis, where they're incredible players like Federer, Murray, Nadal and Djokovic. He spent a really rough time after going through the wrist injuries. He deserves it because he gave it all to keep moving forward."

Another connection for del Potro, from the world of music, is with Andres Ciro Martinez, the ex-singer of Los Piojos rock band, who enjoyed enormous popularity for 20 years. In December of 2016, Martinez offered a show in Luna Park with his current band Ciro y los Persas. In the repertoire of the singer there is a strong song called *Fantasma* that's from the album *Maquina de Sangre*. To set the scene of the song, Ciro usually summons onto the stage "ghost" friends: assistants that appear between the musicians covered in tunics. When the show ended, one of those sympathetic "ghosts" stayed on the stage. They had a hint who it was when the willowy intruder took a racket and started to hit balls into the crowd. Funny, Ciro discovered it was his friend Juan Martín, who was then showered with chants by the audience.

"The great people are the ones who support you during the bad stuff and he and his band filled me with emotion," said del Potro. who received as a present one of the classical harmonicas of the singer.

The music and the lyrics of Ciro inspired del Potro. In Tandil, the chorus "What a pleasure it is to see you again," from the song *Antes y Despues* accompanied him when he was welcomed to the balcony of the Municipal to receive the adoration of thousands of his neighbors after his epic medal-winning performance at the Olympic Games in Rio de Janeiro. During the Davis Cup celebrations, the chords of the National Anthem were executed by the harmonica of Andres Ciro.

Friendship is a key stimulus in the life of del Potro. The people close to him and those who are anonymous are with him always. The true friendships are those who share with him the comfortable but also thorny pillow of popularity.

13

At The Table With Legends

Since Sunday, November 27, 2016, the day when Juan Martín del Potro helped Argentina clinch their first Davis Cup title, the career of the Gentle Giant deserved to be analyzed in a frame against many of the other great athletes from Argentina. It is true that the Davis Cup title is a team event but Juan Martín's input and leadership had basically the same relative importance than that of Diego Maradona during the World Cup in Mexico in 1986. It's that simple. Without del Potro, it was improbable that Argentina would have won the Davis Cup because the team didn't have any other player of stature who would be able to beat Andy Murray in Great Britain or Marin Cilic in Croatia. To undertake that almost impossible mission was fundamental for the Argentine team to maintain some aspiration, and there was no other player who could achieve the task except del Potro.

Argentine sport is, in many senses, miraculous. Far away from the "center" of the world, Argentina is at a geographical disadvantage due to its location and with precarious resources in compared to the more developed countries. However, Argentina produced champions in a variety of rare disciplines. No other nation has enjoyed world titles in tennis, plus the world and Olympic titles in soccer and basketball (probably the sports with the most global fans). This has not been achieved by the United States (still not quite an elite nation in men's soccer) nor Brazil (a nation that has produced some of the greatest tennis players like Maria Bueno, Gustavo Kuerten or the doubles players Marcelo Melo and Bruno Soares, but the highest step Brazil reached in the Davis Cup was the semifinals in 1992 and 2000), or Spain (where they have great potential in basketball but have yet to win Olympic gold), and Germany (still seeking to achieve the highest level in basketball.)

Between Giants

The Argentine sports tradition whose most recent entry here comes from the Gentle Giant from Tandil could start in 1923 with the boxing epic by Luis Ángel Firpo against the American Jack Dempsey at the Polo Grounds in New York but the main comparisons will be from more recent times. The selection of athletes is arbitrary. With that license, perhaps the list could be chaired by the unequaled race car driver Juan Manuel Fangio. Unlike del Potro, Fangio should be recognized as the foundational figure of his sport, although the roots of Argentine car racing have to be explored a few years before in 1901, when the first automobile race was staged in the country in the disappeared racecourse of the Belgrano neighborhood, or in 1937 when Road Tourism was born. For much of the world, Fangio remains the greatest racing driver of all time, despite the fact that one day his incredible record of five titles in Formula 1 had been surpassed by the German Michael Schumacher, or with the appearance of another giant like the Brazilian Ayrton Senna. Two giants, of course, but whose numbers do not come close to the chilling records of the Argentine, who won almost half of his starts on the track in the top category. His summit day was August 4, 1957. That Sunday, Fangio starred in the greatest feat known to a racing driver. In Nürburgring, in the German

Grand Prix aboard a Maserati, he won the race and won his fifth world championship, an unequaled feat.

In the gallery of great names in Argentine sport, the first in the sport of golf is Roberto De Vicenzo. He didn't remember in his long life many contacts with tennis. "Unfortunately I almost never played it in life," said De Vicenzo. "I was at home lots of time and didn't have a real social life, but I remember a lot of Hector Americo Cattaruzza, the No. 1 player in Argentina in 1937 and 1938 and him playing of the Davis Cup and with a versatility that took him to TV.

De Vicenzo's most glorious working day was that of July 15th of 1967 where, at the age of 44 at the Royal Liverpool Golf Club, he beat the golfing giants Gary Player, Arnold Palmer and Jack Nicklaus to win the Open Championship, the most important golf tournament in the world.

De Vicenzo, who passed away at the age of 93 in 2017, said that del Potro certainly deserves to be mentioned among the best ever athletes from their country, perhaps even in a spot strikingly preponderant.

"Del Potro not only won a place in the table of the great Argentinian sports athletes, but could also maybe be the head of it," said De Vicenzo. "His achievements had been phenomenal. He has lots of merit. To be competing again at a great level after so many surgeries isn't something easy. He is a very lovable player and recognized worldwide. It was very emotional what he did at the Olympic Games and the Davis Cup. Also, he managed to get more people to watch tennis in Argentina. He helped spread his sport. In my era, very little people would see me. And years ago not even cats would watch tennis... Now the entire world watches it. It's true that time has changed and there are more options."

De Vicenzo was admired greatly for his talents but gained much respect for his behavior as a gentleman at the 1968 Masters tournament at Augusta National. When the tournament ended, he didn't check his scorecard, where his playing partner, the American Tommy Aaron, recorded that he had scored a par four on the 17h hole, instead of the three that he had achieved. Roberto signed it without looking at it and presented it as such, despite the error that would harm him. In golf, the score that is officially signed is used. If this error had not happened, De Vicenzo would have tied for first and would have played in an 18-hole playoff, but there was no going back. Bob Goalby from the United States was named the winner and the Argentine, now knowing of the error, was just limited to saying what stayed as a memory: "What an idiot I am..." I have never heard a complaint towards Aaron nor for the authorities who applied the rules.

On the courts

Looking back at tennis in Argentina before del Potro, there is one name you can trace back to, the father of tennis in the country: Guillermo Vilas. The date June 5, 1977 is the revered date for the Argentine as on that cloudy Sunday afternoon in Paris, the left-hander from Mar del Plata finished two weeks of overwhelming play. In the singles final of Roland Garros, the American Brian Gottfried resigned to the same destiny that all other challengers faced against the Argentinian during those two weeks in Paris. He barely managed to win three games. To reflect how dominating Vilas was during those two unforgettable weeks, it's enough to say that in his last three matches, he only lost 16 games. He lost eight to Wojtek Fibak of Poland in the quarterfinals, five to the Mexican Raul Ramirez in the semifinals and the last three to the American Gottfried in the final.

More than winning, Vilas was the man who popularized tennis in Argentina. He was the first to win a major title for the nation and was followed years later by Gabriela Sabatini. The great Gaby struggled at first to break through but finally did so on a very warm Saturday on September 8th, 1990 at Louis Armstrong Stadium in Flushing Meadows. On that afternoon, Gabriela, the biggest rock in the shoe of the phenomenal Steffi Graf, beat the world No. 1 from Germany 6-2, 7-6(4) and won the only major of a career that deserved a lot more.

Sabatini, warm and attentive, knew del Potro for more years than many people would guess, from his early years as a young up-and-coming player. "Already at that moment you would appreciate his talent and personality," she said of the young del Potro. "You could tell he was one step ahead by his mentality. Without being too competitive it's difficult to achieve goals and win matches to move up in the tennis world... Physically, you could see he was going to be very tall and that was the only thing that generated doubts where the injuries he would suffer. He grew too fast and feared that he was not strong or muscular enough to sustain all the wear he was doing... For me it's fundamental to have passion for everything because tennis, like any other sport, demands a lot of effort and discipline. On top of that, you have the intensity of the life of a high performance tennis player. Years later, I actually experienced on the court how powerful his game was. In February of 2015, I was in Miami preparing for an exhibition with Monica Seles at Madison Square Garden and Franco Davin (then the coach of del Potro) asked me if I wanted to hit some with Juan Martín at Key Biscayne. I said, 'Of course, why wouldn't I want to?' It was a spectacular experience because there I noticed the real speed of his forehand, the whip that he has in that monster of a forehand."

With the years, Gabriela transformed into a lucky charm as a fan for del Potro. She always held an interest in following the current and up-and-coming Argentinian players. In 2016, she was glued to the television for del Potro's amazing achievements at the Olympic Games in Rio and at the Davis Cup.

"I followed Delpo's matches in Rio from Zurich, where I am living, and I tried to get comfy for the time difference," she said. "What he generated was fabulous. He reached out to everyone. It had been a while since he last competed in important matches and created wonderful results from the first day. I thought that after beating Djokovic in the first round he would be finished but he took strength out from the beyond. He was very tired and, surely, in general pain, but there was nothing that would prevent him from fighting to achieve his medal. That is what I saw. Also for other athletes from other sports to go cheer for you makes you feel really good. All that experience and living together in the Olympic Village is very motivating. I also watched closely all the matches at the Davis Cup Final that were also very exciting. After beating Great Britain in the semifinals I saw the very difficult match against Croatia. It was expected that Argentina would be 1-2 down after Saturday. There Juan Martín appeared again, like when he beat Murray in the semifinals. Cilic played strategically good. He was impeccable. But all of a sudden a small window opened for Juan Martín, and bye. A light appeared and everything changed. That is what usually happens in tennis. Everything that the team did made me feel good. There is no other word than admiration."

Gabriela feels some special identification with del Potro since they both won the U.S. Open and also an Olympic silver medal (del Potro also won a bronze medal in singles in 2012 at the London Games). "We never sat down to talk about that," said Sabatini. "But I heard Juan talk about unique feelings that he got at the Olympic Games and I identified with that. These are feelings that are different from the rest. I put these as the most beautiful and unique experiences in my life. My fist Games were in Seoul in 1988 and I was there in the Olympic Village with all the Argentinian athletes. I remember that I would wake up in the morning and everyone else was already training. That gave me spectacular energy. It was contagious. In that moment there wasn't much technology like now. You had to write a message on a blackboard and then check if someone had left a note. This is how communications worked, it was fun. I left very nourished from the Games and the adrenaline lasted a long time."

Reflective of the pro tennis world that she left in 1996, Sabatini analyzed the past, present and future of del Potro and his respective position in the game. "Someone asked me what would have happened at the top of the tennis world if Juan Martín didn't have so many injuries," said Sabatini. "I don't know. The mind and the constant pressure plays a big role. It's not the same to be in the top 10, than the top three and to know that you could reach No. 1. It's a step further to go that far. The problem is if he wants to go that extra step. He's just human and has his slumps, like everyone. But I have no doubts: he is a No. 1."

Hits and Misses

Another athletic great from Argentina who del Potro earned to right to be compared with is boxer Carlos Monzon. On November 7, 1970, Monzon knocked out Nino Benvenuti, the best Italian boxer in history, in the Palazzo dello Sport in Rome and won the world middleweight title, a title he did not let go of until he retired almost seven years later. Monzon, born in San Javier in the province of Santa Fe, was the ultimate role model for boxing in Argentina.

Monzon's era of glory was parallel to the first part of another Argentine sporting giant Hugo Porta. The rugby star excelled for the national team, the Pumas, for 15 years beginning in the 1970s and included two sublime moments. The first happened on April 3, 1982 in Bloemfontein, South Africa. In reality, the feat of that day wasn't registered in the name of Argentina, but that team, because of political reasons, had to call themselves South America XV. At that time Apartheid isolated South African sport and to be able to compete there and avoid sanctions you had to avoid the presence of official national representations. The South America XV team was made up of almost entirely by players from Argentina. With talent, brains and the magical right foot of Porta, who made 21 points, this team beat the South African Springboks for the first time.

Three and half years later on November 2, 1985, on the field of Ferrocarril Oeste in the porteño neighborhood of Caballito, the mastery of Porta took The Pumas to one of their highest achievements, nearly beating the world-best All Blacks team from New Zealand. It was a tie of 21-21, with all of the points for Argentina coming from Porta.

A member of the Rugby Hall of Fame since 2008, Porta moved into public affairs after his career ended and he was an Argentine ambassador in South Africa. Porta's respect for del Potro is strong as a symbol of sports in Argentina.

"I have no doubts that he is among the top legends of Argentine sports," Porta said. "Also, he will still be a legend when he stops playing and everyone remembers him. What he has achieved, especially with the visibility that sports has today and more people have seen him play, is very important. For him tennis isn't his work. We enjoy this. And he learned to enjoy it."

Porta closely follows del Potro's career and was worried about the dark moment of his career. "During his times of uncertainty, I lived them with some fear," he said. "Seeing the work and the effort he did to come back, and, on top of that, to play at that level was fabulous. He managed to make people identify with his cause and we all wanted him to win. He projected such a positive message. The results of his efforts and his comeback was incredible and most of all, he enjoyed again playing his tennis. He managed to combine his joy along with the responsibility of his position. It's very hard to enjoy what you do if you don't love it. Sports help people heal. Amateur sport is an exercise that prepares a person for the big match of their life. This was reflected in what happened to Juan. Not all moments in life are sweet and you have to learn to overcome and hang on to the values that one has. And to believe in the people who do it out of good faith. In rugby, we say that there is no money to pay for those volunteering to teach in clubs. In the case of Juan, it was very similar in that there was an entire country depending on him at the Olympics and the Davis Cup."

Word from the Ten

In the 1980s, the high point of joy for sports fans in Argentina was the World Cup victory by the light blue and white. It was the peak moment for the "No. 1 fan" in the stands cheering for Argentina in the Davis Cup Final in Zagreb.

Maradona is the name forever linked to the day June 29, 1986, where in Aztec Stadium in Mexico City he dazzled the world and achieved his dream that day and gave Argentina its second World Cup title. Whimsically that day of the final against West Germany did not correspond with his most notable performance of that World Cup campaign. That came against England in the quarterfinals where he scored two famous goals, including the famous "Hand of God" goal.

Passionate about tennis and sometimes controversial, Maradona inevitably is there each time Argentina plays in a big Davis Cup match and has privileged access to the privacy of del Potro in those moments of high concentration where only a few can command his attention.

The journeys of the Argentina Davis Cup team took Maradona to the Zagreb Arena in anticipation that something big could happen in the Davis Cup Final against Croatia. He was there with a broken heart hearing the news of the death of Fidel Castro, the Cuban leader whom he created a relationship with based on mutual admiration.

"When I heard the news it was like receiving a serve of del Potro in the chest," said Maradona. When he was asked for an impression on del Potro for this book, the man who did the magic with his left hand and the No. 10 on his back preferred to turn it into a letter, entitled "Del Potro was Maradona against the English."

"You could say that Martin, because I call him Martin, won my heart the day he won the Davis Cup. But no, man, no... That day he won the heart of all the Argentinians. He won mine when my loved parents passed away, Mrs. Tota and Don Diego, and he was there, present, to accompany me.

"How was I not going to accompany him to Croatia? I would go to the end of the world to cheer for him! For him and the entire Argentinian team. It was the bravest stop, the one to try and win the Davis Cup for the first time in history, as a visitor, against all odds... With everything against us is how I like it! That's why I wanted to be there...

"Many people called me a jinx. Others said I just wanted the visibility and be the center of attention, but the only thing I wanted was to cheer, for all the Argentinians to be supporting them, behind him. The only thing I cared about was being in the grandstands. I didn't even go to the hotel, until they called me. The skinny guy, who is longer than the Eiffel Tower, laughed when he saw me arrive. A phenomenon.

"In that final match, Delpo gave us a lesson to all the athletes and all the Argentinians: If we fight, we can do it. He knew better than anyone that it was a rough spot, but not impossible. What he did was something crazy...Being in a place like this, in a moment like this, it's touching the sky with your hands. I lived that in Mexico in 1986. Martin lived it in Croatia.

"The skinny guy, that day, reached the hearts of the Argentinians, without a doubt. It was like a boiler, I swear. That's how the Davis Cup matches are: lots of heat, lots of battles, adrenaline and screams... A steaming hot boiler. And del Potro turned it off with two big eggs like the rock of Tandil. He had to take and to bring everyone, he had a great responsibility. He was the one who had to take the flag and did it the best way. He beat everyone with hammers. Let it be very clear to all Argentinians, what Delpo was throwing weren't balls, they were hammers! He wanted to destroy the ball each time he hit it. And I swear I was hitting with him.

"That's why, when he invited me to go down to the locker room, when they were already champions and he told me to choose whatever I wanted to take back home as a gift, I choose the racket, because that racket was the weapon he used to win, but I also asked to kiss his hand. Because that hand made us lift the Cup.

"The skinny guy, Martin, Delpo, call him what you want, became a great master that we needed for a long time. He was Maradona against the English. That's why I am going to be grateful for the rest of my life. For making me, making us, so very very happy. And to remember me when I needed it the most."

Legends of Today

This list of legends is completed with two contemporary names of del Potro. The relevance of one of them, Lionel Messi, exceeds all considerations; his immense trajectory still lacks chapters, and the road traveled is too long and bright to choose a single culminating date. From his endless list of individual feats, more than anything because of his emblematic character, he could choose the date of May 27, 2009. On that stifling night in Rome he led for the first time with a leading role his Barcelona team to conquer the Champions League title. His record already included the title for the 2005/2006 season, but in that campaign an injury left him out of the last series. With a header, he helped his team to a 2-0 win over Manchester United and their Portuguese attacker Cristiano Ronaldo, later his arch-rival with Real Madrid.

The other one is someone who del Potro shared moments that he isn't going to forget. Emanuel Ginobili is someone with whom he shares mutual admiration. Ginobili is an example and guide for del Potro, who professes the same respect towards him, the same respect that the entire Argentine sports community have towards the best basketball player in the history of the country. Ginobili enjoyed an extraordinary career that permitted him to shine in European basketball, in the NBA and as a greater star at the Olympic Games who achieved the ultimate on August 28, 2004. Winning the Olympic gold medal in basketball is something that is almost impossible to achieve unless you are the United States, who have only failed in this quest only three times in the history of the Olympics. The first came at the Munich Olympics in 1972 by the hands of the Soviet Union; the second, when the best teams from around the world were absent from the boycotted Moscow Olympics of 1980; the third being performed as a work of art from that a group of amazing Argentine players in Athens in 2004.

Ginobili and del Potro shared many glories, including a memorable walk in the Opening Ceremonies of the London Olympics in 2012 and many talks during the 2016 Rio Games. The 2016 Olympics were important for both as it was the Olympic swan song for Ginobili, highlighted by a tremendous Argentinian victory against Brazil, and for del Potro, winning the unexpected silver medal with wins over Novak Djokovic and Rafael Nadal.

Manu follows del Potro's career closely and would watch his matches on television from San Antonio, where he played for the NBA's San Antonio Spurs.

"I got very excited seeing him and the rest of the team win the Davis Cup and also watching him at the Olympic Games in Rio," said Ginobili. "I know he went through some difficult times because of his wrist injury, when he was going bad and it generated lots of doubts and uncertainties. Seeing him later playing the way he did and enjoying the moment, I loved it. It gave me great joy. With him we didn't see each other so many times but we shared lots of time at two Olympic Games and a few meals in Miami when I would go visit Florida and he was there. We had a great time. We shared experiences and talked a little about everything. He's a very nice guy and his two-year fight with that injury made me value his great 2016 a lot more and get super happy."

Ginobili is a winner of four NBA Championship rings in 2003, 2005, 2007 and 2014, all with the Spurs where he formed a magic trio with Tim Duncan and Tony Parker. He is also one of the best ambassadors ever for Argentina. Comparing him and other national sports heroes with del Potro, he said, is something that is not appropriate.

"I think it's unnecessary to want to rank everything, making lists and that stuff," said Ginobili. "He gave a Davis Cup for the first time to this country and won two Olympic medals. How can you compare that to someone who does a team sport, one that drove cars or whatever? I don't see it necessary. He is a monster and we should feel proud of how he is, how he plays and how he represents us apart from enjoying him on the court."

In a sport like field hockey on grass, which is not as popular as the already mentioned sports, Luciana Aymar created such a legacy in her sport that she deserves some elbow room in the discussion of all-time great sports heroes from Argentina. Some have called her "the Maradona of hockey" for her talent of evading her opponents as if she was the former No. 10 in the most inspired moments of soccer. She was distinguished on eight occasions as the best player in the world (2001, 2004, 2005, 2007, 2008, 2009, 2010 and 2013), won two world championships and won four Olympic medals (silver in Sydney 2000 and London 2012 and bronze in Athens 2004 and Beijing 2008). Her success and influence was so strong that it provoked a surge in participation among a younger generation of girls in the sport. Hockey was cemented as the top sport in Argentina for women and was one of the reasons, among many others, why participation in tennis dropped among young women in Argentina.

Where del Potro stands in the pecking order of Argentine sports greats is not that important. What isn't up for discussion is that the boy who started playing soccer in Tandil, and later left to grab a tennis racket, won a golden chapter in the encyclopedia of Argentine sports.

14

The Second
Grand Slam Final

There was no force behind his groundstrokes. He was crestfallen, dizzy and without security in his serve or in the usual forehand drive that astonished the public. Juan Martín del Potro had enough accolades entering the 2018 Australian Open to be considered as one of the big favorites to win the title. However, he left Melbourne very early. The tower collapsed in the third round when he had a good chance of advancing deep into the tournament. The Czech Tomas Berdych, then ranked No.20, showed no weaknesses and beat him 6-3, 6-3, 6-2, in two hours and 16 minutes. It was a big disappointment.

In 2017, from Flushing Meadows to the 1000 Masters in Paris-Bercy, del Potro built a furious sprint, with 18 wins and four losses (with the Stockholm ATP 250 title and the U.S. Open semifinals included.) He was only one win away from qualifying for the year-end ATP Finals in London. For all these reasons, Australia was expected to be an explosive tournament for him. However, it was far from that huge expectation. At that time, the tennis player was going through a very vulnerable time that directly affected his career. Of course he said nothing and moved on - or so he tried.

Juan José Grande, an owner of a degree in psychology, understands the pressure of competing at high levels. He sailed in regattas and worked with Argentina's first rugby division and with the Uruguayan team Los Teros. Grande is the man who, for example, helped Leonardo Mayer overcome the burden he felt while living in the chaos of the city of Buenos Aires, far away from his native province of Corrientes. Grande began to work with del Potro during the first week of March in 2015, while the Argentine Davis Cup team competed against Brazil in the first round of the World Group. In those days, Grande was accompanying Mayer, one of those chosen by Argentine Davis Cup captain Daniel Orsanic. Del Potro, who was injured, joined the team to encourage his fellow countrymen.

"In one of the sessions we had Juan Martín told me that he saw Leo was doing very well, that he would like to have some conversations with me and that we did," Grande said. "We formed a good relationship."

Of course, the relationship became more professional in February of 2018. Del Potro asked the sports psychologist to accompany him on a tour that, if all went well, would extend for approximately 40 days, through the Delray Beach, Acapulco, Indian Wells and Miami tournaments. And so it happened.

"Everything worked out, the desire of Juan Martín and my availability to travel," said Grande. "I joined a very good group, which included Sebastián Prieto (coach of del Potro since September 2017), the kinesiologist Germán Hünicken and a friend of Juan, nicknamed Perita (Marcos Hernández Olmos, a native of Bolívar, a town located 280 kilometers from Tandil). They were 40 spectacular days. We had been working for a long time. It was a very rich relationship. We spoke with Juan several times a day. They were very productive talks. He is extremely intelligent. I noticed that he has an excellent predisposition and greatly enjoys traveling."

The first stop, Delray Beach, did not turn out as expected. Juan Martín, ranked No. 10 in the world, beat No. 96-ranked Jeremy Chardy in the first round but immediately lost to the American Frances Tiafoe (ranked No. 91) by a 7-6(6), 4-6, 7-5 scoreline.

"For this tournament, honestly, I have not had the best preparation due to personal issues that I have been handling for the past couple of days," del Potro said. "I will surely be better later. I have faith and I trust that I will improve."

On the court in Delray Beach, he acted defeated, with the racket in his hand and the mind in another body.

"As I said, they are not easy days, for personal reasons," he said. "When I can get a little better, I will continue forward and I will surely enjoy much more."

In those days, the magazines pointed out that the tennis player had broken off his passionate relationship with the Argentine actress and singer Jimena Barón. Usually maintaining a low profile in matters related to his private life, during the time that this relationship lasted, del Potro appeared in different publications that had millions of followers. In addition, the death of his 10-year-old Newfoundland dog César, who was a great companion for the family, hit him greatly.

"Juan Martín is very sensitive," said Grande. "He needs a lot of support, his family, his friends, a stable team. He relies heavily on them. When his emotions are steady, he is a more powerful tennis player and plays at his best. When he manages to be emotionally motivated, his tennis becomes practically unbeatable."

After Delray Beach, the entire team headed to Acapulco, Mexico, to participate in the ATP 500. "It was very hot," Grande said. "Juan suffers a lot from high temperatures, but he settled down, gaining confidence. He was finding security as the days went by. His pre-competition ritual is impressive. He is very focused on the match. He is like a samurai preparing for battle."

The German Mischa Zverev was del Potro's first obstacle in Acapulco, although the Argentine's triumph was quick:

6-1 and 6-2. In the round of 16, del Potro had to battle hard to defeat David Ferrer of Spain (then ranked No. 39), 6-4, 4-6 and 6-3. Meanwhile, every night del Potro's team made a habit of playing poker and other card games.

"We played to the death," Grande said. "We were not forgiving. For example, the one who lost had to let himself be dunked in bucket full of ice water. The group climate became very fun. The only problem was the heat, which was impressive. One night Juan was playing, he looked at the bench and asked us to bring him some other sneakers because his shoes were soaked and his foot was slipping. There was a lot of humidity."

If the Argentine had doubts to start the season, Acapulco provided a confidence boost. He became a steamroller capable of overcoming any rival, even crossing tough physical barriers. In the blink of an eye, del Potro eliminated three Top 10s to win the title. He defeated the Austrian Dominic Thiem (ranked No. 6) 6-2, 7-6(7) in the quarterfinals, German Alexander Zverev (ranked No. 5) 6-4, 6-2 in the semifinals and South African Kevin Anderson (ranked No. 8) 6-4, 6-4 for the title. The victory allowed del Potro to climb a spot in the ranking and place himself in the top eight.

"It was a fantastic week. It is a tournament that I give a lot of value for the quantity and quality of players who participated," del Potro said, wearing the Mariachi hat that is usually presented to the champions. The title was the third for an Argentine in Acapulco, after the triumphs by Agustín Calleri in 2003 and Juan Ignacio Chela in 2007.

Until 2018, del Potro had reached three Masters 1000 finals – in Canada in 2009, Indian Wells and Shanghai in 2013 - but had never been able to win a trophy of that caliber. He had always been eliminated in the earlier rounds, for one reason or another. But after triumphing in Acapulco, del Potro arrived in Indian Wells with a different aura.

"The weather in Indian Wells was much drier, more pleasant," said Grande. "There he was trusting tennis. He did not have as many concerns. He was already riding the wave."

Grande continued on with del Potro, Prieto and Hünicken (Perita, Juan Martín's friend, returned to Argentina after the celebration in Mexico.) In the Coachella Valley, a desert area surrounded by mountains in southern California, the routine of each night was to dine at an Italian restaurant that was very popular among tennis players. Launched like a bullet train, del Potro was eliminating rivals one after another. First he defeated the young Australian Alex De Miñaur, then again Ferrer and Leo Mayer, in the quarterfinals over the German Philipp Kohlschreiber and then the Canadian Milos Raonic in the semifinals. Then, in the final, he faced Roger Federer, the world No. 1 who was fresh off winning his second straight Australian Open who held a 17-0 record to start the year. At the age of 29 and after losing almost three whole seasons for various surgeries on his wrists, del Potro finally conquered the first 1000 Masters title of his career. A debt was settled.

The 6-4, 6-7(8), 7-6(2) win against Federer, saving three match points en route, was one of the best victories of his career: for the history, his opponent and for the prestige of the tournament, which had long been considered a sort of fifth Grand Slam tournament. The Argentine became the new No. 6 in the world and, more than ever, he gained momentum to try to fight for No. 1, something unexpected based on his recent history with his battered left wrist that did not allow him to compete and be happy.

"Juan won a sensational mood pulse. He even got Federer to lose his temper," said Grande. "When Juan is connected to the deepest parts of his personality, he achieves a very pleasant coexistence between his tennis and his mood. And so it was in Indian Wells, under an atmosphere of harmony. I have the feeling that he found a lot of depth in himself in those days. He could have a space for his times, reflect, think, not let go of his emotions, keep them present and integrated with his work."

After his win, Delpo went to the on-court camera, where the winner usually signed their name on the lense, and wrote "César" and drew a heart to honor his departed pet. The tournament victory allowed Juan Martín to join the exclusive club of Marin Cilic and Stan Wawrinka as the only ones to win at least one Grand Slam singles title and a Masters 1000 other than the elite "Big Four" group of Federer, Rafael Nadal, Novak Djokovic and Andy Murray.

Del Potro was for a prolonged period without a stable coach. Since July 2015, after breaking his long bond with Franco Davin, he walked alone for quite some time. Specifically, he was without a fixed coach during the second half of 2015, the period of his physical and mood rehabilitation work, throughout 2016 and for eight months of 2017. Del Potro was patching up situations as he could and wanted, week after week, tournament after tournament. Starting in August of 2017, he started to work with Prieto, a doubles specialist when he played on tour who was working with Argentine Guido Andreozzi that year at the U.S. Open. There was chemistry between del Potro and Prieto and for that reason they continued working together.

"Prieto gave me order and peace of mind," del Potro told ESPN. "I spent a lot of time looking for shots, programming my workouts, thinking about what exercises to do, and at the end of the day, he was a big help. Now I am calm. [Prieto] has experience. He was training other players. We went to five or six tournaments together and my level also increased, and that gives me a motivation to continue working together."

Prieto spent his childhood in western Buenos Aires. In 1950, his grandfather started a real estate agency in Ciudad Jardín, which then passed into the hands of his father, Jorge, and then, after his death, to his sister Ana.

"He had a very hardworking, middle-class family with good values," said Willy Franco, who trained Prieto from age 10 to 18. "His parents made an enormous effort so that Seba could travel to compete." Franco was a coach of COSAT (South American Tennis Confederation) teams that traveled to Europe. In one of those groups, he trained outstanding players such as the Brazilian Guga Kuerten, the Chilean Marcelo Ríos, the Ecuadorian Nicolás Lapentti and Prieto himself, who had an outstanding junior career. In fact, in 1991, he was No. 1 in the 16-year category.

"He did it on a tour of Italy and reached about seven finals," said coach Hernán Suárez, who was present on that European tour with another team. "At that age in juniors he won everything. He was a terrific worker, professional and mature for his age. He was just as physical until 10 o'clock at night. He didn't care about the time." In 1993, Prieto won the doubles title at the Orange Bowl in Miami with partner Jimi Szymanski, the Venezuelan who also worked as a coach of del Potro. When he traveled to Europe, he used to buy CDs that were not sold in Argentina and he dressed in T-shirts from Guns N 'Roses.

"He was a fan of the band," said Franco. "His mother forbade him to go to one of their first concerts in the country because she was afraid of it."

As a professional, Prieto could not replicate the same individual results he had earned as a junior and instead focused on a career in doubles. He was ranked as high as No. 22 on the ATP in 2006 and No. 137 in singles and won 10 doubles titles: four with Mariano Hood, four with José Acasuso, one with Martín Rodríguez and one with Horacio Zeballos.

"When you are not so strong in singles and you do not have so much ease to stand out, you try to find other weapons, specialize in how to take advantage," said Hood, his doubles partner and friend. "It forces you to think much more, to study rivals more. That happened to the players who were not as dominant. Sebastian is intelligent and he knows how to read the game very well. He understands it. He has lived around high-level tennis as a coach and has a lot of knowledge. He is methodical, tidy. And he learned a lot from Alejandro Gattiker, who was a sub-captain of the Davis Cup in 2016."

A meticulous, assiduous reader and a lover of Argentine rock music, he cultivates a low profile that deepened since he began training del Potro. He no longer speaks to the media.

"We shared a room for a long time," said Hood. "It was tidy. He folded everything in the closet and put the dirty clothes in a bag and his shoes in boxes."

Prieto also worked as a coach for José Acasuso, Diego Schwartzman and Juan Monaco. He debuted as a member of the Davis Cup team for Argentina in 1999. In total, he participated in four Davis Cup series, his last in April of 2007 in the 4-1 loss to Sweden in Gothenburg in the quarterfinals. It was there where he was teammates with del Potro. A month before, they played doubles together and reached the final of the Challenger in Sunrise, Fla. The turns of life brought them together again in dissimilar circumstances.

Del Potro grew up playing on red clay courts. However, that surface is far from being his favorite. After winning the titles in Acapulco and Indian Wells as well as reaching the semifinals in Miami, del Potro rested and then faced the European tour on slow courts with some optimism. In the first two tournaments, he did not receive good news. In Madrid, he lost in his second match against the Serb Dusan Lajovic. In Rome, he had to retire when he lost to Belgian David Goffin at 6-2, 4-5. What happened? As he reported without giving too many details, he suffered a "Grade 1" tear in his right abductor. Of course, it was striking that a few days later he was seen at the Real Club de Tenis in Barcelona doing different exercises. There, he visited doctor Ángel Ruiz Cotorro, a trusted professional of most of the Spanish players.

"Red clay is the part of the year that brings me the most difficulties. I already knew that," del Potro said in Paris on May 26, just before the start of the French Open. "In Madrid, I played very tough matches. In Rome, I felt that little tear during my match with Goffin. And it still has me in full recovery. It still makes me doubt if I will be recovered to play this tournament. It is the last tournament on clay and then comes the grass swing, which gives me great enthusiasm. Therefore, I take all the necessary precaution for recovery."

If one took into account that Roland Garros' matches are the best of five sets and on a surface on which the players constantly slide and, therefore, demand the adductors, everything made one suspect that the Argentine would not play. However, he did. He managed to recover in record time for the usual demand for a tear (many doubted that this was really the diagnosis of his injury) and appeared in the first round against the Frenchman Nicolas Mahut, whom he defeated 1-6, 6-1, 6-2, 6-4.

What would happen from there? It was another example of resilience, that fuel that feeds del Potro's fire. The Argentine player went from almost withdrawing from the event to reaching the semifinals in Paris for the second time in his career (the first, in 2009). It was unthinkable madness, really. The Frenchman Julien Benneteau (No. 62), Spaniard Albert Ramos-Viñolas (No. 36), American John Isner (No. 10) and Croatian Marin Cilic (No. 4) fell like sand castles. Rafael Nadal, who at that time was No. 1 in the world, was the one who ended up defeating del Potro 6-4, 6-1, 6-2.

"I entered into the tournament unexpectedly, playing well, winning good matches," del Potro said to *La Nación*. "Everything that is happening to me in my career is surprising. And I like it that way, without planning the goals so much at every step. I want life to surprise me. Then I enjoy it more...The effort I made to return is known by very few people. At the end of 2015, I played without coaches and was accompanied by friends. And being alone, fighting alone, with people who helped me not to lose, so that I didn't lower my guard. It was about what everyone is looking for in life... trying to be happy."

Del Potro had a few opportunities to be No. 3 in the world. He had it within reach of his forehand. However, physical difficulties and injuries prevented him, again and again, to reach the ranking podium. Moreover, many believed that after so many health problems, the Argentine wouldn't arrive at that place. After reaching, in the first days of August, the final of the ATP 250 of Los Cabos, Mexico, where he fell to the Italian Fabio

Fognini 6-4, 6-2, del Potro withdrew from the Canadian Masters 1000 in Toronto because, as he said, his left wrist "should rest." The tennis player had felt discomfort in that area, which had been operated on three times and he preferred to take a break. This apparently meant a disadvantage in his career towards being ranked No. 3 in the world. However, Alex Zverev, who at the time held that ranking, fell in the quarterfinals of Toronto (he won the title the previous year in 2017.) The German could not defend the amount of points required to maintain his ranking and, automatically, del Potro made history. The official ranking, published on August 13, showed del Potro at 5,410 points, with only two players ahead of him: Roger Federer (No. 2 with 6,480 points) and Rafael Nadal (No. 1 with 10,220 points.)

If del Potro looked at himself in a mirror and, with his career, his titles and his personality, he already saw a tennis superhero reflecting back. Climbing to No. 3 in the world brought him to a place of excellence that in Argentina, in conventional tennis, only Guillermo Vilas had achieved. Vilas was officially only recognized as the No. 2 in 1975, although there is some debate that he should have been ranked No. 1, due to some controversial missing results, it is alleged. Gabriela Sabatini (1989), Guillermo Coria (2004) and David Nalbandian (2006) are Argentines who also reached as high as No. 3.

"There are people who feel jealous," said Vilas, said to *La Nación* of the high ranking. "Everyone thinks as he likes. What we do is make our footprints, with our own style. The absence of other champions does not make us bigger. Greatness is in the titles you win. Depending on the amount of titles you have, you are bigger than others, so you cannot be envious. You have your place, a place that nobody can change. You have a number and all who have obtained that number are by your side in history; those with more numbers are above and those with less are below. And nobody fights for places that do not belong to him."

In Argentina, the world No. 1 honor belonged only to Gisela Dulko and Paola Suárez in doubles and Gustavo "Lobo" Fernández in wheelchair singles.

For the Magician Coria it was an honor to have been ranked No. 3. "You have many privileges when you are hold that ranking," he said. "You have a driver available in almost all tournaments, the largest hotel room, the court you want available and the schedule you want to train. I enjoyed it much more and I valued it more once I retired, because at the time my goal was No. 1."

"I didn't want to settle," said Gaby Sabatini. "It is a great achievement that Juan Martín has reached No.3 in the world and it is also an honor for him to share that podium with two tennis legends, Nadal and Federer."

Nalbandian did not agree with the symbolic and prestigious effect of reaching the Top 3:

"The podium is more symbolic than anything else," said Nalbandian. "In tennis there is no podium of 1, 2 and 3. That is for the press. We, or at least I, do not see much difference between being world No. 2 and being No. 4. There is no podium, at least from my point of view. It is just a statistic."

Between Monday, September 14, 2009 and Sunday, September 9, 2018, 3,282 days passed. Actually, a life passed. And it was said by del Potro, that between his first Grand Slam title and reaching his second Grand Slam final he lived all moods, his mouth was sweetened with successes and he was distressed with failures and injuries. Before the 2018 U.S. Open, expectations were high for the Argentine. The tournament was the launching pad for del Potro's career from the moment he posed with the U.S. Open trophy on top of the Empire State Building in 2009. From that moment, del Potro became a magnet for sponsors and attention, especially in the United States. In 2018, he was chosen for an unprecedented promotional experience for the tournament: the Argentine gave "tennis tips" to Andrew Feustel, a NASA astronaut.

The contact between del Potro and the astronaut came through a computer located in the Arthur Ashe Stadium in Flushing Meadows, N.Y. The talk, which was very friendly, revolved around tennis and the last big event of the year, which was del Potro's favorite.

"Can you see me from up there?" joked del Potro. The astronaut explained to the tennis player the "game" that he would then play with his teammates and how complex he moves in space.

"I congratulate you on the ranking," said Feustel, wearing a shirt from the U.S. Open. The NASA representative asked del Potro what he felt when playing in New York and he replied, "It is an incredible city to play tennis, but also to go to the theater, watch concerts, watch basketball, baseball. In addition, there are many Argentine fans who come, especially to see me. It is my favorite tournament. I hope I can win it again." Del Potro, in that last sentence, showed what he dreamed of...

Fourteen friends of the tennis player, all of them schoolmates in Tandil, were with Juan Martín during the U.S. Open. They called themselves "The band of the salamín," which is the sausage of the city where del Potro grew up. The boys said that it was the first trip they could do together and that the preparations required special logistics. Everyone stayed in Brooklyn and had to organize their vacation schedules to make sure it coincided with the U.S. Open.

"We didn't know how much longer he will be competing at the highest level, so we wanted to be here with him at a tournament," said Manuel, one of the tennis player's friends. "We asked Juan which one he wanted us to come to and obviously he chose the U.S. Open, his favorite."

The group did not go unnoticed during the tournament as they created a "football" climate during Delpo's matches, with songs typical of the most popular sport in the world. Even in the press conferences, del Potro talked about them. When asked how much the extreme heat affected him, he responded: "They are difficult conditions to play, for fans and for my friends who drink beers. They are also in dangerous heat conditions (he smiled). They have fun, I think they are respectful watching this event and create a fun environment for fans."

Americans Donald Young (No. 246) and Denis Kudla (No. 72), Spaniard Fernando Verdasco (No. 32), Croatian Borna Coric (No. 20) and American John Isner (No. 11) stood in the way of del Potro. Of all of them, only Isner managed to get a set. In addition, with those wins, del Potro became the 21st ATP tennis player to pass 300 wins on a hard surface.

Under the lights of Arthur Ashe Stadium, del Potro had to measure up to then-No. 1 Rafael Nadal in the semifinals. And, while the battle lasted, the Argentine proved to be more than prepared to subdue the Mallorcan, who would end up retiring after losing the first two sets, 7-6(3) and 6-2. A discomfort in the right knee pushed Rafa to decide to leave the match. After a tight first set that lasted for 70 minutes, the following games had a similar score line. But very soon after, Nadal felt a jab in the knee at 2-2 and 15-0. Just 20 minutes into the match and the Spaniard was already hurt. At 4-3, he requested the assistance of the physiotherapist, who provided him with a bandage that he removed two games later. Up 2-1 in the second set, Nadal again requested treatment. And this time, after a medical timeout, his participation in the match began to be questioned. He had less and less mobility and he ended up shaking hands with del Potro at the end of the second set. With the victory, his 10th against a world No. 1, the Argentine became the tennis player with the most victories against a world No. 1 without having reached that position, followed by the American Michael Chang and the Dutchman Richard Krajicek, who each had seven wins.

Del Potro waited nine years to play the U.S. Open final again. This time, Federer would not be his opponent since the Swiss had unexpectedly lost in the fourth round to the Australian John Millman, who at that time was ranked No. 55. It was Novak Djokovic, during those days ranked No. 6, who stood in the Argentine's way. He ended up defeating Juan Martín 6-3, 7-6(4), 6-3 after three hours and 16 minutes. The Serbian represented, for del Potro, a higher demand. This was evident from the first groundstrokes. Both players' strategies were exposed: Djokovic hit cross courts to corner the Argentine on his weaker side. And that tactic worked perfectly for him. He managed to annoy del Potro, who gradually ran out of defensive shots and yielded to the Serbian's forehand. Of course, many of those shots Djokovic managed to put back into play, which frustrated the Argentine.

Del Potro did everything to continue and posed a greater challenge to Djokovic in the second set. In fact, there was a key game, the eighth, with Djokovic trailing 3-4. Del Potro had three chances of breaking serve, which would have put him up 5-3 and serving, but after 22 minutes, the Serbian held his serve. The set ended up being defined in the tie-breaker. After losing it, del Potro was practically out of breath. With little energy in the legs, he had no choice but to take more risks and he ended up deflating.

"Sometimes, one can win or lose a tournament, but the love of all people is worth the same as that cup and I already have it. Today I take the love of all of you," del Potro stammered, as soon as the final was over. Later, he would expand his feelings. "I have been crying since the end of the match, but Novak deserved the trophy," he said. "He played well and played a smart match. I had my chances. We both played to the limit, I was forced to go for winners because he returned from everywhere. He is a great champion."

Said Djokovic, a friend of Delpo, "I really like Juan Martín, not only as a player but as a person. He is a close friend, someone whom I appreciate a lot. He is a kind giant. He is tall, has a great game, but at the same time, nourishes the right values of life. He is interested in his family, his friends, respects everyone, fights in each match from start to finish. I think people link him with that and appreciate everything he gives to tennis. That's why they love him as he is."

There was an instant, which was very emotional, after the match when del Potro broke down in his seat and Djokovic approached him, hugged him and said something in his ear.

"I was very anxious and needed to rest," said del Potro. "I found it hard to endure. Then, in the locker room, I was quite sad for quite some time. But on the court he approached me, he told me that he understood the moment, but that I was a great champion, that he was proud of where I was, what I was achieving and all the effort I had made to be there, that I would stay calm and I had to be happy."

The boys at the Tandil Independent Club's tennis school, where del Potro used to train, gathered in the clubhouse to watch the U.S. Open final on a giant screen. "He's scared, Nole is scared!" they sang, excited, waving Argentine flags and red-and-black club shirts. In the end, with the defeat, the boys shouted "Boooo!" when the TV showed Djokovic. Anger ran through them. But immediately they sang again for their idol: "Olé, olé, olé, Delpooo, Delpooo!" And for del Potro, in the distance, tears became caresses of the soul.

On September 23, 2018 del Potro turned 30. After celebrating his birthday with his friends in Buenos Aires, he set out to continue his career on the tour. He traveled, along with his team, to Asia. In his first tournament in Beijing, he reached the final, but lost to Georgian Nikoloz Basilashvili 6-4, 6-4. Regardless of that result, he earned entry to the year-end London Masters, the exclusive tournament he hadn't played since 2013.

"I am happy to have entered the Masters after five years. It will be an incredible moment for me," said del Potro, who earned his spot after beating Karen Khachanov in the second round of Beijing to clinch his position.

Everything was going well for del Potro. He made the second round of the Shanghai 1000 Masters after beating Richard Gasquet. But, as if it were a horror movie that is repeated again and again, on October 11, del Potro got injured in his match against Coric. And he did it in an unusual way, even awkwardly. The Argentine, still with a little cough from a flu that affected him in Beijing, was up 5-4. At 40-40, when the Argentine tried to run forward, he stumbled and fell with his weight above the right knee. After doctors bandaged the area, he returned to play, but his game was hindered. Coric held his serve, broke the Argentine's service, and sealed the first set 7-5 with another hold. Immediately after, del Potro took off his headband, approached the net and shook hands with his rival. He could not continue.

The tennis player returned to Argentina and confirmed the worst. He had fractured his right kneecap, but it was not displaced, so he did not need surgery. The injury is unusual in tennis and even more common in elderly people with osteoporosis. Although del Potro was excited to be playing in top form, he had to face another obstacle. But undoubtedly, it would serve as another test to show the enormous resilience of a fabulous athlete.

ALSO FROM
NEW CHAPTER PRESS

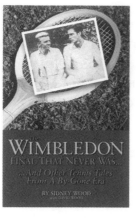

The Wimbledon Final That Never Was... And Other Tennis Tales From A Bygone Era
By Sidney Wood with David Wood

Sidney Wood tells the entertaining and fascinating tale of his Wimbledon title win 1931, capped with a strange default to his best friend, doubles partner, roommate and Davis Cup teammate Frank Shields ordered by the U.S. Tennis Association! Also included in this volume are a compilation of short stories that deliver fascinating anecdotes of old-school Hollywood and the styles of play of all 20th-century tennis legends.

The Greatest Tennis Matches of All Time
By Steve Flink

Author and tennis historian Steve Flink profiles and ranks the greatest tennis matches in the history of the sport. Roger Federer, Billie Jean King, Rafael Nadal, Bjorn Borg, John McEnroe, Martina Navratilova, Rod Laver, Don Budge and Chris Evert are all featured in this book that breaks down, analyzes, and puts into historical context the most memorable matches ever played.

Sport of a Lifetime: Enduring Personal Stories From Tennis
By Judy Aydelott

Enriching and motivational stories about those who love and participate in tennis over the age of 50. This is a volume of senior tennis through the stories and experiences of senior tennis players, from Gardnar Mulloy and Betty Eisenstien and Mayor David Dinkins to unknowns such as Chuck Niemeth.

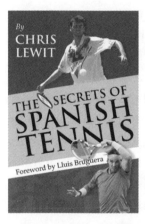

The Secrets of Spanish Tennis
By Chris Lewit

What makes Spanish tennis so unique and successful? What exactly are those Spanish coaches doing so differently to develop superstars like Rafael Nadal and David Ferrer that other systems are not doing? These and other questions are answered in *The Secrets of Spanish Tennis,* the culmination of five years of study on the Spanish way of training by USTA High Performance Coach Chris Lewit. He visited many of the top Spanish academies and studied and interviewed some of the leading coaches in Spain to discern and distill this unique and special training methodology.

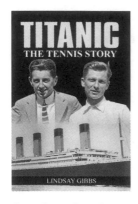

TITANIC: The Tennis Story
By Lindsay Gibbs

A stirring and remarkable story, this novel tells the tale of the intertwined life of Dick Williams and Karl Behr who survived the sinking of the *Titanic* and went on to have Hall of Fame tennis careers. Two years before they faced each other in the quarterfinals of the U.S. Nationals – the modern-day U.S. Open – the two men boarded the infamous ship as strangers. Dick, shy and gangly, was moving to America to pursue a tennis career and attend Harvard. Karl, a dashing tennis veteran, was chasing after Helen, the love of his life. The two men remarkably survived the sinking of the great vessel and met aboard the rescue ship *Carpathia*. But as they reached the shores of the United States, both men did all they could to distance themselves from the disaster. An emotional and touching work, this novel brings one of the most extraordinary sports stories to life in literary form. This real-life account – with an ending seemingly plucked out of a Hollywood screenplay – weaves the themes of love, tragedy, history, sport and perseverance.